CW01263220

Hoaxers and Their Victims

HOAXERS AND THEIR VICTIMS

NICK YAPP

Robson Books

First published in Great Britain in 1992 by Robson Books Ltd, Bolsover House, 5-6 Clipstone Street, London W1P 7EB

Copyright © 1992 Nick Yapp
The right of Nick Yapp to be identified as author of this work has been asserted by him in accordance with the Copyright, Designs and Patents Act 1988

British Library Cataloguing-in-Publication Data
A catalogue record for this book is available
from the British Library

All rights reserved. No part of this publication may be reproduced, stored in a retrieval system, or transmitted in any form or by any means, electronic, mechanical, photocopying, recording or otherwise, without the prior permission in writing of the publishers.

Typeset by EMS Photosetters, Thorpe Bay, Essex
Printed in Great Britain by
Billing and Sons Ltd, Worcester

To Jacob,
whose hoax threw me more
than it did the victim

Contents

Acknowledgements	ix
Introduction	1
1 — The Inspiration and Origins of Hoaxes	9
2 — Puffers and Bluffers	24
3 — Never Give a Sucker an Even Break	49
4 — Habitual Masquerade	64
5 — Not What They Seemed	90
6 — The Fairy Tales of Science	103
7 — True Colours, False Canvases	125
8 — There Must Be a Man Behind the Book	138
9 — Growing Weary, Growing Wary	157
10 — The Psychology of Hoaxers	167
11 — Victims	180
12 — The Psychology of Victims	193
13 — The Prevalence of Hoaxing	205
References	211
Index	221

Acknowledgements

I am grateful to all those hoaxers who have allowed me to interview them in the preparation of this book, assuming, that is, that what they told me was true. I should especially like to thank Brian Bethell, Ken Campbell, Sophie Lloyd, Victor Lewis-Smith, Zad Rogers, Paul Sparks, and Jenny Winstanley.

I'm also most grateful to Gwyneth Lewis for permission to read and to quote from her unpublished PhD thesis.

Nick Yapp, Catford

Introduction

'Everything that deceives may be said to enchant.'
Plato

'Plato is dear to me, but dearer still is truth.'
Aristotle

In September 1991, an Algerian runner named Abbes Tehami finished well ahead of the field in the Brussels marathon. He was not awarded the £4,500 first prize. Journalists and spectators noticed that Tehami appeared to have grown during the twenty-six mile race, and that although he had started the race with a fine moustache, he had ended it clean-shaven. Swift inquiries revealed that Tehami's coach and trainer had run the first ten miles of the race and had then swopped running vests with Tehami, who had been hiding behind a tree along the way. A senior IAAF official was quoted as saying: 'In my time I have not come across such an incident in an international race.'[1]

There is, however, nothing new about hoaxing. The Bible suggests it is the oldest profession of all, for chapter 27 of the Book of Genesis tells the tale of what may well be the first recorded hoax. Isaac believes he is near death, and sends Esau, the older of his twin sons, to fetch him savoury meat, in return for which Esau will receive Isaac's blessing. Rebekah, mother of the twins, overhears this and decides that the younger twin, Jacob, should have the blessing . . .

And Rebekah took the goodly raiment of Esau her elder son . . . and put them upon Jacob her younger son: and she put the skins of the kids of the goats upon his hands, and upon the smooth of his neck: and she gave the savoury meat and the bread, which she had prepared, into the hand of her son Jacob.

Jacob then takes the meat to Isaac and receives the blessing that was intended for Esau. The forty verses of the Old Testament that describe these events contain all the essentials of a hoax. There is a hoaxer (Rebekah) and an accomplice (Jacob). There are two victims (Isaac and Esau). There is the element of playing on the credulity of the victim: Isaac believes Jacob is Esau because his hands are hairy and because he smells Esau's raiment which Jacob is wearing, 'the smell of my son is as the smell of a field which the LORD hath blessed'. There is also the unpleasant element present in so many hoaxes, where the hoaxer plays upon the victim's weakness or handicap – for Isaac is blind. There is even the very common component in all hoaxes, the part played by the victim in his own downfall, since Isaac unwittingly colludes with the hoaxers in the way he baits the trap. He asks for savoury meat, strongly flavoured, and is therefore unable to distinguish goat from venison. Jacob and Rebekah play on the expectation in the mind of the victim: Isaac has asked Esau to bring him a dish of meat, so when a dish of meat is brought to him, he naturally assumes that it is Esau who brings it. And, perhaps above all, the hoax is a product of the age in which it is perpetrated. The death-bed blessing of the oldest son was an entrenched part of the structure of Ancient Hebrew society, and Jacob was prepared to act in an underhand and undergloved manner to obtain it.

What is a hoax? According to the Oxford English Dictionary, a hoax is 'a humorous or mischievous deception with which the credulity of the victim is imposed upon'. The word 'hoax' is probably a late eighteenth-century contraction of 'hocus-pocus', which in turn was derived from *hoc corpus est*, words uttered at that point in the Catholic Mass when the bread changes into the body of Christ. The word 'prank' comes from a Middle English verb 'prankon', and is probably related to the Spanish word *picar*, meaning 'to wound slightly', or the German word *prunk*, meaning 'an ostentatious trick'. We tend to think of hoaxes as lightweight, more humorous than mischievous, and even the word 'mischievous' may now carry a lightweight or even light-hearted meaning, but not all hoaxes are comic. Some of the best hoaxes often have a more serious side to them. All hoaxes are ruthless, and some of the worst are very cruel.

In July 1953 a young man named Edward Watters, of Austell, Georgia, bet a friend ten dollars that he'd get his photo in the local paper within two weeks. To win the bet, Watters bought a monkey for fifty dollars, chloroformed it, shaved it from top to bottom, killed it with a blow to the head, and cut off its tail. With two accomplices, he then drove the monkey to a lonely stretch of Highway 78 outside Austell, made skid marks on the road and placed the monkey in front of the truck he had been driving to simulate an accident. A little later, a patrolman reached the scene and discovered the dead monkey, with Watters wandering around in an apparent state of shock, mumbling something about Martians.

The hoax initially succeeded. The local authorities were informed, and representatives of the Georgia Bureau of Investigation, the FBI and the US Air Force were all summoned to the scene of the accident. There was extensive TV coverage and Watters's name duly appeared in the local paper. Watters told a story of a 'glowing thing, settling down and covering half the highway', and of these 'manlike objects' that had emerged from it, one of which he had run over. It was not long before the autopsy revealed that the Martian was a Capuchin monkey, but Watters won his bet. (It should be noted that Watters lost money on the hoax, for setting it up cost considerably more than the ten dollars staked on the bet. Most hoaxers and practical jokers don't seem to mind the expense involved in a hoax such as this.)

On a slightly less cruel note, Harry Reichenbach proudly recorded the story of how he 'trained' his dancing ducks when he operated a fairground booth at the Mardi Gras celebrations in New Orleans just before the First World War.

> We had three ducks in a frame of wire netting on a floor of tin, elevated on a dry goods box. As the spieler, I explained to our audience how many years we had laboured to train these aquatic *aves* in the terpsichorean art. What a problem it was to teach mere ducks the proper mental and muscular co-ordination and to make them acquire a sense of rhythm and an ear for music. During my oration the ducks would be sitting on the tin floor as though unconcerned and indifferent to the praises I showered on them. But at one point in my talk they seemed to respond with the alertness and spirit of true artists and rose to their feet.[2]

The ducks rose to their feet because an associate of Reichenbach turned up the wick of a lighted lamp under the tin floor on which the ducks had been sitting.

> As the temperature gradually increased, the ducks would raise first one foot, then the other in lively unison while King Carlos (another associate) played 'Turkey in the Straw' on his fiddle. The Dancing Ducks were the wonder of the Mardi Gras. They grossed us over a thousand dollars on the week.[3]

There is little that is humorous in hoaxes such as these. We have to accept that, with very few exceptions, hoaxers are not 'nice' people. Hoaxing is not one of the caring professions. No hoaxer seeks to bring comfort or joy to anybody. His motives are often vengeful or greedy. Most hoaxers have large and belligerent egos, have little thought for others, and are capable of immense self-deception, often construing a criminal act as simply 'a bit of fun'.

Once we start examining hoaxes, we are examining and questioning the concept of truth. A hoax is by definition not a truth. Hoaxers don't tell the truth – neither do some of those who write about hoaxers, many of whom dip their pens in exaggerating ink. We need to be very suspicious even when dealing with primary source material. The memoirs of hoaxers are not modest works. The situation becomes more complicated when we have to look at secondary sources, accounts of hoaxes in the newspapers or in books about hoaxes. For newspapers like to print a good story, which isn't always the same as the truth.

But it is never easy to know what is true. If we see someone dressed as an army officer, talking and behaving like an army officer, then we assume that person is an army officer, rather than a lorry driver or an escaped convict or a professor of linguistics. If I walk into a Park Lane reception wearing a dinner jacket, I am greeted with trusting smiles. If I walk into the same reception in a suit, but without a tie, I am greeted with can-we-help-you looks and very guarded smiles. If I walk in wearing a T-shirt, combat fatigues and DMs, I am greeted with no sort of smiles at all. I am the same person, but it is what I seem to be that matters, and hoaxing is about what seems to be.

Many hoaxers and commentators on hoaxes believe that a true hoax doesn't have to be funny, but should, rather, be satirical. They cite the invitation to the Coronation of Edward VII, received by several hundred leading citizens of Chicago in 1901, purporting to come from the Earl Marshal of England, but sent by Charles Dennehy and Company. 'Those honoured with invitations to the Coronation are expected to give particular attention to their attire. . . . ' There followed regulations for the dress of the English aristocracy:

> Titled nobility from America, such as merchant princes, coal barons, trust magnates, lords of finance with their ladies, must appear in costumes typifying the origins of their titles, and they may carry tape measures, coal scuttles, oil cans, stock tickers, and may wear stick pins, clothes pins, scarf pins, coupling pins, hair pins, rolling pins, cuff buttons, shoe strings, picture hats, turbans, handcuffs, overcoats, imitation lace scarfs, celluloid collars, hose or half hose as the case may be, rhinestones, collar buttons of silver gilt, and golf capes edged with two and one half rows of rabbit skin. . . .

The whole purpose of this wordy spoof was to invite people to drink their toast to His Majesty in any kind of drink as long as its base was 'old underhoof rye, manufactured by Charles Dennehy and Company of Chicago, USA'. The satire on the wealthy upper echelons of American society is in there, though it takes a little digging out.

The desire to fool the experts is often at least part of the motive behind a hoax, and it's a more attractive motive than sordid financial gain. 'All the world loves to see the experts and the establishment made a fool of, and everyone likes to feel that those who set themselves up as experts are really just as gullible as anyone else.'[4] But there are many hoaxes that serve no satirical purpose. For there are those hoaxers do not want their hoax ever to come to light: there is no humorous side to what they do, but plenty of mischief. On some levels, hoaxers have a lot in common with the more light-hearted anarchists. They have little or no respect for the generally accepted laws and practices of the society they live in. They delight in creating a sense of confusion and disorder. They find the routine of everyday life humdrum, boring and frustrating. They believe that what they do is morally sound and that they are asserting the rights of the individual.

To most of us many hoaxes are barely distinguishable from fraud, but not all frauds are hoaxes. If a man offers to sell me double glazing, takes my deposit and runs, he is hardly a hoaxer. If he offers to sell me the Brooklyn Bridge or the Eiffel Tower, however, he almost certainly is. The difference is that thinking I can buy double glazing is a reasonable action, thinking I can buy the Eiffel Tower is a foolish one.

Some hoaxes are very similar to straightforward practical jokes, but reveal a method and planning that goes beyond the banana skin on the pavement. Traditionally, it is the fat man or fat woman who is supposed to trip on the banana skin, the idea being that fatness is a condition that deserves to have fun poked at it. This isn't much of a joke: it certainly isn't a hoax. A much better practical joke, and one that may well qualify as a hoax, was that staged by Jonathan Routh some twenty-five years ago on a television series called *Candid Camera*. An attractive young woman stood at a street corner with a suitcase resting on the pavement. The suitcase was full of lead, and weighed half a ton. The victims were all men, who, as they came along, were asked by the woman if they would kindly carry her case across the road. As each gushingly accepted the invitation, the woman walked briskly across the road, leaving the man impotently struggling even to lift the case. The joke was at the expense of male gallantry (perhaps an unfair target) and male chauvinism (always fair game).

For the purposes of this book, the definition of a hoax will be widely construed. A hoax is a trick or deceit that must contain at least some of the following elements:

- extreme gullibility or credulity on the part of the victim
- an attempt to expose pomposity or hypocrisy
- an attempt to exploit the greed or over-lofty ambition of the victim
- a desire to amuse
- an attempt to defeat those in positions of considerable wealth, power or status
- an intention to satirize some aspect of the society in which the hoaxer lives

To these may be added a desire on the part of the hoaxer to heighten his sense of self-importance – some, indeed, quite simply want to be famous – or to gain financially. There is room here for jokes and cons, fraudulent deception and outright swindles, and for the life stories of those who have spent their entire existence donning false identities and trying to trick the world. We return to the notion that few hoaxers are attractive figures, though there may well be something attractive about the idea of most hoaxes. The best hoaxes have been greeted with acclaim by the world at large, and some have achieved a merry immortality. Many of us are fascinated by the idea of walking out one morning and becoming somebody else – the great lover, the millionaire, the international spy, the seer, the prophet, the Emperor, the discoverer of life on the Moon, the confidant of the world's richest eccentric. Folk tales abound with hoaxers, always cast at least semi-heroically: Lieutenant Kije, Háry János, Baron Munchausen, Till Eulenspiegel. The human race has shown a great reluctance to abandon a hoax. We like to cling to our pranks, even when they are discredited or repeated as often as the Cabbage Hoax.*

The more hoaxes are examined, the more clearly patterns in hoaxing emerge. While hoaxers come in all shapes and sizes – slim and slight, flabby and fat, mean and medium – most, but not all, have a sense of humour; most, perhaps all, have considerable courage, often of a delinquent variety. All pick their victims carefully: premeditation is another essential feature of a hoax. Many employ softening-up techniques on their victims, frequently using the press or other media to do this. Many have considerable understanding of human psychology, and know when to add fresh bait to the trap, when to cast doubts on the authenticity of their own hoax, and when to admit defeat. Those who make a study and practice of hoaxing are often surprised, however, at how easy it is. 'I never cease to be amazed at how seriously people take themselves, unable to see the funny images we all reflect in everything we say or do,'[5] remarks Adrian Stephen, accomplice to Horace Cole of *Dreadnought* fame (see page 15).

It is highly probable that we hear only of the successful hoaxes, of course, for no hoaxer would want to tell of the times his plans have

---

* The Cabbage Hoax takes the form of a verbal joke. 'The Lord's Prayer,' it goes, 'has fifty-six words. The Gettysburg Address has two hundred and sixty-eight. The Declaration of Independence has one thousand three hundred and twenty-two. So how come it took the Federal Government of the United States twenty-six thousand nine hundred and eleven words to issue a Regulation of the Sale of Cabbages?' The hoax is that there has never been any such Regulation.

blown up in his face. The apparent high incidence of susceptibility and gullibility among victims should be seen in this context. However, we have to be careful here. Many writers on the subject of hoaxes and hoaxers are carried away in intoxicated enjoyment of the hoax they are describing. Exaggeration is rife, invention not unknown. Some stories are clearly too good to check. Two Yale professors appear as dupes in accounts of several different hoaxes. In one case they have been named as Marsh and Silliman. Initially, that last name seemed to me too good to be true, but there really was a Benjamin Silliman. At the time of the hoax in question, he was in his mid-forties and was professor of chemistry at Yale Medical School and Yale College. Othniel Charles Marsh was professor of palaeontology at Yale and later became President of the US National Academy of Sciences.

One strange pattern that emerges is that of a weave made up of strands in the lives of hoaxers and victims. The activities of one are knitted into the activities of an other, though they have seemingly nothing in common and may not even be contemporaries. Horatio Bottomley (MP, 'Hater of the Hun' and dodgy entrepreneur) sat in the same House of Commons as Trebitsch Lincoln (MP, spy, and Buddhist Abbot). Bottomley (as self-styled 'Tommy's Ambassador') later met Percy Toplis (self-styled 'General' in charge of British Army deserters), to negotiate an agreement between the British Army and the thousands of mutineers at the Étaples camp in 1917. Trebitsch Lincoln was almost certainly fed information by Sir Edmund Backhouse (fraudulent business operator and pornographer). Backhouse's Diaries form much of the source material for Hugh Trevor-Roper's *Hermit of Peking: The Hidden Life of Sir Edmund Backhouse*. Trevor-Roper (historian and author) is one of the major victims in the Hitler Diaries hoax. Konrad Kujau (perpetrator of the Hitler Diaries hoax) is probably responsible for the spurious suggestion that Hitler and Trebitsch Lincoln met in 1920. Thus the loom of hoaxing sweeps to and fro, weaving them all together.

Another pattern that emerges clearly is that hoaxes are the products of the age and society in which they are perpetrated. We may not get the governments we deserve, but we certainly get the hoaxes we deserve. And, if suckers are born every minute, then hoaxes must be, too. Indeed, some hoaxers seem to travel in convoy, like buses.

1

The Inspiration and Origin of Hoaxes

'No one who is not conscious of having a sound memory should set up to be a liar.'

Montaigne

'Horace Cole and I,' wrote Adrian Stephen, 'were sitting in his rooms in Trinity one evening and I suppose we must have been feeling depressed for I remember that we set ourselves to think out some plan of amusement. We had both already played a few hoaxes on a small scale, and it occurred to both of us that it might be amusing to do something more elaborate.'[1]

Stephen put up the first idea in 1906, that he and Cole should 'acquire' the uniforms of German army officers and travel to Alsace-Lorraine. There, they should don their uniforms, take command of a detachment of German troops and march them across the frontier into France.

> Once we got across what happened would naturally have depended on circumstances. I had no doubt, of course, that the French would stop us before we had gone a kilometre. We should have surrendered immediately, and perhaps been interned. There would, I hoped, have been what is called an 'international incident', the Kaiser would have made gestures and sent telegrams, and other people might have been amused.[2]

Stephen's plan was turned down in favour of Cole's, which was easier and cheaper. It does not seem to have occurred to either of them that the Alsace-Lorraine plan could have led to their own deaths and those of innocent French and German soldiers. To them, as Stephen put it: 'There had just been some trouble near the French frontier.'[3] They were wealthy undergraduates with nothing else to do.

Cole fancied a hoax nearer home: 'It happened that at this time the Sultan of Zanzibar was in England; what could be simpler than to impersonate him and pay a State Visit to Cambridge?'[4] This initial plan was modified after a photograph of the real Sultan appeared in the English newspapers. Cole became, instead, the Sultan's uncle and, accompanied by Stephen and three other friends, set off to a theatrical costumiers. Once suitably attired, the party sent a telegram to the Mayor of Cambridge, telling him to expect an official visit. All went well at first. They were driven in a carriage to the Guildhall, visited a charity bazaar, at which Cole made an enormous number of purchases, and were conducted on a tour of the colleges. The Town Clerk then took them to the Great Eastern part of Cambridge station to put them on a train for London. Cole and Stephen had no desire to return to London, so they lifted their skirts and bolted. It was an ignominious end to a State visit.

The motive for this hoax, and the subsequent *Dreadnought* hoax, appears to be partly relief from boredom, but for Stephen there more to it than that. 'It had seemed to me ever since I was very young, just as I imagine it had seemed to Cole, that anyone who took up an attitude of authority over anyone else was necessarily also someone who offered a leg for everyone else to pull.'[5] For a couple of Cambridge undergraduates, once the offer had been made, it was impossible not to accept it. But, in the case of Cole, there appears to have been something else that drove him to play practical jokes for almost the whole of his life – a kind of lunacy, daredevil madness, extrovert lack of self-control that didn't always amuse even his friends. 'No practical joker myself, I would have preferred to view such activities at a certain distance,' claimed Stephen. 'It was embarrassing to find myself, without warning, in charge of an epileptic in convulsions on the pavement and foaming at the mouth; or to be involved in a collision between a whooping lunatic and some unknown and choleric gentleman who had been deprived suddenly of his headgear, and who had all my sympathy.'[6]

It has been argued by some writers that the trouble with Cole and his friends was that they had nothing to do. They were Edwardian gentlemen for whom there was no occupation, and who had to rack their brains each day to think of something on which it was worth expending energy. Cole himself was denied the place in *Who's Who* to which he was entitled by birth because he insisted on putting his recreation as 'f-----g' (Cole's spelling). But not every young man-about-town in the 1900s spent the greater part of his day planning and practising hoaxes. To find out what inspired or motivated Cole and Stephen, we need to see what they have in common with other hoaxers from other times, other places, and other social backgrounds.

One of the commonest practices among hoaxers is that of assuming an identity different from their own. Cole and Stephens did this for fun. Archibald Belaney, raised by two maiden aunts in Hastings during his childhood in the 1890s, assumed the identity of Grey Owl because he was fascinated by the Indians of North America. 'What with his camping out, his tracking of all and sundry, and wild hooting, he was more like a Red Indian than a respectable grammar school boy.'[7] Percy Toplis, the 'Monocled Mutineer', changed rank and uniform with bewildering frequency, as far as the military authorities were concerned, to stay one jump ahead of nemesis. Stanley Weyman, who pretended to be a Romanian consul-general, was also in turn a bogus lawyer, doctor, lieutenant-commander in the US Navy, an accredited United Nations official, journalist and night manager of a motel. Frank Abnagale was a bogus airline pilot, but also a bogus paediatrician, a bogus graduate of Harvard Law School, and a bogus sociology teacher. While in gaol he wrote his autobiography, *Catch Me If You Can*, in which he said of himself. 'I was simply a poseur and swindler of astonishing ability.'[8]

Coupled with the desire to wrap themselves in alternative identities, to say nothing of the necessity thereof, most hoaxers have an astonishing ability to take on another role, another personality. Clifford Irving, perpetrator of the Howard Hughes autobiography hoax, excelled at presenting himself as a man of great honesty. The press release from the publishers McGraw-Hill, announcing the forthcoming autobiography (or, more accurately, authorized biography), explained that Mr Hughes had selected Irving as his go-between 'because of his sympathy, discernment, discretion and . . . his integrity as a human being.'[9] The words may well be Irving's own, few hoaxers are modest, but for a considerable time he was able to persuade his publishers that he lived up to them.

Cole and Stephen also had this ability. By the time they reached the *Dreadnought*, Cole was not far from believing he really was the person he was pretending to be, while for Stephen, 'the expedition had become . . . almost an affair of every day. It was hardly a question any longer of hoax. We were almost acting the truth.'[10] Other hoaxers have noted this slide into a situation where the hoax takes on a replacement reality, like a cuckoo that has pushed the legitimate occupants from the nest. 'There always comes a time when you find yourself getting in too deep,' as Demara said, 'You've made good friends who believe in you, and you don't want them to get hurt and disillusioned. You begin to worry about what they'll think if somebody exposes you as a phoney.'[11] To insure against exposure, many hoaxers have behaved outrageously, on the age-old principle that fraud and hoaxing are easy, provided they are carried out with sufficient panache and on a grand scale. In the words of Tertullian: 'I believe, because it is impossible.' In the words of the Duke of Wellington: 'Possible? Is anything impossible? Read the newspapers.'

Which brings us to another trait shared by many hoaxers: love of publicity. Adrian Stephen was a modest and unassuming man who imagined that once the *Dreadnought* conspirators arrived home, the whole incident was finished.

> We had decided not to tell the newspapers and, though something was bound to leak out, we did not expect what happened. We had had a photograph taken of ourselves in our fancy dress as a memento, and one day walking in the street I saw this reproduced on the poster of the *Mirror*. I believe that was how I first realized that someone had given the story away.[12]

The 'someone' was Cole. The others felt that they had been charmingly entertained on board His Majesty's warship, treated with such kindness that they felt rather guilty. For them, the joke had gone far enough, 'but not for Cole: he had always wanted fame, and here was his chance of it. Without telling his confederates, he went to the newspapers'.[13]

A professional hoaxer, such as Alan Abel, makes his living through publicity. Rogues, such as Trebitsch Lincoln, thrive on it. Scientists, such as Sir Cyril Burt, are so conscious of the importance of publicity in a professionally competitive world that they fudge results to obtain it. Hugo Baruch, aka Jack Bilbo, after the success of his fictitious autobiography *Carrying a Gun for Al Capone*, loved posing for publicity pictures, dressed in a raincoat with the collar turned up and a hat with the brim snapped down, and carrying a gun. McGraw-Hill were perhaps too well aware of the publicity that would attach to an authentic Howard Hughes autobiography not to be drawn into Irving's net. Irving himself certainly enjoyed the limelight, and there are those for whom it is everything. On 18 July 1988, John Vidal reported in the Diary column of the *Guardian*:

> Donald Trelford, editor of the *Observer*, will heave a sigh of relief some time this afternoon when Rocky Ryan, a chap who, in the words of his solicitor, 'has achieved a moderate degree of celebrity as a perpetrator of harmless hoaxes upon newspapers by persuading them to print totally bogus stories', agrees to be bound over at Wells Street Magistrates' Court not to pester the paper. The problem arose when the *Observer* published extracts of a book by Bob Woodward of the *Washington Post* suggesting that an Englishman was behind the 1985 Beirut Massacre. The trail, in fact, led straight back to Rocky who is somewhat amused by the *Observer*'s attempts at silencing him now, seeing, he says, that they have used his services so often. 'The binding over won't cramp my style', he says – referring, of course, to other papers.

There is nothing any newspaper likes as much as the discomfiture of another newspaper, but the tone of the *Guardian*'s report illustrates another aspect of hoaxing: that it meets with a generally sympathetic response from the public (of which more in a subsequent chapter).

Although, as we shall also see later, there is a very clear distinction between those hoaxers who seek only money and those who seek only fun, all hoaxers seem to enjoy the feeling of having power over others that hoaxing gives them. For some this power is exercised to gain revenge: they feel they have been slighted, insulted, ignored by society or members of it. For some (Alan Abel, Hugh Troy, Horace Cole), the joy is in being able to turn the world momentarily upside down, deflating the pompous, exposing the ridiculous. For some (Louis de Rougemont, 'Caraboo', Psalmanazar of Formosa, Karoly Hadju aka Michael Karoly), it is a manner of forcing the world to take notice of them by inventing exciting lives that they have never lived. Many seek to bamboozle the experts, including almost all those whose hoaxes have been in the field of music, painting, sculpture and literature. For some (Trebitsch Lincoln, Maundy Gregory, Horatio

Bottomley, Clifford Irving), hoaxing is clearly a means of generating increased self-esteem through self-deception, making it seem, in their eyes if nobody else's, that they have an importance on the world stage that does not exist in reality.

This power over others may be maintained for a long time – years or even decades. The Piltdown Hoax was perpetrated in 1912, but not uncovered until 1953, by which time some of the hoaxers and many of the victims were as extinct as Piltdown Man. The Cottingley Fairies were photographed in 1917, articles about them appeared in *The Strand Magazine* in November 1920 and March 1921, but the two girls responsible for the hoax (Frances Wright and Elsie Griffiths) waited another fifty-five years before admitting their deception. Both the Piltdown and Cottingley hoaxes suggest that, even among the hoaxers who are out for fun rather than profit, there are those who do not feel the need to be present when their work is exposed and their victim ridiculed. Those out for profit, of course, never wish to be around when the hoax is exposed.

The more we look at hoaxes, the more it is apparent that there is often an element of luck that enables the hoaxer to succeed beyond his original estimate. Time and again experts (many of them from high in the realms of Academia) vouch for the authenticity of the false; crucial details are not checked; the victim shows an unexpected urge to collaborate in his own downfall*; someone who would have been able to expose the hoax is unaccountably absent when the trick is pulled. When Clifford Irving presented two forged letters to executives at McGraw-Hill, there was no genuine sample of Howard Hughes's handwriting with which to compare them. Irving was able to take the letters away and re-forge them twice more before McGraw-Hill were in a position to place them side by side with the genuine article. Ironically, it was a McGraw-Hill executive who had told Irving where he could find a lengthy example of Hughes's handwriting. But, luck apart, most hoaxers have done their homework carefully and prepared the ground for the wicked seeds they wish to sow. More than that, they have identified a time and a place where conditions are fertile for such seeds to be sown.

---

* Forgive the concentration on the masculine in this book. Most hoaxers happen to be men, as do most victims. Quite what this tells us about the male gender, I don't know.

THE INSPIRATION AND ORIGIN OF HOAXES

Most hoaxers, then, have a lust for power, a thirst for publicity, a delight in assuming a false identity, and considerable audacity. To this list we can add at least two more qualities: a ruthlessness towards their victims – whether the hoax is for material gain or not – and an element of luck. The time has come to put all these ingredients together and to examine one of the most famous hoaxes of all time.

The inspiration for the *Dreadnought* hoax came from a young naval officer who was a friend of Horace Cole, and who wished to embarrass William Fisher, a brother officer then serving aboard HMS *Dreadnought* and a cousin of Adrian Stephen. Early in 1910, *Dreadnought*, flagship of the Home Fleet, was lying at Weymouth, and Cole and his fellow conspirators fixed the date for the hoax as 10 February, the fourth anniversary of the launching of the ship by Edward VII. The planning was skeletal, the preparations hasty. Stephen and Cole invited Anthony Buxton, Guy Ridley and Duncan Grant to join them, and, with forty-eight hours to go, added Stephen's cousin Virginia Stephen (later Virginia Woolf) to the party, as it seemed a little small for an Emperor's suite. Cole was to be Herbert Cholmondeley of the Foreign Office. Stephen – tall, thin, and almost impossible to disguise – was to be the interpreter, called 'Kauffman'; Anthony Buxton was to be the Emperor; the others were to be members of the Emperor of Abyssinia's entourage. Looking at the photograph taken of the group after their visit to Clarkson's, the theatrical costumiers, and after the application of false beards and moustaches and various skin-darkening ointments, powders and greasepaint, it is hard to believe that they got away with it. Only Buxton and Cole appear the genuine article. Stephen, in his own words, looks 'like a seedy commercial traveller'.[14] Ridley and Grant look like refugees from a provincial production of *Aladdin*, and Virginia Stephen looks as though someone had been using Edith Sitwell to sweep a chimney. In the photograph, an aura of mental subnormality hangs over the group.

On the morning of the hoax, Cole and company put on their costumes and make-up, took taxis to Paddington and caught the 8.30 train to Weymouth. At the same time, an accomplice sent a telegram *en clair* to Vice-Admiral Sir William May, Commander-in-Chief Home Fleet. The telegram warned the Admiral that he was about to be paid a visit by the Emperor of Abyssinia and his suite, and was signed 'Hardinge': Sir Arthur Hardinge was permanent head at the Foreign Office. Apart from an attempt to teach Stephen a smattering of Swahili (from a grammar supplied by the Society for the Propagation of the Gospel) in the luncheon car on the way to Weymouth, that was the extent of their preparations. The hoaxers had not even taken the trouble to find out whether Swahili was the appropriate language. It wasn't.

For Stephen, the arrival at Weymouth Station was the plunge into the cold bath. Apart from Cole, the entire party had the deepest misgivings. Cole, however, was happy and confident, and had the true hoaxer's determination to succeed. 'As the train slowed down ... we were all agog. I think I half expected that no notice would be taken of us at all, and we should just have to slink back to London but no, there on the platform stood a naval officer in full uniform, and the hoax had begun.'[15]

A red carpet led to a line of taxis that took the Emperor's party to the quayside. Here a small launch awaited them, with steam up, and they were taken to HMS *Dreadnought*. As the launch came alongside, the ship's band struck up the national anthem of Zanzibar. Like Stephen's Swahili, it was the nearest the British Navy could get to the real thing. Cole was first to climb aboard, followed by the Emperor and his suite, with Stephen bringing up the rear. The Admiral and his staff officers (among them Stephen's cousin) were in full dress uniform. Lines of marines were drawn up on deck.

Cole then introduced the members of the party, completely throwing Stephen by introducing him as 'Herr Kauffmann'. 'We had all chosen our own names coming down in the train and Cole, who was rather deaf, had misheard me. I had chosen an English name that sounded rather like Kauffmann.'[16] Stephen was particularly worried as there had recently been a great many German spy scare stories and he was afraid of 'extra close scrutiny', or worse. Some accounts of the hoax allege that, as interpreter, Stephen was then informed by one of the officers that there was a man in the fleet who could speak fluent Abyssinian, but that this man was unfortunately on leave. This sounds too good to be true, but, if it was true, it is another example of the extraordinary luck that clings to hoaxers.

> Then I became aware of another source of danger that was quite unexpected, for the captain of the ship also turned out to be a

man with whom I was personally acquainted. I belonged at that time to a small club which took long country walks on Sundays, and the captain had several times joined in and spent whole days in our company. I knew, of course, that he was a Captain in the Navy, but did not know his ship.[17]

Poor Stephen later wrote that from that moment his memory of the visit was rather 'scrappy'. Other accounts say that it then began to rain, and Cole decided he must get his Abyssinians below deck before their stained faces began to run. There was also trouble with Duncan Grant's moustache, which had come unstuck on one side and was slowly slipping down his face. They were offered luncheon but refused, being not too sure what foods were permissible to their religion – whatever that was. The rain stopped. They went back on deck and the tour of inspection was completed. Stephen's powers as interpreter were taxed by Sir William May's insistence that he should explain to the Emperor why there were two different uniforms for the marines in the guard of honour. Stephen promised he would try to get this information across, turned to Buxton (the Emperor) and said: 'Entaqui, mahai, kustufani.' All his life, Stephen remained unsure as to whether these were genuine words of Swahili, learnt on the train, or whether they simply came to him by divine inspiration. For the rest of the visit he relied on bastardized Latin and Greek, particularly from the Fourth Book of the *Aeneid*.

The Admiral then asked the Emperor, through Stephen, what would be the correct number of guns to be fired in salute to the Emperor.

> I took the course which I think at any rate most of us approved of and said that it was not necessary at all. The French Fleet had not saluted us at Toulon, why should the English? The real fact was that I understood that firing salutes meant cleaning guns afterwards, and it seemed too much of a shame to cause such unnecessary trouble – besides, it was almost as grand to refuse a salute as to accept one.[18]

Some accounts suggest that Cole didn't agree, and was very disappointed when no salute was fired. This would seem to fit in with his character and with his callousness as a hoaxer.

Other accounts, however, differ. Some say that a salvo of guns was in fact fired as a salute to the Emperor, and that each percussion was greeted by the Abyssinians with shouts of 'Bunga-Bunga!' This version passed into popular contemporary mythology. Music Hall comedians made many 'Bunga-Bunga' jokes, along the lines of:

Comedian: I say, I say, what did the Abyssinian prince say to the Admiral?
Audience (in delighted unison): Bunga-Bunga!

After details of the hoax were leaked to the press, poor Sir William May was pursued through the streets of Weymouth by urchins shouting 'Bunga-Bunga!' wherever he went. But Stephen makes no mention of a salvo of guns, and suggests that 'Bunga-Bunga' was an invention of one of the assistants at Clarkson's, who jumped on the bandwagon and falsely represented to newspaper reporters that he knew a great deal about the hoax.

The hoaxers disembarked in the same steam launch that had brought them to the *Dreadnought*, and headed for shore. Some accounts say that another vessel crossed the bows of the launch, a gross breach of naval etiquette, and that the officer in charge of this ill-mannered vessel was subsequently reprimanded. Stephen does not say the story is true but that 'it ought to be'. There is always the worry that many details in accounts given by hoaxers 'ought to be true'. Back on the quayside, Cole tipped the sailors who had accompanied them, and attempted to pin a 'fancy-dress order' on the breast of one young officer. This was shyly refused. Taxis took the party back to Weymouth Station, and they slumped into the London train, completely exhausted and ravenously hungry. They maintained the hoax only so far as to insist that the waiters wore white gloves to serve them dinner on the train. This resulted in more work for the innocent, as these white gloves had to be specially purchased. The hoaxers returned safely to London.

Had Cole not leaked the story to the press, matters might have ended there, reasonably peacefully. But Cole was an extrovert who liked the world to know of his existence and of his inventive powers as the Prince of Practical Jokers, in which capacity Virginia Stephen found him 'bumptious and boring'. He went to the *Daily Mirror* and gave them both the photograph and the story. It was a dangerous thing to do, for 'the object of their excursion [had been] to hoodwink the British Navy, to penetrate its security and to enjoy a conducted tour of the . . . most modern and the most secret man o' war then afloat'.[19] Cole and Stephen had picked the British Navy as their target because it was pompous and authoritarian and lacked any sense of humour. Anyone willing to exercise prudence or foresight would have avoided such a target for those very reasons. But hoaxers are not prudent and their foresight is sometimes blinkered.

The story spread from the *Daily Mirror* to the *Express* and *Daily Telegraph*. The papers tended not to see the funny side of the joke, or at least gave the impression that what had taken place was reprehensible, and pointed out that those responsible had committed a criminal offence in sending a telegram under a false name. Questions were asked in the House of Commons:

> *Colonel Lockwood* asked the First Lord of the Admiralty, whether a hoax had been played on the naval authorities by the pretended visit of some Abyssinian prince; and, if so, whether he will take steps to prevent such conduct in future?
>
> *First Lord of the Admiralty (Mr McKenna)*: I understand that a number of persons have put themselves to considerable trouble and expense in pretending to be a party of Abyssinians, and in this disguise visited one of His Majesty's ships. The question is being considered whether any breach of the law has been committed which can be brought home to these offenders.
>
> *Mr William Redmond*: Will the Right Hon. Gentleman include in this inquiry an inquiry as to whether or not it is a fact that this gentleman conferred the Royal Abyssinian Order on the Admiral, who wrote to the King to know whether he could wear it, and will he wear it?
>
> *Mr McKenna*: I shall be relieved from the necessity of inquiring into that matter because I know it not to be true.
>
> *Colonel Lockwood*: Does the Right Hon. Gentleman think with me that the joke was a direct insult to His Majesty's flag?
>
> *Mr McKenna*: I think I have answered the question fully. The Hon. and gallant Gentleman will not ask me to go further into a matter which is obviously the work of foolish persons.[20]

Shortly after this exchange, Stephen heard that some form of reprimand was to be administered to Sir William May. This may have been merely a rumour, but Stephen claimed it reached him from Mrs McKenna, wife of the First Lord of the Admiralty. What had started as a prank was beginning to get out of hand. Stephen decided it was time to apologize, to take some of the heat out of the situation. He was unable to contact Cole, who was ill, but persuaded Duncan Grant to go with him to the Admiralty. The doorkeeper there clearly knew all about the *Dreadnought* hoax, and they were ushered upstairs to McKenna's private room. A stiff interview then took place. McKenna assumed that Stephen and Grant had come to beg for mercy, and adopted a hectoring tone, saying that at least one of the foolish persons involved was liable to go to gaol. Stephen attempted to point out that all they wanted was to find a way of smoothing things over. 'We had come absolutely gratuitously to make what seemed a generous offer, and I did not see why this politican should treat us *de haut en bas*, not even if he had rowed in the Cambridge boat before he was First Lord of the Admiralty.'[21] In a paper presented to the Women's Institute at Rodmell in the summer of 1940, Virginia Woolf wrote: 'The truth was I think that Mr McKenna was a good deal amused, and liked the hoax, but didn't want it repeated. At any rate he treated them as if they were schoolboys, and told them not to do it again.' The hoaxers may have had their own legs pulled.

From this point the whole affair sank to the level of prep-school politics and power struggles. Two naval officers arrived at Cole's house, armed with canes with which they proposed to beat him to avenge the honour of the Navy. Nobody has yet explained how this retribution was supposed to work. Cole received them calmly, hinted that he was prepared to fight them, and that his manservant would join in, but added that he was recovering from illness and violent exercise might be dangerous for him. If we believe Stephen's account, the naval officers then said that this was the third weekend they had journeyed up to London to avenge the Navy and that they were jolly well not going to be disappointed this time.

A bizarre agreement was reached. Cole assented to being caned if he was allowed to reply in kind. He and the naval officers then crept round the corner to a quiet back street, where Cole and one of the naval officers ceremoniously, but gently, caned each other, and then shook hands. Honour, that worn-out prop from the theatricality of

Victorian and Edwardian England, was satisfied. A few days later, another group of naval officers, also armed with canes, called at Duncan Grant's house, and bundled him into a taxi. 'Mrs Grant, who was looking out of the window, saw her son disappear head foremost and turned back in alarm. "What on earth are we to do?" she asked her husband. "Someone's kidnapping Duncan." Major Grant, who had been in the army himself, merely smiled and said, "I expect it's his friends from the *Dreadnought*".'[22] There appears to have been little paternal concern on the part of the Major. Duncan Grant was taken to Hendon, then a leafy hamlet on the fringe of London. Here another ceremonial caning took place, the officers being disappointed when Grant refused to put up a fight and further refused a lift home from them afterwards.

And then, at last, the furore died down and the hoax was laid to rest. Virginia Stephen was relieved, 'although she feared that it would mean they would see even more of Horace Cole'.[23] She had originally joined the Abyssinian adventure for the fun of the thing. When it ended she felt she had discovered a new sense of the brutality and silliness of men. Subsequently she made use of the incident in a short story called 'A Society', which she published in 1921.

Alone among the hoaxers, Cole was delighted. The *Dreadnought* hoax was his finest achievement. The others had had enough of it, and it had left a nasty taste in their mouths. Stephen thought that the Navy had no need to seek revenge. 'As for revenge, if they wanted any they had already had plenty before the hoax was over. They treated us so delightfully while we were on board that I, for one, felt very uncomfortable at mocking, even in the friendliest spirit, such charming people.'[24] It is this sense of consideration for those who are being hoaxed that sets Stephen apart from Cole and from most hoaxers.

Although, once he stepped on to the red carpet at Weymouth Station, Stephen felt that they were not so much perpetrating a hoax as 'almost acting the truth', there were several moments when he might have come clean: when Cole introduced him as Herr Kauffman, when he saw his cousin staring at him from a few yards off, when he was wrestling with the problem of speaking fluent impromptu gibberish, when Duncan Grant's moustache began to peel off. There seems never to have been a moment when Cole was assailed by doubt.

In this Cole was a true hoaxer, the others merely followers. He may have played for fun, but the hoax was always carried through to the bitter end. All his hoaxes had a very clear goal, which had to be reached regardless of the cost to others. Stephen may not have wanted extra work for the ship's crew, Cole had not a thought for them. McKenna's statement in the House of Commons, that the hoaxers had 'put themselves to considerable trouble and expense', was totally inaccurate. The conspirators had spent little time and less money on the hoax. The real cost was to the ship's company on board HMS *Dreadnought*, who would have been ordered to put in a great deal of extra work to make the Emperor's trip a success. Someone had to scrub the deck, clean and press the Admiral's dress uniform, roll out the red carpet, and run through the streets in search of white gloves in which to serve the Emperor's dinner *en route* to Paddington. It is a fairly safe bet that these someones were not people with an overbearing attitude of authority 'offering a leg for everyone else to pull'. It is possible to admire the nerve of the *Dreadnought* hoax, but to come away feeling that bright young things have dropped their clothes and belongings on the floor and left someone else to pick them up.

This is perhaps a little unfair. In every successful hoax someone has to suffer, but we tend to regard snatching someone else's money as a much wickeder act than snatching their time. There may be moral and legal distinctions between a hoax that deprives someone of his dignity and one that deprives him of his cash, but, in hoax terms, the main difference seems to be that the practical joker often gives very little thought to the consequences of his actions, the conman usually gives a great deal of thought to them. Cole and his friends sit in their rooms in Cambridge or London, decide on a good wheeze, and set off almost immediately to put it in action. Where money is involved, weeks, months, even years of planning separate the initial inspiration from the final operation. There is a vast difference between the 'what shall we do today?' approach of Horace Cole, and the unsought seed that drops into the nidus of van Meegeren or Clifford Irving, takes root, and slowly grows into a confidence trick of sequoian proportions.

But every hoax is a product of the age and society in which it is conceived or planted. Circumstances come together that allow the most daring and complicated of hoaxes a comparatively easy passage.

McGraw-Hill knew and trusted Irving. The publishing world in general was greedy for an authorized biography of Howard Hughes. McGraw-Hill needed a boost to their reputation. *Time-Life*, who bought the magazine rights for a quarter of a million dollars, were desperately in need of such a scoop. Hughes had totally withdrawn from public view.

The same pattern surrounds the art forgeries of van Meegeren in The Netherlands of the 1940s. Though very little was known about Vermeer's life, experts had argued that there must be other paintings of his hidden away, and, specificallly, that there must somewhere be a Vermeer painting on a biblical subject. The discovery of such paintings would return some pride to an occupied nation. Van Meegeren had access to a seventeenth-century canvas, and in the words of Lord Kilbracken, his biographer, 'in the case of a truly old canvas, there must often be no way of establishing who painted it, the expert can only inspect it and say what he thinks, and *indeed the very continuance of the market depends on such decisions being generally respected*'[25] (my italics). There was a vast potential market for more Vermeers at the time van Meegeren painted them. In the 1970s, when Count Alain de Villegas claimed he could dowse for oil, it was the resource that the French Government most needed. When James Shearer presented his Delineator to the British military authorities in 1916, the Allies were sinking in the mud of the Western Front and prepared to grasp anything that might keep them afloat. The acclaim the greeted the discovery of the Piltdown skull in 1912 has to be seen against a background of industrial and military rivalry with Germany, and the blow to British patriotic pride when early human fossils were unearthed at Heidelberg in 1907.

And while circumstances provide fertile ground for hoaxes, technological advances – particularly those that spread information far and wide – have rendered some ground barren. How many people would today fall for the yarns about foreign lands spun by the likes of Psalmanazar, Mandeville, or de Rougemont, for instance? And yet, everything has potential, especially for the hoaxer . . .

2

Puffers and Bluffers

'I never cease to be amazed at how seriously people take themselves, unable to see the funny images we all reflect in everything we say or do.'

Alan Abel

'There is a strong tendency in the human mind to flatter itself with secret hopes, with some lucky reservation in our own favour, though reason may point out the grossness of the trick in general.'

William Hazlitt, Puffing

The printed word and more modern means of mass communication have done much to banish ignorance and give people the security of knowledge. Even though books might have spread fantastical tales, they also spread learning; newspapers, radio, then television – all became trusted sources of information. Through two world wars the wireless gained massive credence. And by the late 1950s television had become accepted as a respectable and reliable medium, BBC Television matching BBC Radio's high quality. Come 1957 the Panorama programme was established as serious and trustworthy; the journalist Richard Dimbleby had gained an unrivalled reputation for utmost integrity in his reportage, when, over pictures of Swiss spaghetti orchards, his totally dependable voice supplied the commentary:

> Spaghetti cultivation here in Switzerland is not of course carried out on anything like the scale of the Italian industry. Many of you, I'm sure, will have seen pictures of the vast spaghetti plantations in the Po Valley. For the Swiss, however, it

plantations in the Po Valley. For the Swiss, however, it tends to be a family affair . . .

He went on to talk of the spaghetti weevil, and to explain why spaghetti was of such uniform lengths. An enormous number of viewers were persuaded that what they were watching was genuine; engrossed, they were oblivious to the date – 1 April. As James Thurber said, 'You can fool too many of the people too much of the time',[1] and for this hoaxers are profoundly grateful. The Spaghetti Hoax has become legendary, but do people ever learn?

Twelve years later, on 1 April 1979, Capital Radio in London broadcast a story that Britain was out of synchronization with other countries because of the constant changing to and from British Summer Time. It was explained that this discrepancy had occurred gradually since 1945, and that as a result Britain was some forty-eight hours ahead of the rest of the world. The Government had, therefore, come up with a scheme – Operation Parallax – to put the clocks back to immediate post-war settings. To do this, the Government had decided to cancel 5 and 12 April. That Capital Radio then received hundreds of anxious calls isn't perhaps surprising. Radio and television have both manoeuvred themselves into positions where whatever they say is believed. Not everyone is aware of April Fools' Day when it arrives. What is surprising is the depth of anxiety aroused and the alacrity with which listeners projected how this would affect their lives. Among the worried callers to Capital Radio was a man who was due to sell his house on one of the cancelled days, and who wished to know what would be his legal position.

Thus have mass communication and mass information created the very means by which far bigger – or, at least, wider-ranging – hoaxes and practical jokes are accomplished. The news reporter and the newsreader give authority to almost any statement. 'It must be true,' we used to say. 'It was in the newspapers.' Now, a little more guardedly, we say, 'It's probably true – I saw it on television.' We accept as the truth so many things that are in print: our bank statements, our telephone bills, the claims of most advertisers, railway timetables (despite experience to the contrary), the captions to photographs and, still, what the papers say. It stretches even the imagination of the staff at *Sunday Sport* to come up with a story that no one will accept. The headline 'WORLD WAR TWO BOMBER FOUND

ON MOON' may have been too much to swallow, but there were those who believed a report a couple of years earlier that the Russians were responsible for Britain's bad weather. In the words of Edmund Bergler: 'Nobody so far has been able to explain by conscious logic the ridiculous respect for printed matter in the average adult.'[2]

Perhaps we have this respect because we want to believe what we are told. Normal life could not go on if we didn't trust most of the people most of the time. We may not actually believe that nine out of ten cat owners said that their pets preferred a certain brand of cat food, but we don't seek to challenge this claim. Indeed, the law of contract has incorporated within its framework a tolerance of what it refers to as an advertiser's 'puff'. We are content with what we see as the truth, or a near approximation to it. So the ground is beautifully prepared for those who wish to hoax us. It only needs a little extra stupidity or ignorance or vulnerability to be added to the basic trust in our society for the hoaxer to be in business. And, once believed, some hoaxes never seem to go away. In 1917 H L Mencken wrote an article called 'A Neglected Anniversary' which was published on 28 December in the New York *Evening Mail*. It was a light-hearted piece, intended to raise a laugh or two during the dark days of the First World War. It purported to be a history of the US bath-tub, beginning with the arrival of the first bath-tub in Cincinnati in 1842. Mencken provided an inventor, one Adam Thompson, who was supposed to have got the idea from Lord John Russell, and described the struggle that had taken place to establish the bath-tub in American society. Virginia, he wrote, had introduced a special bath tax. Doctors had claimed it threatened public health. In Boston a by-law had been passed banning bathing on all but medical grounds. The fact that these two statements are mutually contradictory didn't alert readers to the possibility that this was a hoax. The article was taken at face value.

Nine years later, Mencken tried to undo what he had done in another article, 'Melancholy Reflections'. This was published in over thirty newspapers, and in it Mencken admitted that his history of the American bath-tub was totally spurious. The hoax refused to go away. The original article was still accepted as genuine. 'Facts' taken from it were used by President Truman in a speech he made in Philadelphia in 1952, as illustrations of the great advances that had been made in public health.

Many a dishonest buck has been earned by selling fiction as fact. Ralph Delahaye Paine was a young reporter in the United States in the 1890s. He invented a French immigrant named Pierre Grantaire, and wrote an article in which he described how Grantaire ran a spider farm. Grantaire, according to Paine, had invented a new industry – the breeding and selling of special spiders. His buyers were wine merchants who wished to 'cobweb' new wine bottles to give them the appearance of great age. Paine claimed that Grantaire had four thousand spiders of the species *Nephila plumipes* and *Epeira vulgaris*. This was another hoax that refused to go away. It was still being reported as genuine in the 1930s.

In *The Pleasures of Deception* Norman Moss has written: 'Time and again in looking at hoaxes, we find that people have accepted the most unlikely things because to question them would be to question something they have already accepted as true.'[3] Moss cites several examples of this. In one case a man described as 'a highly intelligent scholar' was persuaded to stand in his socks, striking a telephone with a fountain pen, and then to lower the phone into a bucket of water. It was possible to manipulate him in this way because he was convinced (wrongly) that his telephone was out of order and he was impatient to have the fault traced and rectified. The manipulator on this occasion was R V Jones, a much respected professor of physics. Jones made a study of practical joking, and published a paper on it. He believed that 'we are hoaxed when we fail to distinguish the evidence of our senses from the conclusion we draw from it'.[4]

One simple example of this is a hoax played by Harry Reichenbach on a leading motion picture studio back in the 1920s. Reichenbach was a friend of an actor named Francis X Bushman, subsequently best known for the villainous role he played in the silent version of *Ben Hur*. At the time of the hoax, Bushman was comparatively unknown. He had been acting in Chicago at a salary of $250 a week, when Reichenbach brought him to New York to sign a contract with Metro Pictures. Reichenbach met Bushman off the train and walked with him to the offices of the film studios. He had already stuffed his pockets with two thousand pennies. As the two men walked along the streets, Reichenbach dropped fistfuls of pennies at regular intervals. Children snatched up the pennies as they fell and began following Reichenbach and Bushman. A large crowd gathered, adults followed the children to see what all the fuss was about. By the time they reached the Metro offices, the crowd was enormous. The Metro people were impressed at Bushman's apparent fame and offered Bushman $1,000 a week. The evidence they had before their eyes was a crowd of people following an actor. The conclusion they drew was that the crowd was there *because* the man was a famous actor.

After his early career as a fairground barker, Reichenbach became a successful New York press agent who repeatedly played on this human weakness. Although he played for money, it is perhaps fairer to regard him as a practical joker rather than a conman. His targets were the mighty and the powerful, and it was their arrogance that he attacked rather than their wallets. His most famous hoax is called *September Morn*, the name of a painting by Paul Chabas, a French artist who worked in the early 1900s. This painting depicts a nude young girl, standing at the edge of the sea on a chill September morning. Reproductions of this painting came to the United States around 1902 but didn't sell, even at ten cents a copy. One Brooklyn shopkeeper was left with hundreds (some accounts say two hundred, some say two thousand), and offered Reichenbach $45 if he could find a market for the pictures. Reichenbach told him to place a copy of the painting on display in his shop-window.

Reichenbach telephoned the head of the New York Anti-Vice League, a man named Anthony Comstock, and complained about the picture in the shop-window. Comstock took no notice and refused to be drawn. Reichenbach then elaborated the hoax. He paid a group of 'urchins' to goggle and leer lecherously at the picture in the window, and went himself to the office of the Anti-Vice League. Here he shouted at Comstock and demanded that something be done. Comstock agreed to take a look at *September Morn*, and was suitably horrified. The shopkeeper refused to remove the picture from the window and Comstock took him to court. The subsequent legal battle made the painting famous overnight. The shopkeeper sold all his reproductions, and the original was sold for $70,000 many years later.

Early in his career, Reichenbach had worked for a shyster psychic medium who styled himself 'The Great Reynard', a significantly foxy name. On one occasion, to bolster a sagging reputation, Reynard bribed a mother to part with her baby for a while. He told Reichenbach to hide the baby in a nearby barn. The alarm was then raised that the baby had disappeared. When neither the parents nor the police could find the missing infant, Reynard used his psychic powers to 'discover' where the child lay, and led them to the barn. It was Reichenbach's job to create and promote the myth that Reynard had these special powers, and he gradually made an important discovery about the workings of the human mind and the insatiable appetite of many people's egos.

> Reynard's faculty of gradually believing the flattering fictions that I built around him struck me as rather peculiar. But later on, when I handled famous movie stars like Rudolph Valentino, Wallace Reid, Barbara La Marr and others, I realized this was the irony of all publicity. No matter how fantastic the ruse by which an unknown actor is lifted to fame, he'd come to believe it was true, and the poor press agent would be shocked to find that he had never told a lie.[5]

The problem is that there seems to be a ready market for lies, exaggerations, fantasies, for what Phineas T Barnum called 'humbugging', and for the sort of stories that pad out newspapers during the silly season. In 1898, E J Stroller White was working as a journalist in Dawson, Alaska. He was asked by the editor of the *Klondike Nugget* to come up with tall stories when news was slow, which it was quite often in Dawson. After a violent snowstorm, White wrote a piece about the arrival of ice worms from nearby glaciers. These creatures were attracted by the sudden drop in temperature to intense cold. 'The little critters,' wrote White, 'come to the surface to bask in the unusual frigidity in such numbers that their chirping is seriously interfering with the slumber of Dawson's inhabitants.' The ice worms, which do exist, are still remembered at an annual Ice Worm Festival in Cordova, Alaska every February when a 150-foot, multi-legged ice worm marches in a parade down Main Street.

In Winsted, a small town about a hundred miles north of New York, near the state line that separates Connecticut from Massachusetts, a town sign was erected many years ago in honour of a man who spent much of his adult life inventing lies about the town, some of which were believed by some of the people, some of the time.

WINSTED

Founded in 1779, has been put on the map by the ingenious and queer stories that emanate from this town and which are printed all over the country thanks to L T Stone.

Louis Stone became known as The Winsted Liar. His stories took the form of outrageous claims made in respect of the people of Winsted. The town was supposed to have a man who painted a spider on his bald head to keep away flies; a deaf and dumb pig; a chicken that laid red, white and blue eggs on Independence Day; a cow that gave hot milk after grazing on horseradish; a farmer who plucked his chickens with a vacuum cleaner; a cat with a harelip that whistled 'Yankee Doodle'; a modest cow that would let only women milk her; and a tree that grew baked apples. Of course, it is all quite ridiculous, except that in the light of what we know about factory farming, isn't it possible that some farmers do pluck their chickens with vacuum cleaners? And if one of Louis Stone's stories could be true, maybe the others could be, too – as true, that is, as the report that there is now a bridge in Winsted that bears Stone's name and crosses Sucker Brook.[6]

The lies of Stroller White and Stone were harmless. They were merely items of fun, sufficiently far-fetched not to upset the status quo in either Dawson or Winsted. And, so long as a joke or a hoax doesn't upset the status quo, so long as it is relatively ineffective, nobody needs to investigate it, to push it and prod it, to hold it up to the light, or to take it to pieces. Most hoaxers, however, very much want their skulduggery to have impact. Hoaxing is about exercising power over other people, about making them abandon the truth and put their faith in the false. What is surprising is not that there should be such power-seekers, but that they should spend so much time and trouble over the exercise of a power that may exist for little longer than a mayfly, and that they should include in their ranks those who seem already to be in sufficiently powerful positions.

An example of this is my own favourite hoax and hoaxer. Morris Newburger was a conservative and wealthy New York stockbroker and a partner in the firm of Newburger, Loeb and Company. He was a great fan of American football, but it annoyed him that coverage was given in the press to teams from the backsticks and beyond – the example that is usually cited is a team called Slippery Rock. In 1941 Newburger decided to invent a team of his own, the Plainfield Teachers. He then phoned the *New York Herald Tribune* to give the paper a report of the Teachers' most recent game against Beacon Institute, whom they had beaten 20-0 (some accounts say the game was against Scott and that the Teachers won 12-0). His phone call was so well received that Newburger then contacted the *New York Times*, United Press and Associated Press and gave them similar match reports.

Newburger's hoax was a simple flight of fancy. He conjured something out of nothing, created a team that didn't exist, drew up a fixture list of matches that were never played, and invented a new persona for himself as sportswriter Jerry Croyden. Every report that he filed to the papers that season was by-lined 'From the Desk of Jerry Croyden'. He covered the Plainfield Teachers with glory, letting them win a high percentage of their games. The star of the team was Johnny Cheung, 'The Celestial Comet', a two-hundred-and-twelve-pound, 'full-blooded' Chinese American, who gulped down bowls of rice between halves of each football game. Croyden heaped praise on Cheung, predicting that the guy had an All American future. Other (genuine) sportswriters picked up this story. Herb Allen of the *New York Post* wrote a feature article on Cheung – a man he had never seen and who didn't exist.

The Teachers' coach was Ralph 'Hurry Up' Hoblitzel, famed for his unique W information, using a special five-man backfield. Newburger allowed himself a slice of fabricated glory by including one Morris Newburger in the team as tackle. With such stars the Teachers went from victory to victory. Newburger was preparing them for a crack at the Blackboard Bowl Championship, but the hoax fell apart. Some say too many people knew about it, among them a couple of real sportswriters. Others say Newburger was betrayed to Caswell Adams of the *New York Herald Tribune* by a friend who worked for the phone company and who overheard Newburger admitting the hoax during a private phone call. Adams broke the story of the hoax on 14 November 1941, and it was passed to *Time* Magazine who told Newburger they were about to expose him. Newburger is said to have begged *Time* to hold off until the end of the season, but the magazine took a strict and truthful line – *Time* has never been an easy target for hoaxes, as Clifford Irving was to learn thirty years later.

There was time only for one last report 'From the Desk of Jerry Croyden'. Sadly, wrote Newburger, six of the Teachers, including Johnny Cheung, had been declared ineligible for the team after failing their mid-term exams. Coach 'Hurry Up' Hoblitzel had been forced, therefore, to cancel the remaining games of the season.

The media are magnets for hoaxers, and the motivation behind a great many hoaxes is the desire to get into print or at least to get one's name in the papers. Early in his life, Hugh Troy bet his sister that he could get a poem of his printed in the *New York Times*. He wrote a letter to the paper requesting information about a poem he was trying to trace. It was, wrote Troy, 'by an American, I believe, with some particularly moving stanzas about a gypsy maiden abandoned on the trail by her tribe'. Troy signed the letter 'Titus Grisby' – hoaxers like names with a sense of atmosphere. He waited until his letter was published by the *New York Times*, and then wrote a second letter to the paper, under a second assumed name, G Claude Fletcher. This letter picked up the query of the first letter. 'Titus Grisby must be referring to the beautiful "Curse of the Gypsy Mandolin", written in 1870 by the celebrated Poet Laureate of Syracuse, New York – Hugh Troy.' The second letter, quoting the poem in its entirety, was also published. Troy won his bet.

Troy was a man who indulged in hoaxing for much of his life, although professionally he was in the CIA until his death in 1967. That an Intelligence Agency should employ a hoaxer may surprise no one, but, unlike the CIA, most of Troy's hoaxes were harmless. One winter, while he was a student at Cornell University, Troy 'borrowed' a waste-paper basket that was reputedly made out of the foot of a rhinocerous. With this, one night, he made tracks in the snow leading down to a lake which was frozen save for one large black hole in the ice. The next day, the public drew the conclusion that Troy had wished them to – that a rhinocerous had blundered through the campus and had drowned in the icy waters of the lake.

In November 1935 there was an important and popular exhibition of Van Gogh's paintings at the Museum of Modern Art in New York. 'Those who had perhaps begun to think that the art of Vincent Van Gogh was perhaps over-rated,' reported the *New York Times* of 11 November, 'are pretty certain to find such misgivings set at rest. Here was an art gallery packed like a popular department store on the

Saturday before Christmas. These people had come just to look at paintings. It was another sign that the champions of American culture need not despair.' Among the crowd was Troy, who became annoyed when he found that they made it very difficult to see the paintings. So he bought a piece of beef, which he trimmed and modelled to resemble a bloodstained human ear. This he placed in a velvet-lined box on a pedestal in the Museum with an accompanying card, which read:

> THIS IS THE EAR WHICH VINCENT VAN GOGH
> CUT OFF AND SENT TO HIS MISTRESS, A FRENCH
> PROSTITUTE – 24 DECEMBER 1888

The aim of the hoax was to draw people's attention away from the paintings to view this horrific exhibit. According to Troy, it worked, and he was able to view the paintings at his ease. But then, if we are to believe hoaxers, their hoaxes always work.

Troy's most successful hoax, and one whose results have been authenticated by others, was also connected with paintings. In his spare time Troy was a writer – in 1947 he published a children's book called *Five Golden Wrens* – and he was therefore aware of the phenomenon of ghost-writing, where a person puts his or her name to a book that has been written by someone else. Troy took this a stage further, and invented ghost-painting, placing this advertisement in the *Washington Post*:

> TOO BUSY TO PAINT?
> CALL ON GHOST ARTISTS, 1426 33rd STREET, NW
> WE PAINT IT – YOU SIGN IT!
> PRIMITIVE (GRANDMA MOSES TYPE), IMPRESSIONIST,
> MODERN, CUBIST, ABSTRACT, SCULPTURE...
> ALSO, WHY NOT GIVE AN EXHIBITION?

If anything, the hoax worked too well. The Thirty-third Street address was flooded with applications, and ghost-painting became a reality rather than a joke. There are still those making a living practising the art.

After the cruelty to animals displayed by Watters and Reichenbach (see pages 2 and 3), it's a relief to come across an animal hoax played by another American, Brian Hughes, at the end of the nineteenth century. Hughes was a journalist who came to the conclusion that there was a large element of chance in the distribution of prizes at the New York City Annual Cat Show. He bought an alley cat for ten cents, fed it sirloin steak for a number of weeks and had it expertly groomed. He then entered the cat in the Show as an example of the rare 'Dublin Brindle' breed. The cat won first prize.

The most fecund American hoaxer is Alan Abel, who now makes his living by creating hoaxes to order as part of publicity campaigns for many American firms. Abel has spent time developing a philosophy of hoaxing. He believes that laughter is healthy and that most of us, especially the media, have insatiable appetites for practical jokes and hoaxes. He also believes that there are an enormous number of potential victims. 'People will swallow anything at all, providing you give it to them with a serious demeanour. A serious manner implies serious intent.'[7] But he draws an important distinction between the acceptable and unacceptable hoax. To think crazily and act seriously is wrong (e.g. to plant a bomb on a plane while appearing to be a legitimate baggage handler). To think seriously and act crazily is right (e.g. offering $100 bills for rent, so that people can impress their friends).

Most of Abel's hoaxes have begun with the despatch of a totally unreliable press release. This launches the falsehood down the slipway into the trusted waters of the media. If the papers climb aboard, then the hoax is half-way to achieving credibility. In 1967 he sent out a release that announced the arrival in the United States of the Topless String Quartet, 'France's first gift to America since the Statue of Liberty'. The Topless String Quartet was thus presented from the beginning in a slightly off-beat, light-hearted way, making it far more credible as a phenomenon than if it had been presented too seriously.

The Quartet consisted of a cellist and three violinists. All were, of course, women, and their names were Madeleine Boucher, Michele André, Maria Tronchet and Gretchen Gansebrust. Gansebrust, said Abel, was Swedish for 'goosebreast': in reality it isn't Swedish for anything. Abel explained that the Quartet played topless as that enabled them to produce 'unhampered' tones, a pure sound not damped down by clothing. He stressed, however, that the Quartet would perform only for 'private concerts under strict conformity to local laws'. The *New York Post* phoned for more details. Abel then hired four models and paid them for a photo session at which they appeared as the Topless String Quartet, clad in white, formal length skirts with cummerbunds. A pianist named Jacques Goldetsky was produced to accompany them. Abel sent the photographs to twenty leading papers and magazines across the United States. The *San Francisco Chronicle* (an old victim of Abel) was interested. *Life* Magazine, four years away from falling for Irving's hoax, printed an article about the Quartet. The hoax took off. Abel received hundreds of requests for autographed photographs of the Quartet, agents contacted him wishing to promote recitals, Frank Sinatra wanted the Quartet to sign a recording contract with his Reprise label.

Three years earlier, Abel entered a candidate in the US Presidential Election. He was bored with the official candidates and with the expectation that Lyndon Johnson would have a runaway success. The press were hungry for stories about the small-time candidates. Abel introduced Yetta Bronstein as one such candidate on a phone-in radio programme in which he was taking part. Yetta's ideas including postage stamps of a nude Jane Fonda, to help the US Post Office raise money and 'also to give a little pleasure for six cents to people who can't afford *Playboy*', and the posting of a suggestions box on the White House railings. Her campaign headquarters were in New York, where she became instantly popular. Handbills appeared in the streets: 'VOTE FOR YETTA AND WATCH THINGS GET BETTER'. Callers to Yetta's office were greeted with a recorded message: 'So why are you calling me? Isn't there something better you have to do?' Publicly, Yetta admitted that she knew nothing of foreign policy, but that, if she was elected, she would force the State department to publish details about US relationships with every other country in the world, in language which everyone could understand, including herself. She provided a welcome change from the campaign proper and was revived by Abel in the elections for Mayor of New York City in 1968, under the banner 'NEW YORK NEEDS A MOTHER'. Yetta was always presented as an archetypal mother figure. In reality, she was Abel's young wife, Jeanne.

In the 1950s Abel created his most famous hoax. The inspiration for it came one day when Abel was stuck in a traffic jam. In a field bordering the road, two horses were copulating. Abel noticed how strong, and how varied, were people's reactions to this as they sat imprisoned in their cars while the horses performed. Most found it embarrassing, and either laughed or turned away in outraged indignation. So Abel invented G Clifford Prout Junior and the Society for Indecency to Naked Animals, or SINA for short. The aim of the Society was to clothe all animals, and their slogan was: 'Decency Today Means Morality Tomorrow'.

SINA was originally conceived not as a hoax, but as a satirical short story, which Abel wrote but never published. Then he realized that it would be possible to turn it into 'a living social satire, an allegory cloaked with the absurd purpose of putting panties on pets, half-slips on cows, and Bermuda shorts on horses'.[8] Sadly, SINA's true intention failed, because, Abel said, 'hardly anyone recognized it as satire'. The trouble was that too many people took it seriously. There were those who thought that G Clifford Prout was a crank, and those who thought he was a saviour. Few thought he couldn't be real. The part of Prout was always played by Buck Henry, an actor who worked in New York, subsequently perhaps best known for his role as the hotel receptionist in *The Graduate*, a film of which he was also the co-writer.

Henry and Abel began their campaign quietly. Mr Prout Junior, it was said, had inherited a great deal of money from his father, and it was Clifford Prout Senior's wish that this money should be used to educate the masses so that they would cover the indecent parts of brute creation. Abel told NBC that Mr Prout planned to build up membership of the society before opening offices and going nationwide with membership drives and big publicity campaigns. This was a subtle and effective approach. By suggesting that he didn't want big publicity, Abel was almost certain to get it. In May 1959 Mr Prout appeared on NBC's *Today* programme, preaching that all animals over four inches tall should be clothed for the sake of decency. 'Why do cows have their heads down in fields? Not because they're grazing, but because they're hanging their heads in shame.'

Prout was an immediate success. Abel ordered thousands of propaganda leaflets, hired pickets to march to and fro outside the White House, and engaged a full-time telephone answering service on MOrality-1-1963. SINA became big news, and Henry had to make several more radio and television appearances as Prout: *The Jack Paar Show* on 2 and 4 June 1959, NBC Radio's *Dave Garroway Show* on 14 June. Garroway was suspicious and realized it was a hoax, but chose not to expose it. SINA went from strength to strength. The society managed to get a giant papier-mâché horse removed from the window of the New York office of Northwest Orient Airlines, after Prout complained to the Fifth Avenue Business Committee that displaying even a model naked horse was offensive to right-minded people. Prout complained about the RCA Victor dog 'Nipper', who still adorns HMV records, and ordered Brigadier-General Sarnoff, head of RCA, to clothe the beast.

Abel organized parades at which the SINA Marching Band appeared, playing a weird variety of instruments in whatever key suited them. 'It was horrible to hear and ridiculous to see, but because we were carrying the American flag and looking serious, everyone along the way applauded.'[9] Prout visited farms and zoos, gaining more and more publicity for SINA. The hoax became almost too successful. The Internal Revenue Service wrote demanding back taxes on the $400,000 that Prout Senior had bequeathed to his son, and, not satisfied with the written replies they received, paid a visit to SINA's office. This was a broom cupboard that Abel rented in a New York office block, large enough only for the mail that was regularly thudding in. The IRS then suspected fraud and threatened to prosecute SINA. Abel, as Prout's manager, persuaded them to grant a six-month extension on their demand and then played for more time as the hoax ran its course. Eventually, the Department accepted that it was all a hoax and left Prout and Abel alone, not wishing to appear stupid or lacking in a sense of humour.

Meanwhile, Prout was talking to groups of supporters from coast to coast across the United States. Forty thousand letters were delivered to the broom cupboard in New York. The *Los Angeles Chronicle* printed an in-depth interview and article about Prout. Walter Cronkite interviewed Prout on television, giving the society seven minutes of prime-time television. Abel was ecstatic. But the end was nigh. Buck Henry's career as an actor was prospering. He became too well known after being given a role in a TV soap. He was identified as Prout and SINA's head gave no more television interviews. Nevertheless, six years later there were those who still believed the society was genuine and who still wished to pledge their support. In 1966 Abel wrote:

After six years with SINA I realize now that some people who were taken in will never forgive me. Others will never see anything funny about the spoof. Far too many will never be able to dismiss SINA as a hoax because the indelible print of the newspaper stories and the sound of my determined voice on radio and television linger on and on . . . From an unpublished short story to a gag, to a 'social experiment', and, finally, a game to see how long it could last, SINA seems to have achieved an enigmatic state of immortality.[10]

Abel's approach to hoaxing has always been professional, which is perhaps why he nowadays makes his living supplying hoaxes to order. British-born hoaxes have tended to be less carefully prepared and to be more class-based – they are performed by the middle classes on the middle or upper classes. Cole's Sultan of Zanzibar and *Dreadnought* hoaxes were both aimed at the British Establishment, and most of his other hoaxes sought to puncture the pompous and the proud. Only once did he select working-class victims, and that appears to have been very much a spur-of-the-moment hoax. He bore a strong resemblance to Ramsay MacDonald, then leader of the Labour Party, and one day a group of workmen digging up a road did indeed mistake him for MacDonald, put down their shovels and went up to him to shake his hand. Cole, whose sister married Neville Chamberlain and whose politics were well to the right, is said to have delivered a lecture to them on the evils of socialism and then gone on his way, leaving the men puzzled and angry. Cole had no witnesses to this hoax, but his friends readily believed it was true. Nowadays, Labour leaders deliver their own lectures on the evils of socialism.

Cole is also credited with the invention of the piece-of-string hoax. He picked a victim at random off the street, and asked him to hold one end of a length of string. Cole then took the other end of the string and went round the corner. Here he gave the string to another victim and then walked away. In every account of this hoax, the men are said to have stood there, holding the ends of the string, for a considerable length of time. One authority even suggests half an hour.

Better authenticated is the trick that Cole pulled on a Conservative MP and old friend, Oliver Locker-Lampson. Locker-Lampson was a man of little compassion for the poor and the unfortunate, whom he believed deserved every trial and tribulation that came their way.

Cole argued that the humiliation of arrest and incarceration would turn even an innocent man against society. Locker-Lampson would have none of this, and averred that 'A truly innocent man would no sooner be arrested on a London street than I.'[11] This sort of remark was the equivalent of smacking Cole in the face with a glove, and Cole decided to teach him a lesson.

He slipped his watch into Locker-Lampson's pocket and then suggested that they should have a race. Locker-Lampson was a man who loved a challenge, no matter now witless, and the heavyweight pair started to sprint towards Bond Street. Cole waited until Locker-Lampson got ahead and then shouted: 'That man's stolen my watch!' Locker-Lampson was collared as he panted along Bury Street, and a policeman was summoned. Sure enough, Cole's watch was found in Locker-Lampson's pocket. Cole explained that it was all a joke, but the policeman arrested the pair of them on the charge of 'using insulting words and behaviour whereby a breach of the peace might have been occasioned'. Cole was imprisoned overnight and fined five pounds the following day. On learning of this incident, Winston Churchill is reported to have said that Cole was 'a dangerous man to his friends'.[12]

Cole married twice, each time to a woman half his age. His first marriage was in 1919 when he was thirty-six and he and his bride spent their honeymoon in Venice, where Cole appears once again to have become bored. On the eve of April Fools' Day, he persuaded a gondolier to take him to the mainland where he bought a load of horse manure from a riding stables. Under cover of darkness, he returned to the canal city and deposited the manure in small heaps over the Piazza San Marco. In the morning, Venetians were puzzled as to how horses could have crossed the canals, paraded round the Piazza, and then disappeared. Cole's first wife, Denise Daly, frequently corroborated that this hoax took place, but never suggested that she derived any joy from it. She may well also have been bored while on honeymoon. They were divorced a few years later.

Pranks of this nature have long been practised in England. In 1810 Theodore Hook made a wager with one Samuel Beazley, for a guinea, that he could make any 'unassuming house' the most talked-about address in England. The 'unassuming house' Hook chose was 54 Berners Street, in the West End of London, a very middle-class interpretation of 'unassuming'. The house belonged to Mrs

Tottenham, and a few days later, on 10 November, she was woken early in the morning by the first of many visitors. Some coalmen had arrived with a delivery. They were immediately followed by a furniture van, confectioners with a wedding cake, costermongers with vegetables, an organ carried by six men, flowers, bread, fish and meat. Chimney sweeps arrived, doctors, lawyers, dentists, coach and cabinet makers, opticians, clockmakers, coachmen, footmen, wig makers, housemaids, gardeners, nursemaids, ladies' maids, undertakers (complete with hearse and coffin), and a brewer's dray. The Governor of the Bank of England arrived, in expectation of a generous endowment from a wealthy widow, followed by the Chairman of the East India Company, the Archbishop of Canterbury, the Lord Chief Justice, the Duke of Gloucester and the Lord Mayor of London.

Hook duly collected his guinea from Beazley. He had won his wager, but he had written over four thousand letters in the process. How long this took him and how much it cost him, we do not know.

Cole and Abel became public figures through the stunts they pulled, but there is a sprinkling of people who achieved considerable reputations in more legitimate occupations and who occasionally turned to hoaxing for light relief. In the early 1960s a letter appeared in *The Times* on the subject of the Anglo-Texan Friendship Society. The letter said that this society had been established out of the desire to strengthen '... cultural and social links between this country and the State of Texas'. The letter stated that a special relationship existed between Britain and Texas though it failed to show exactly what this consisted of, and nobody subsequently asked. The letter was signed by John Sutro and Graham Greene.

Greene was at that time in his late fifties and in the middle of a prolific period in his career. *Our Man in Havana* had been made into a film in 1959, his novel *A Burnt-Out Case* had been published in 1961, and Michael Redgrave had opened in *The Complaisant Lover* on Broadway in the same year. It was perhaps time for a little fun. The *New York Times* was suspicious: 'We feel scepticism, like a calcium deposit, residing right in our bones ... We wonder whether Mr Greene doesn't have some insidious plot underfoot.' Others, however, took the letter at face value and Sutro and Greene received sixty genuine replies, including one from the Attorney-General (Sir Hartley Shawcross) and another from Samuel Guinness, a leading merchant banker.

As in the case of the Society for Indecency in Animals and Hugh Troy's Ghost Artists, what started as a joke became a serious proposition. A genuine Anglo-Texan Society was formed, a meeting was called, officers were elected (among them Samuel Guinness), and a programme of social and cultural events was drawn up. The United States Air Force organized a giant barbecue at which the US Ambassador presented Sutro with the Texan flag. The Duke of Edinburgh attended a cocktail party and reception held in London. A plaque was unveiled on the site of the old Republic of Texas Embassy in Pickering Place off St James's Street. Sutro and Greene left the Society but it continued to flourish.

How far hoaxing is a worldwide phenomenon is difficult to assess, as almost all the examples that we hear about come from Europe or North America – perhaps it's more a product of an industrially advanced society. In the 1960s and 1970s, hoaxers were particularly active in New York and California. Although they were called 'pranksters' rather than hoaxers, their aims were serious and their methods often dangerous. Many of the pranksters were painters, sculptors, performance artists or writers. Many of them had leanings towards anarchism. They were strong on philosophy, and many subscribed to a Pranksters Creed: 'A prank should have a resonance and ring to it. It should speak of the higher aspirations of human activity. It should go far beyond the limitations one should expect it to have.'[13] How far strewing the streets of a city with tin tacks, or taping fireworks to one's body and exploding oneself at a class reunion, or donning a doctor's gown and touring a hospital giving women unscheduled pelvic examinations achieves these lofty aims isn't too clear. The trouble is that hoaxes often get lumped with any old anti-social act, simply because a true hoax also has an inconvenience factor.

A lot of the American hoaxes made use of the telephone. One of the best was an off-the-cuff response to a wrong number call. If the caller asked 'Is Jack there?' the response wasn't 'I'm sorry, you have the wrong number', but 'Hang on. Who's calling?' This was followed by a pause, and then 'I'm sorry, Jack doesn't want to talk to you. Jack is still very angry with you and he doesn't want to discuss it'.[14] Another phone hoax was to phone a supermarket and report an escaped racoon in the fresh food warehouse. A more complicated trick was to call a number taken at random from the phonebook and report to the receiver of the call that the line needed repairs. The victim was told on no account to use the phone for the next five minutes, as to do so would endanger the life of the repairman. The hoaxer would then immediately phone the victim again. After the phone had rung and rung, most victims would eventually give up and answer, to be greeted by a scream down the line as though the repairman had been electrocuted.

Other hoaxers make use of animals, not always as cruelly as Watters and Reichenbach. Jeffrey Vallance bought a frozen chicken in a supermarket, and then took it in a shoebox to a pet cemetery in Los Angeles. He explained that the chicken, which he christened 'Blinky', had been a great friend of the family and that he wished it to be buried with due care and ceremony. The staff at the cemetery were at first suspicious, but co-operated enthusiastically once Vallance showed that he had the money to pay. Blinky was placed in a powder-blue coffin with pink lining, on a bed of paper tissues since he/she was still thawing. There was also a little pillow for Blinky's head, which, alas, was not present. Pallbearers lowered Blinky's coffin into a shallow grave in the astroturf and the ceremony was over.

While at university in 1969, Paul Mavrides and others staged an anti-Vietnam war protest by announcing that they were going to napalm a puppy publicly in Akron. The aim had been to bring a crowd together and then tell them that no puppy would be harmed, but that hundreds of innocent Vietnamese were being napalmed. The hoax backfired, simply because the crowd that gathered was so large, and so incensed, it was impossible to make any sort of announcement. Joey Skaggs, of whom more later (see page 168), persuaded United Press International that he had developed a strain of nuclear-proof cockroaches, whose extracted hormones could be made into a pill that would cure arthritis, acne and anaemia, and would also protect those taking it from nuclear radiation. Though the story smacks of the quack medicine men of the nineteenth century, this took place only twenty years ago.

These were short-term hoaxes, played largely to cock a snook at some aspects of society. They may have been serious, but their effect was transient. There are, however, hoaxers who are altogether more rapacious, and several of them have been Members of Parliament. Thomas Cochrane (1775-1860) was the tenth Earl of Dundonald. He was a sailor, with the forceful personality and independence of spirit that we associate with Captains in the Royal Navy during the time of Hornblower. In 1806 he was elected MP for Honiton in Devon. Cochrane had already crossed swords with the Admiralty, and other superiors several times, when in 1813 he met Captain de Berenger, a French refugee and an officer in one of the foreign regiments attached to the British Army. Late in February 1813, de Berenger sent word to London that Napoleon Bonaparte had been killed, that the Allies were in full march on Paris, and that peace was imminent.

De Berenger then posted up to London and headed straight for Cochrane's house in Green Street. Here he changed into civilian clothes which he borrowed from Cochrane. Meanwhile, the National Fund had risen dramatically on the Exchange, following the news of Napoleon's 'death'. Once it was established that this news was false, the Fund fell again, but not before de Berenger and Cochrane's uncle had made a great deal of money. Once he learnt of the hoax, Cochrane gave information that led to the arrest of de Berenger and his own uncle. But Cochrane was also arrested, convicted and sentenced to an hour in the pillory, a year in the King's Bench prison and a fine of £1,000. He was also struck off the Navy List and expelled from the House of Commons, only to be enthusiastically returned as MP for Westminster while in prison.

From this point Cochrane's story becomes an adventure tale. He escaped from prison, but was recaptured. His imprisonment was now made 'cruelly severe'. The authorities feared a popular rising in Cochrane's support, and offered him his liberty if he would pay the £1,000 fine. He did so, with a bank note, on the back of which he wrote: 'My health having suffered by long and close confinement . . . I submit myself to robbery to protect myself from murder, in the hope that I shall live to bring the delinquents to justice.'[15] The note is still preserved in the Bank of England. Cochrane's enemies had not finished with him. He was fined a further £100 for escaping from prison. He refused to pay, and was again imprisoned. This time the fine was raised by public 'penny' subscription and Cochrane was finally released after sixteen days.

The hoax was the work of de Berenger and Cochrane's uncle. Cochrane was that rare creature, an innocent politician. Jabez Balfour, however, was an MP and a rogue. In 1892 this description of him was sent by Lord Rosebery, Foreign Secretary in Gladstone's fourth cabinet, in a despatch from the Foreign Office.

> Age 50, looks 55; height 5'6"; broad shoulders; very corpulent; hair dark, turning grey, parted centre, thin top of head; eyebrows dark; nose short; face full; complexion florid; straggling beard; dark, slight whiskers, turning grey; dark, slight moustache; appearance of having weak legs; usually dressed in dark jacket; gentlemanly appearance.

There was little of the gentleman in Balfour. He was born in 1842, the son of a marine store dealer and a mother who wrote books of a moral nature, notably *The Women of Scripture* and *Moral Heroism*, said by some to be the inspiration for Samuel Smiles's *Self-help*.

Balfour's version of self-help was to pocket the savings of the poorer members of the community through the Liberator Society – motto *Libera sedes liberum facit* ('A free house makes a free man'). At first glance, Balfour was a pillar of respectability, a regular chapel-goer, a man with a reputation for generosity, and from 1880, an MP.

He was at his most seductive in the privacy of the humble homes of his investors. There he would persuade them to part with their tiny savings, with promises of fat capital growth and juicy dividends. The dividends, initially, were forthcoming. Balfour's simple trick was to pay interest and dividends out of new investment. There was no capital growth. As long as new funds flooded in, he was safe: A could be paid with B's money, B with C's and so on.

For a while, it worked. He became the first Mayor of Croydon, and the owner of a grand estate at Burcot Manor House near Oxford. He was described as 'a man of business turned squire . . . There was an air of genial ruffianism about him . . . and an open joviality'.[16] In the City, this 'joviality' vanished, and he got his way by hectoring and bullying. It is hard to like what one learns about Balfour. The best that can be said is that his was a consummate performance: bombastic, confident, single-minded, merciless.

He foresaw the end. When the Liberator crashed in 1892, he had already salted away some £40,000. He stayed long enough to be re-elected to Parliament, boasting that he expected high office in Gladstone's government. A couple of weeks later he scuttled to Argentina, 'the one country with any pretence of civilization where a criminal can live without fear of extradition'.[17] Two years later, detectives arrived from England, with a strong case for extradition. On the voyage back to Southampton, Balfour believed that he had won the hearts of Captain, crew and fellow passengers, who crowded the rails and wished him good luck when he was loaded into a police launch and whisked up the Solent. To avoid the crowd of waiting pressmen at Waterloo, Balfour was bundled out of the train at Vauxhall and taken to Bow Street. Here he was invited to rent a cell room in Holloway, where he could order any food or drink he liked, and where he paid another prisoner sixpence a day to clean his room.

A year later he was sentenced to two terms of seven years' imprisonment for fraud. The moment sentence was passed, Balfour's counsel rushed from the court, returning minutes later with bottles of champagne and some cakes. As a result, Balfour arrived at Wormwood Scrubs with a splitting headache. It was no more than he deserved. Under the twin banners of 'philanthropic finance' and the Temperance Movement (from which he sought many of his 'investors'), Balfour's Liberator Group had picked its targets with wicked deliberation. His was a masterly and disgraceful hoax.

Horatio William Bottomley was cast in a similar mould. Orphaned at the age of five, and placed by his uncle, G J Holyoake, in the Sir Josiah Mason Orphanage at Erdington, Bottomley's start in life was hard. At fourteen he was an errand boy, and then solicitor's clerk and shorthand writer in the Supreme Court of Judicature. For Bottomley was extremely intelligent, and his extraordinary self-confidence enabled him to pick up a variety of skills with ease. He was a demagogue in an age of demagogues. In ten years, from 1895 to around 1905, he promoted over fifty companies, with a total capital of over £20 million. Bottomley himself is estimated to have made over £3 million. He rang a string of racehorses, bought a country estate at Hailsham in Sussex, a flat in Pall Mall and a villa in the south of France. In 1906 he founded *John Bull*, a fervently patriotic magazine, and was elected Liberal MP for South Hackney. When the First World War broke out, he became 'The Tommies' Friend' and 'The Hater of the Hun', a man of high profile, delivering recruiting speeches and perorations to raise money for the war effort. He charged £50 a time for these speeches, slapping the notes into his pocket as he declaimed a poem that ran:

This is more than a war, mate,
It's a call to the human race . . .[18]

Set against this triumphant career were sixty-seven bankruptcy petitions between 1901 and 1905, the liquidation of his joint stock company in 1907, and a charge of fraud in 1909. Bottomley defended himself, skilfully and successfully – he was always at his most glibly brilliant with his back to the wall. In his financial dealings, he was more conman than hoaxer, but as a politician and journalist he had all the attributes of a hoaxer – histrionic talent, powers of persuasion, the ability to entice people into a world of his own making, and an adamantine determination to force his hoax through. When he finally fell from grace in 1922, receiving a seven-year sentence for fraudulent conversion, he said that fifty thousand ex-Servicemen would march on Westminster in his support. It was one of the few prophecies that he couldn't fulfil.

Arthur John Peter Michael Maundy Gregory was a hoaxer and conman who used his acting talent on the stage. His first professional acting role was in a play appropriately called *The Brixton Burglary*. For, like Bottomley, Maundy Gregory was a man of humble origins but rich appetite. He was born in 1877, began his career as an assistant master at a prep school, became a 'drawing-room entertainer', and then opened a theatrical agency. Here he answered the door dressed and made-up as an aged butler, shuffled away, and reappeared moments later as the debonair proprietor.

Like so many aspiring hoaxers, Maundy Gregory's luck began to change during the First World War. He had spent the pre-war years collecting information on what he described as 'foreigners and undesirables'. Once the war broke out, some of this information was considered valuable by security services. Maundy Gregory obtained an introduction to Whitehall. 'His subsequent activities are less certain, but it can be said that his remarkable genius and delightful manner won him a high place in the opinions of men of experience and probity.'[19]

The collapse of the Austro-Hungarian Empire, the Revolution in Russia, and the turbulent restructuring in the Balkans presented Maundy Gregory with further opportunities after the war. He began to specialize in the care of unthroned royals: King George of Greece, the Montenegrin Royal Family, Prince Davrilo of Serbia, and many White Russians. The decrepit butler was gone for good. Maundy Gregory wore elegant clothes, many rings on his fingers, and sported a heavy gold watch-chain with a large jewelled watch on the end. In his button-hole there was always an orchid. He carried gold cigarette cases. He rented magnificent offices at 10 Parliament Street. This enabled him to leave messages to the effect that he was 'over at Number Ten' with satisfactory deception. He had a London home in Hyde Park Terrace, a flat in Brighton, a bungalow on an island at Thames Ditton. He owned the Deepdene Hotel at Dorking, and two river launches. He had a fine library, a large wine cellar and several hundred statues of Narcissus. He bought the Ambassador Club in Conduit Street, and founded *The Whitehall Gazette*, a half-crown monthly whose ostensible object was to expose Moscow and all its wicked ways, 'while at the same time stressing all that a citizen of the British Empire could regard as natural and patriotic'.[20]

To keep all this going, he sold honours: £10,000 for a knighthood, £35,000 for a baronetcy. There was nothing new in such dealings. In the early 1920s the Coalition between Lloyd George's Liberals and the Conservatives had raised approximately £6 million by such sales. It was legal for a political party to sell honours. It wasn't legal for an individual to do so. Things began to go wrong. One of Maundy Gregory's customers paid £30,000 for a baronetcy, but didn't live long enough to receive it. The deceased's executors demanded a return of the money. At the same time, Maundy Gregory was being blackmailed by someone threatening to expose him as a homosexual.

In December 1932, he approached Lieutenant-Commander E W B Leake of the Royal Navy, telling him that the government were prepared to recommend Leake for a knighthood, but that the charge would be £12,000. Leake was at first curious, and then suspicious. He wanted to know where the money would go. Maundy Gregory gave him some vague answer that it would be used to fight socialism. Leake went to the police. On 16 February 1933, Maundy Gregory was tried by magistrates at Bow Street under the Honours (Prevention of Abuses) Act of 1925. He pleaded guilty on the advice of his counsel, Norman Birkett. He was fined £50 and sentenced to two months' imprisonment. It was the end of the high life.

Balfour, Bottomley and Maundy Gregory were all hoaxers of their times. Balfour traded on the humble investors' desire to participate in the economic boom of late Victorian Britain. Bottomley made and lost fortunes, taking advantage of gold, war or patriotic fever. Maundy Gregory sold titles while patricians and aristocrats all over Europe creakily joined together in the face of socialism. All three wrenched money from the grasp of thousands, but it eventually slipped through their own fingers.

3

Never Give a Sucker an Even Break

For every kid born with fifty dollars there's twins born on the other side of the street scheming to take the fifty from him.
Doc Crosby

In the late 1950s, the sunny suburban calm of Cheam Cricket Club, on the fringe of south-west London, was disturbed by the arrival, and later dramatic departure, of Brigadier Maxwell. He was always known as 'The Brigadier', and he had the instant respect of the entire membership. He was portly and of average height, with a well-tanned complexion that made the inhabitants of Cheam think Poona, Peshawar or Phagwara, rather than Wallington, Waddon and West Croydon. For much of the summer he wore a khaki shirt and khaki drill shorts of an unbecoming length, and occasionally carried a swagger stick. But it was his upright bearing, his powerful authoritarian voice, and the obvious expectation that he would be obeyed with military alacrity and precision, that made the entire suburb comply with his wishes. He took over the Colts team, frequently umpired 1st and 2nd Eleven matches, and marched round the grounds of the Club as though they were his own. Every Saturday afternoon, he was to he heard shouting at the little boys whose job it was to put up the metal number plates on the cricket scoreboard.

'Telegraph!' he would bellow, and there was a desperate clattering noise as the wrong numbers were taken down and the correct ones hastily displayed.

After a couple of years as CO, he disappeared, leaving a bundle of dud cheques, some ill-will, a baffled police force, and a Cricket Club whose members said that they had known all along there was something fishy about the Brigadier. But they hadn't, any more than they had known that he was not Brigadier, but Colour-Sergeant Maxwell. He had tricked everyone, for he had come down, like the Assyrian, on an innocent community, with a thoroughly plausible persona. In the outer suburbs, in the late 1950s, an ex-Indian Army Brigadier was a figure to be respected and to be proud of. Malden Wanderers Cricket Club didn't have a Brigadier, neither did the Beulah Bohemians, nor Southern Railway. For a few sunny seasons, he was Cheam Cricket Club's glory.

Colour-Sergeant Maxwell was able to hoax the entire population of a middle-class suburb because he was larger than life. A mere confidence trickster would have been content to present a respectable front and lull his victims into a false sense of trust simply by being ordinary, run-of-the-mill, unremarkable, even humdrum. Maxwell chose to make his hoax into a piece of theatre, giving himself the leading role and occupying centre stage all the time. There was nothing hole-in-the-corner about him: he strutted into the community and barked his presence and his pretence. Not for one moment did anyone suspect that he wasn't what he claimed. No one quizzed him about India or his military career (Where had he served? What had been his job in the Army? What regiment did he come from? What had he done in the War?). No one pressed him for verifiable information that might have led to awkward half-answers and eventual disclosure. Not until cheques began bouncing all over Sennacherib did it occur to anyone that the Brigadier should not have been taken at his well-bronzed face value.

Maxwell wasn't unique as a hoaxer. He was but one of a long line of conmen, impostors and humbugs who have happily operated in the glare of the spotlight, men of charm and persuasion, who smiled as they stole or as they deceived. These are hoaxers with a sense of theatre and a sense of humour, for the line between showbiz razzmatazz and hoaxing is seldom in clear focus, as the career of Harry Reichenbach illustrates.

Reichenbach (whom we have already met) was born in 1894 at Frostbury, Maryland. His father was an easygoing man who ran a small grocery store. His mother was spirited and active, the driving force in the family. Neither had much influence over their son, and

Reichenbach left home as soon as he could to join travelling circuses, fairs and medicine shows. Doc Crosby, who made his living peddling cures for a disease he called 'haemoglobin', impressed upon the young Reichenbach that 'It's dog eat dog all along the line . . . So the only way to make a ten strike is to strike up the band!'[1] Reichenbach was an apt pupil and was soon making a few dollars exhibiting a bowl of water containing 'The Only Living Brazilian Invisible Fish'.

When the United States entered the First World War, Reichenbach went to France and Italy, where he got to work on enemy morale. He claimed to have projected silent films from Italian trenches onto snow-covered mountains, for the benefit of the enemy troops in opposing trenches. The films were interspersed with anti-Austro-German propaganda. 'To me,' he wrote later,

> . . . the most striking piece of propaganda we devised was a diploma that we dropped over the German lines. This diploma qualified any German private who picked it up to come unmolested into the Allied trenches, surrender himself and immediately receive promotion to an officer's station. This meant that he would be treated as a prisoner of rank and be given the rations and considerations due an officer. On the back of the diploma we enumerated the different things he would get. So many grams of bread per meal, so many orders of meat per week, so many choices of vegetable, and so many packs of cigarettes. But the two items that proved to be the greatest inducements to surrender were the promise of 24 sheets of toilet paper per day and a delousing comb.[2]

In this, as in all Reichenbach's ploys and strategies, the real hoaxer was at work – according his victims a special status, holding out the promise of good things to come, taking advantage of the current situation, coaxing people from their harsh reality into his appealing fantasy. 'The whole difference between the things one dreamed about and reality was simply a matter of projection,'[3] he wrote. He became a publicity agent and headed for Hollywood. Here he worked with the founding fathers of the film industry: Sam Goldwyn, Harry Cohen, Adolph Zukor, and Carl Laemmle. According to Reichenbach, he *made* Metro Pictures. They hadn't released a single film when he began his publicity campaign for them based on the slogan 'CAN

THEY KEEP IT UP?' People assumed Metro must have been making films, and films of a high quality. Reichenbach even persuaded the judges at the Los Angeles Exposition to present Metro with a gold medal for Best Production, surely one of the only incidents of a film gaining an award before anyone had seen it.

For ten years Reichenbach pulled the most effective stunts in Hollywood. One of them, to coincide with the release of a somewhat shoddy film called *The Virgin of Stamboul*, involved the arrival in the States of a dashing young Turk and entourage, supposedly seeking his bride-to-be who had been abducted and whisked across the Atlantic. Reichenbach kept the story in the newspaper headlines day after day with details of the quest of the young man for the young woman. This culminated in a happy ending when the bride-to-be was found in a hotel bedroom. The public lapped up the story and, according to Reichenbach, believed (or at least wanted to believe) every word. 'There was the quality of fascination about the incident that made it almost better than truth. It had become romance, illusion. It was one of those episodes that gave public and press alike the feeling that if it didn't happen, it should have happened!'[4] Reichenbach here identifies one of the truths about many hoaxes. If what we are being offered isn't real, it should be. The only problem is to find the right hoax for the right victim. If the Emperor of Abyssinia didn't want to visit HMS *Dreadnought*, he should have. If Howard Hughes didn't want to sell McGraw-Hill his authorized biography, he should have. If it wasn't true that there were fairies at the bottom of the garden in Cottingley in 1917, it should have been true.

Reichenbach's hoaxes were part of the legitimate ballyhoo of the film industry, where publicity has always been larger than life, and where extravagant claims and promises are made in a special *lingua franca*. We may be disappointed when we go to see *The Greatest Motion Picture Ever Made*, as we were when we saw another film similarly hyped a couple of years ago, but we have at least seen a film, we have had something for our money. Reichenbach, with his Dancing Ducks, his Invisible Fish, and his Virgin of Stamboul, always gave the public something for their money. He practised deception all his life, but his 'pirouettes from reality to fantasy'[5] always kept on the right side of the law.

Oscar Merril Hartzell produced a single hoax in his lifetime, but it produced over two million dollars and, when it was exposed, almost all his seventy thousand victims refused to believe it was a hoax. Of all the tricksters who have fleeced the public, Hartzell, more than anybody else, managed to hold the loyalty and the credulity of his victims. If what he told them wasn't true, it should have been.

He was born in Madison County, Iowa, the son of a farmer. In 1913 he left home and moved to Des Moines where he came across Mrs Sudie B Whiteaker. Sudie Whiteaker is that rare specimen, a female hoaxer, and Hartzell borrowed her hoax and improved upon it. Hoaxes can often be recycled: the fake 'Mussolini Diaries' were offered for sale some ten years before the fake 'Hitler Diaries'; David Stein and Elmyr de Hory were producing 'Sexton Blake' Picassos and Renoirs long before Tom Keating; Horace Cole paid an unofficial state visit to a warship long before Stanley Weyman.

The hoax that Hartzell borrowed from Sudie Whiteaker (after her indictment) was simple. He offered for sale shares in the estate of the late Sir Francis Drake, seadog and freebooter during the reign of Elizabeth I and one of the most famous figures in English history. But Hartzell worked for eight years to make many improvements on the original hoax. First, he moved to England, a much better place from which to supervise operations. Secondly, he sent all his correspondence by American Express, knowing that it was a federal offence to use US mails for fraudulent purposes. Thirdly, he picked his targets with greater care. Sudie had ripped off anyone that cared to come along: Hartzell aimed at those people who could be persuaded that they were possible descendants of the Elizabethan hero.

He began the hoax by sending a letter (via American Express) to friends back in Iowa, the Shepherds. Adna Shepherd's maiden name was Drake, and she was particularly interested in the contents of Hartzell's letter. He wrote to say that he had made an extraordinary discovery. The clever hoaxer never tries to pretend that his 'discoveries' aren't extraordinary. Hartzell said he had proof that Sir Francis Drake had had an illegitimate son who had been shut up in gaol to avoid scandal and had been robbed of his rightful inheritance, the Drake estate. Hartzell claimed he had traced the true heir to this estate, which was worth $22,000,000,000. The problem was that Hartzell needed money for the legal fight to prove the justice of the descendant's claim. The heir had authorized Hartzell to collect this money by selling shares in the estate. Once the claim had been approved in 'the Secret Courts of England', shareholders would be paid at the rate of $500 for every dollar invested. Hartzell stipulated that only those people named Drake, or direct descendants of others named Drake, would be permitted to invest in the scheme.

Those who send junk mail through the post know the importance of stressing that we as recipients are somehow privileged to receive their rubbish. The clause in any offer that excludes other people is the most effective in snaring those to whom the offer is made. 'YOU, YES YOU! MR XYZ of Chingford, have been specially selected . . . ' etc. etc. The Shepherds were hooked. They mortgaged their home to invest $5,000, and other Drakes from Iowa invested a further $166,775. Hartzell, still operating from London, appointed the Shepherds the first of several agents he soon had working for him in the United States. In all he appointed eleven agents in seven states, and demanded that they raise $2,500 a week to cover the cost of his investigations and the impending legal action. The agents had to swear that they would send the money only by American Express and that they would maintain 'secrecy, silence and non-disturbance'. Every contributor to the funds had to promise that he or she would not disclose what was going on. Anyone who broke this promise would forfeit their right to share in the pay-out when that wonderful time came.

A settlement was always imminent. Hartzell had a natural aptitude for thinking of ways to keep his victims happy and expectant. He said that the English Government was offering to negotiate, since such a vast sum of money had implications for the entire British economy. This was during the early 1920s when Britain was in the grip of a recession. Hartzell suggested that every tremor in the British economy was linked to his legal battle. 'An innocuous item in the Chicago *Journal of Commerce* about a slight fluctuation of the pound was accepted as proof of things soon to happen.'[6] Hartzell increased the size of the Drake estate: it was now said to be worth $400,000,000,000. Rumours multiplied with the bonanza. Britain was on the point of bankruptcy, President Hoover was in cahoots with the British, the mother of Sir Francis's illegitimate child was Queen Elizabeth, the Royal Family were involved in the negotiations.

The last hoax lasted eleven years. Hartzell himself fathered an illegitimate child in England, but avoided nemesis by allowing the mother's father to invest over £500 in the Drake Fund. Then came the first slip. In 1932 several of his agents were arrested in the United States for using the US Mail. Those agents who remained free held secret meetings of the faithful and hopeful; sometimes as many as four thousand people attended. Hartzell sent cable after cable from London. Supporters were urged to write to their congressmen, to the Attorney-General, to the President (by this time Roosevelt). In January 1933 Hartzell was deported from Britain, arrested on landing in New York and charged with fraud in Iowa. Agents and investors were told that this was proof of the legitimacy of his claim, and that Washington was in league with the British Government. Money continued to pour in. Hartzell received another $130,000, enough to pay his bail bond and live comfortably until 1 July, when he promised the estate claim would finally be settled.

It wasn't. Hartzell was brought to trial, accused of defrauding 270,000 people. The prosecution had no difficulty in finding witnesses prepared to swear that they had given money to Hartzell, but all these witnesses wished to attest on his behalf. Drake's will was located in Somerset House. An English barrister travelled to Iowa to explain the Statute of Limitations and how it operated with respect to the will of a man who had been dead for well over three hundred years. He also read a letter to the American court purporting to come from an Englishwoman who alleged that Hartzell had swindled her out of her jewels shortly after he had been made 'Duke of Buckland' by George V. The letter may have been no more genuine than Hartzell's promises. Hoaxers both dispense and attract calumny.

Hartzell was sentenced to ten years' imprisonment and began his sentence in January 1935. For three months the operation hung fire, and then agents revived it, taking greater care to avoid using the US Mail. Rumours circulated that Hartzell was in hiding from the British Secret Service who were out to assassinate him. Money for Hartzell and for investment in the Drake Fund continued to arrive. Many of the victims of the hoax went to their graves convinced that the scheme was honest. Agents went on collecting thousands of dollars for a further eighteen months. Hartzell's former US headquarters were raided and it was discovered that $350,000 had been contributed since Hartzell's conviction. In the three days that followed the police raid, a further $25,000 arrived.

Witnesses remained reluctant. A post-office inspector seeking information in Houston and Galveston was told a boat lying off Galveston was filled with gold sent from England as first payment. He got half a dozen Hartzell backers to accompany him to the boat to see for themselves that it was loaded with oil-well pipes. They saw and were unimpressed. They knew a government trick when they saw one. The gold must have been removed during the night.[7]

In all, forty-two others (including Hartzell's brother, Canfield) were indicted for taking part in the Drake estate hoax. The hoax was never completely exploded. As Francis Bacon wrote in his *Essay, Of Truth*: 'It is not the lie that passeth through the mind, but the lie that sinketh in and settleth in it, that doth the hurt.'

Hartzell was a faceless hoaxer, using the post to communicate with his victims, but a large proportion of hoaxers like to perform in public and many of them have trained for the theatre. Arthur Furguson (or Fergusson) was an erstwhile actor who specialized in the classic kind of hoax – selling well-known public buildings or monuments. Speed is of the essence in this kind of transaction: it doesn't do to hang about, as even the most gullible discover that they have been fleeced within a short time of parting with their money. So Furguson made what he could in his *annus mirabilis*, 1925. He sold Nelson's Column to American tourists, giving them receipts and the names of reliable demolition companies who would dismantle it and ship it to the United States. The going rate was about £6,000. He also 'rented out' Buckingham Palace, the Palace of Westminster and the Tower of London, for prices that ranged from £1,000 to £2,000. After a few successes, he sailed to America. In Washington he convinced a visiting Texan that the Administration was strapped for funds and the President was, therefore, having to move to smaller premises. The White House was available to rent at $100,000 a year. The Texan is said to have paid a year's rent in advance. Furguson proceeded to New York, where he met an Australian tourist. The story this time was that the entrance to New York Harbour needed widening and that the Statue of Liberty was on offer. Again, the price was $100,000. The Australian became suspicious, told the police, and Furguson was arrested. He was sent to prison, but some authorities believe that he had most of his money stashed away and that he was able to live on his ill-gotten gains happily ever after his release.

Stanley Weyman, born Stanley Weinburg, was that rare phenomenon, a 'costume' hoaxer from the working class, and a hoaxer who shunned aliases. He was born in 1891, the son of an impoverished immigrant family who lived in the Bronx area of New York. Weyman was a small man who was attracted to uniforms, insignia and all the trappings that indicated special status. He was blessed by nature with several of the gifts that every hoaxer needs – a quick wit, powers of persuasion and an air of authority. While still very young, he ran up bills in smart New York restaurants, claiming to be the US Consul-Delegate to Morocco. These jaunts were undress rehearsals for his first major success. In 1915 he emulated Cole's *Dreadnought* hoax and paid a visit to the USS *Wyoming*, dressed in the pale blue uniform of the 'Romanian Consul-General'. The visit had many parallels with Cole's trip to the British flagship at Weymouth five years earlier. A launch was sent to the quayside to greet him. Weyman inspected a guard of honour and was entertained in the officers' wardroom. The Romanian flag was flown alongside the Stars and Stripes. He so appreciated the hospitality that the United States Navy gave him on this trip, that he booked a private room at the Astor Hotel in New York to repay them. He then sent out a press release to this effect. The expensive dinner was interrupted when police officers arrested Weyman half-way through the entrée.

Weyman spent most of his life assuming different professional roles, not merely to con victims, but more as a means of earning his living. In between these professional engagements, he would spend a few months in prison. On his release from prison following the Astor fiasco, Weyman became a hospital assistant, a naval officer, and then 'Doctor Weyman'. As a 'doctor' he successfully applied for a job as medical officer to an oil exploration company. He was sent to Peru as a consultant on an engineering project, where he quickly became very popular, both as a doctor and as host at the many lavish parties he threw. Like many successful and audacious hoaxers, he believed that the way to keep ahead was to maintain a high profile, and not to appear to be trying to hide away.

After a couple of years in Peru, Weyman returned to the States where he became Rudolph Valentino's doctor. Presumably he wasn't very effective in this capacity, as all we know about this period is that

Weyman helped to arrange Valentino's funeral. He then became Pola Negri's personal physician, until he tired of the life of a medical practitioner and decided to become a lawyer. He was less successful in this profession, and was twice sent to prison for practising while totally unqualified. He found it easier, and safer, to obtain employment as a lecturer in either law or medicine. What that tells us about the institutes of higher education I'm not sure.

During the Second World War Stanley Weyman became a 'selective service consultant'. For a small fee, people were advised on how they could best dodge the draft. Weyman and nine of his clients were imprisoned for this, but he was free by the time the war ended, and he became a journalist. As might be expected, this was a job that suited him above all others, for 'Journalists say a thing that they know isn't true, in the hope that if they keep on saying it long enough it *will* be true,' as a character in Arnold Bennett's play *The Title* remarks. Many hoaxers have plugged away at this principle as the basis on which to operate. In 1948 Weyman was employed by a News Agency as their United Nations correspondent. He became a familiar figure at UN headquarters, and was subsequently offered the post of press officer to the Thai delegation there. Here Weyman made one of his few mistakes. He contacted the State Department to ask if accepting such a post would affect his rights as an American citizen. The State Department discovered they had a thick file on Stanley Weyman, and his journalistic career came to an end. From this point, life was all downhill.

His greatest moment of glory had taken place in 1921, when he was twenty-six. In that year, an Afghan princess was on a private visit to New York. She was rich. Weyman obtained the uniform of a lieutenant-commander in the United States navy and visited the Princess in her suite at the Waldorf Astoria. He told her that he was the State Department's chief protocol officer, and that he had been told to arrange an official visit to Washington, where President Harding wished to receive her. Weyman then phoned the State Department and told them that the Princess was anxious to visit the President. The State Department told him to make the necessary arrangements. Weyman went back to the Princess and explained that it was the custom in America for the protocol officer to be given a cash present for making such arrangements – this present would be shared out among the many minor officials involved.

Weyman took the Princess and her three sons to Washington and found them hotel accommodation. Then he accompanied them to the White House and introduced them to the President. It was a formal occasion such as Weyman loved. The President was in a dress suit, the Princess was in white robes, Weyman was in his gleaming naval uniform. Photographs were taken on the White House lawn. When it was all over, Weyman collected more money from the Princess, to pay the Washington hotel bills, and then disappeared.

Two other holders of fake positions – who certainly did not shun aliases – were Martin Hewitt and Ferdinand Waldo Demara.

Hewitt was born in 1922 and was a very able child with a special aptitude for mathematics. While at college he came across another student, Julius Ashkin, who matched his age and ability. Ashkin had been appointed to a teaching post at the University of Rochester. Hewitt 'borrowed' Ashkin's name and CV, and applied for a teaching post at a college in Philadelphia. Unfortunately, the Head of the College recognized names and places on Hewitt's false CV, and Hewitt had to move hurriedly to St Louis University, where he taught nuclear physics to graduate students, still under the name of Ashkin. The real Ashkin then published a paper which was read by members of staff at St Louis University. Hewitt was unable to explain how he could be teaching at two universities at the same time, when they were over a thousand miles apart. Hewitt moved on to the University of Utah, where he was made a full professor. Ashkin tracked him down and Hewitt scuttled back to Philadelphia.

Eighteen months later, Hewitt applied for a post at the University of Arkansas, with a recommendation from one of the vice-presidents of RCA Records. The recommendation was all Hewitt's work: he had no contact with anyone at RCA. Hewitt got the job, but his run of unfortunate coincidences continued – he was one of the few hoaxers to have such bad luck. The real vice-president of RCA visited the University of Arkansas. Once again, Hewitt fled back home to Philadelphia. He then became, in turn, Clifford Berry at the New York State Maritime College, and Kenneth Yates at the University of New Hampshire. By then, Hewitt, had at least five false PhDs. He was again exposed, and was too well known to keep going.

Demara, also an academic hoaxer, was born in Massachusetts in 1921 and early in his career became known as 'The Great Impostor'.

He dropped out of high school, and spent the next thirty years of his life moving from hoax to hoax. One of his first efforts was to borrow a dummy from a clothing store, stick a pair of boots on the feet and shove it upside down in a snow drift by the roadside. Passing motorists screeched to a halt to hurry over and rescue the poor victim. As a young man, Demara joined both the army and the navy, and deserted from both in quick succession. He then joined a Roman Catholic order as a trainee priest, with a phoney PhD in psychology, which enabled him to gain entrance to the St Paul University to study scholastic philosophy.

He lay low for a while, and re-emerged as Robert Linton French, Professor of Psychology. He taught at Pennsylvania College, Gannon College California, and St Martin's School, Washington. 'There's no mystery about psychiatry,' he said. 'Anybody with common sense could practise it.' He then joined a Catholic teaching order in Maine as a graduate biologist and physician, moved on to cancer research at the Cancer Institute, Seattle, and became a recreational officer in a Texas maximum security gaol, but his big break came during the Korean War in the early 1950s. There was a great shortage of doctors in the Royal Canadian Navy. Using false certificates stolen from a Dr Cyr, Demara – as 'Dr Cyr' – was commissioned as an officer and posted to the *Cayuga*. The first patient he treated on the warship was the captain, who had raging toothache. Demara is said to have sat up all night reading textbooks on dentistry before extracting the captain's tooth the following day.

Once the ship reached Korea, business was brisk. He attended nineteen badly wounded Korean civilians. 'I had to keep one basic principle in mind. The less cutting you do, the less patching up you have to do afterwards.'[8] His surgery became more ambitious. He operated on a Korean soldier who had a bullet lodged near his heart, and on another whose lung had been lacerated by a dum-dum bullet. 'I couldn't have been nervous, even if I felt like it,' he said. 'Practically everybody on the bloody ship was watching me.'

Demara's success under the name of Dr Cyr caused his own downfall. The navy released details of the remarkable work performed by their surgeon-doctor. The real Dr Cyr read of them and recognized Demara's photograph – he had been the local doctor when Demara had been living as Brother John in the Catholic Monastery, and had admired Demara's treatment of Brother Boniface's arthritis with bee venom. Demara was exposed and sent back to Canada. Accounts vary as to what happened here. There are those who say that Demara was discharged with honour, but the alternative and more likely account is that he was asked to leave the navy and Canada with the pay that was owing to him. His former shipmates sent him a Christmas card:

> He may be six kinds of a liar,
> He may be ten kinds of a fool;
> He may have faults that are dire,
> And seem without reason or rule . . .
> But we don't analyse, we just love him,
> Because – well, because he's our friend.

Demara had a couple of careers left. He was appointed as a teacher in a high school in Maine, but was sacked and charged with false pretence when it was discovered that his alleged qualifications were totally fraudulent. On his release from prison, he became a hot gospeller, but then slipped from the public gaze. By the late 1970s, his whereabouts were unknown.

The doyen of the conmen in the first half of the twentieth century was Count Victor Lustig, alias Robert Miller, George Duvan and twenty-two other names. He was born in 1890 in Hostoun, Czechoslovakia, not far from the German border. His father was the local burgomaster and a respected figure in the community, but, like so many hoaxers born in small towns, Lustig sought the bright lights and the big cities. He was educated at a boarding school in Dresden. By the time he was nineteen years old, he had a record as a petty thief in Paris. Physically, Lustig 'had a square handsome face with a clipped moustache, and was clothed in elegance by a Savile Row tailor'.[9] He also had a quick mind and a flair for languages, becoming fluent in Czech, German, English, French and Italian – if you're going to assume a couple of dozen aliases, it helps to have several languages at your disposal. He was also reckoned to be one of the best amateur billiards players in Europe and a dangerously competent card player. Before the First World War, he worked the transatlantic liners, picking up a living as a professional card player. Here he met a professional gambler named Nicky Arnstein, who taught him one basic principle: 'You *always* let the sucker suggest the game'. By 1914, Lustig was back in Paris, but in the early 1920s he left to try his luck in the United States, where he reckoned the pickings would be richer.

He visited Hollywood, briefly, at a time when Harry Reichenbach was busy running his many hoaxes there; it's tempting to think that they might have met, but there is no evidence. While in Hollywood, Lustig met and seduced Estelle Sweeny, a former runner-up in a Miss Illinois contest. Promising her a career on Broadway (his bluff would have been swiftly called if he'd promised her a career in the movies), Lustig took her to Havana, Cuba. Here he posed as the big Broadway producer who was looking for a backer for his next show. His mark, or victim, was Ronald Dredge, a forty-five-year-old New England businessman with a passion for the theatre. Lustig told Dredge that he needed $70,000 for a Broadway show. Dredge was eager to lend it to him, but Lustig insisted that he wouldn't dream of taking Dredge's money until he had raised at least 51 per cent himself. Dredge returned to his home in Providence, Rhode Island, to sweat out the wait.

Lustig let him stew for weeks before returning to the United States, leaving Estelle behind. Lustig contacted Dredge, and invited him to come to New York, saying that he had raised his 51 per cent and would now permit Dredge to invest his 49 per cent, some $34,000. Lustig arranged that they should meet in a speakeasy, where Lustig left his case, supposedly containing $36,000, while he took Dredge's $34,000, allegedly to count it. He was gone a long time. Dredge became worried, then uneasy, then suspicious. He finally opened Lustig's case and found a few dollar bills covering a wad of old newspaper. Lustig took off by train for Canada, but later stole a car to cross the border. He then returned to Europe. Poor Estelle, left penniless in her hotel in Cuba, ended up doing bumps and grinds as a stripper in a club in Havana.

Lustig is most famous for selling the Eiffel Tower. It was a clever hoax, with some masterly touches. In the 1930s there were reports in the French newspapers that the Eiffel Tower needed repairs. Lustig posed as a high-ranking civil servant, attached to the Ministère des Postes et Télégraphes. In this capacity, he sent invitations to five leading scrap-metal merchants in Paris, one of whom, André Poisson, he had already identified as his victim. Lustig and the five met in a room in the Hôtel Crillon, where Lustig swore them to secrecy and told them that what they were about to hear was a matter touching the reputation of France. He explained that the Eiffel Tower needed repairs, but that the Government was not in a position to finance these repairs. It had been reluctantly decided that the Tower must be scrapped. He took all five contractors to the Tower in limousines, and wined and dined them. He then told them that they were invited to send in their sealed bids for the contract to demolish and remove the Eiffel Tower, pointing out that the scrap-metal value of the monument was staggering. The sealed bids were to be sent to him, at the Hotel, within the next five days. He would inform them of the Government's decision.

Five days later he contacted Poisson and told him that his bid had been successful. Poisson agreed to bring a certified cheque to the Hôtel Crillon. There was one further point, said Lustig. Where such large contracts were being awarded, it was customary to pay a fee to the civil servant involved, as proof of appreciation for his work as go-between. Poisson, who had previously had doubts about the whole affair, breathed a sigh of relief. If a bribe was involved, he was convinced the deal was genuine. He met Lustig and parted with two cheques – one for the contract and one for the bribe. Lustig shook Poisson's hand, showed him out, nipped round to the nearest bank, and was away before any alarm had been raised. There are those who say that Poisson was too embarrassed to admit what had happened, and that this enabled Lustig to sell the Eiffel Tower a second time, but there is little proof of this.

Lustig returned to the United States, cabling the FBI ahead of his arrival to say that he had information that touched on the safety and welfare of the President in order to forestall any interest they might have in him. He was questioned by the secret service for eight hours on disembarkation in New York, but was then released. He perpetrated several more frauds or hoaxes in Canada and the United States, including selling a box that printd money for $25,000 and conning money out of a punter by establishing a false bookie joint in Montreal. However, the FBI were again on his trail, and Lustig was finally arrested in December 1935. He was accused of distributing $1,340,000 worth of counterfeit notes. On 7 December he pleaded guilty, and three days later he was sentenced to fifteen years in the State Penitentiary in Alcatraz. Count Victor Lustig (alias Robert Miller, alias George Duval, alias twenty-two other names) had at last come to rest.

4

Habitual Masquerade

'Everything is mortal – except human gullibility.'
Jack Bilbo

Popular culture has always found a place for the hero with more than one identity, the little guy (it is nearly always a man) who drags out a humdrum existence for much of the time, but who, when the occasion demands, bursts from his drab attire to stand revealed as The Scarlet Pimpernel, Zorro, Superman, Batman, The Incredible Hulk. In stories and in dozens of films there have been those thrilling moments when the hero leaps upon his enemies, crying 'Not the village simpleton . . . but Robin à Locksley!', or Scaramouche or The Lone Ranger or whoever.

It is an appealing prospect – that in each of us there exists some bold adventurer, patiently waiting for the moment when we can drop (or don) the mask, unsheathe our gleaming swords and ride out to right wrongs. For in our popular culture, such figures are always goodies.

In the world of hoaxers it doesn't work like that. If a hoaxer takes on a second identity, it is at best for mischievous reasons. Most, perhaps all, hoaxers feel the need to bolster their sense of self-importance, and creating a new and more effective identity is one way of doing this. What makes it exciting and satisfying for them, is what makes it daunting for us. It's one thing to daydream about suddenly turning into The Caped Crusader or The Masked Avenger; it's quite another thing to see the metamorphosis through. Even on a much humbler level, the histrionic skill and raw nerve to turn the daydream into a living deceit, are beyond most of us. If we can't summon up courage to remonstrate with dog owners whose pets we see fouling the pavement, or to ask smokers to extinguish cigarettes in non-smoking areas, we are unlikely to be able to cling to a false identity that we have adopted in public, once it is tested or challenged.

What many hoaxers appear to have, to see them through such tough times, is a touch of obsession, of ruthlessness, of madness. Percy Toplis came close to madness towards the end of his short career. There was little that was wholly sane about Trebitsch Lincoln, both in his private life and in the bizarre professional roles that he adopted. Judged by his writings, Louis de Rougemont, who, as we shall see, claimed to be the Robinson Crusoe of Australia, was a deeply disturbed man. Arthur Orton, the Tichborne Claimant (Chapter 5), floated in and out of a state of self-deception, of believing that he really was Sir Roger Tichborne. It may not be possible to live so fundamental a lie for any length of time without the strain that is imposed on the brain doing some damage. Once the pretence is under way, the hoaxer has to lose himself in it, leaving reality as far behind as possible. The hoaxer lives by enticing us into the fantasy world he has created, but he has to take up residence there first. As remarked earlier, Adrian Stephen had barely set foot on HMS *Dreadnought* before 'the expedition had become for me almost an affair of every day. It was hardly a question any longer of a hoax.'[1] Cole and company were no longer actors; they *were* the Emperor of Abyssinia and his entourage.

Hoaxers who have masqueraded under new identities fall into three groups: those whose 'acting' was habitual or permanent, those who repeatedly assumed new roles, and those who tried it for a while and gave it up.

This last group is the smallest - Buck Henry as G Clifford Prout, Cole as the Foreign Office representative, Victor Lewis-Smith as Clint Rees-Bunce, Sophie Lloyd as Raymond Lloyd (see page 67), Humphry Berkeley as H Rochester Sneath (see page 69) - and also the most innocent of any criminal intent. These are the true hoaxers: men and women who were out to expose pomposity and indulge in social satire.

Victor Lewis-Smith is a writer and broadcaster who invented Sir Clint Lucioni Rees-Bunce as a kind of many-headed scourge of the modern media. Rees-Bunce could change sex, age, religion and social status at will, simply to suit whatever situation his inventor found himself in. Lewis-Smith, as Rees-Bunce, wrote to radio and television programmes, communicating outlandish opinions and offering eccentric personae for interview. Often radio and television responded positively to these communications, and Rees-Bunce appeared on television as a gynaecologist who dressed as Batman, and as an Arab sheikh who ran an Islamic musical group. In radio phone-in programmes he was a man who had run up £200,000 in credit-card bills and whose house was being invaded by loan sharks while he was on the air, and a driver whose windscreen was totally obscured by cactus plants growing from the dashboard of his Ford Capri. Lewis-Smith's speciality is the telephone hoax. He has phoned experts in a variety of guises – as the owner of a Picasso that he had found in the loft and sawn a piece off as it was too large for his uses, as an aspiring DJ on Vatican Radio, and as a paraplegic who could play 'The Sailor's Hornpipe' in three seconds flat on the bass trombone (for *That's Life*). These phone calls are always delivered at a fast pace, so that the victim is swept along, hurled into the mad world that Lewis-Smith creates.

Some of the hoaxes appear cruel in that they take advantage of people's ignorance (what hoax doesn't?); he has phoned reception at BBC Television and at London Weekend Television, requesting that they page, respectively, Marcel Proust and Emperor Haile Selassie. By using the phone, Lewis-Smith may also be catching victims very much off guard, but that isn't how he sees it. 'Rees-Bunce played away, on opposition territory, and his victims always had the opportunity to exercise free will.'[2] Maybe every hoaxer would make the same claim, but Lewis-Smith takes great care always to present himself to his victims as a man of lesser intelligence. He cultivates situations where his victims feel that they are in a position to be kind, patient and tolerant towards someone to whom they are superior in intelligence and social standing. 'It's a version of the woman whose car has broken down on the motorway, standing on the hard shoulder and using her sexuality to get help.'[3] Another part of the technique is to use flattery. The recipient may allege that he doesn't really want to hear this, but most of Lewis-Smith's victims come from the world of showbiz, where flattery is a *lingua franca*.

Some of the hoaxes created by Lewis-Smith and his fellow hoaxer, Paul Sparks, are variations on the theme of the Henry Root letters. At one time they fired off a series of letters of complaint, mainly to food production companies – in return they received a great deal of free food. One letter, however, had less pleasant results: they wrote to a soup company complaining that they had found a condom in a tin of soup. For once they didn't have the hoaxer's habitual good luck – their timing was bad. There had recently been a spate of sabotage in the food industry, and the soup company shut down their production line while they investigated Lewis-Smith and Sparks's complaint. The hoaxers received a visit from the police. 'But it was all right,' said Lewis-Smith. 'They were pissing themselves when they left.'

'And you,' countered Sparks, 'were shitting yourself when they arrived.'[4]

Lewis-Smith decided to kill off Rees-Bunce in November 1990. The problem was that it was becoming increasingly difficult to think of something so ludicrous or in such bad taste that the media would turn it down. For his last spoof he telephoned the Associate Producer of the TV programme *Beadle's About*.

> 'I've got a great idea for your programme. Jeremy goes to Death Row at Maryland State Penitentiary, and you film one of the prisoners playing that fairground game – you know, moving the loop along the wiggly copper wire, without making contact. If he manages it, he goes free, but if he doesn't, it's not a bell that rings. The whole circuit's connected to his electric chair and he gets 20,000 volts through his frontal lobes.'
>
> There was silence, followed by a horrified 'Oh dear, no. No, we couldn't *possibly* do that.'
>
> 'Why not?' Rees-Bunce asked.
>
> 'Our budget. It doesn't extend to foreign trips.'[5]

Sophie Lloyd's hoax was performed to obtain entry to the Magic Circle in 1989, a time when the Society was an all-male preserve. It was a brilliant hoax, the work of months of planning and preparation, in partnership with her agent, Jenny Winstanley. The hoax arose out of Jenny Winstanley's anger that women were not admitted to the Magic Circle, no matter how competent they were as magicians. She was too well known to members of the Magic Circle to disguise herself, but she had for some time performed as a double act with her partner, Sophie Lloyd, the latter in the guise of a twelve-year-old boy. Together they invented Raymond, a not very academic, not too intelligent, non-athletic sixteen-year-old lad obsessed by his hobby –

magic. Lloyd studied how young men walked, talked, carried themselves, used their eyes, ate, drank, leant against walls. Winstanley both coached her and studied her appearances in public as Raymond. Raymond was taken into shops, on buses and tubes, pubs and restaurants. An entire family, school and social history were invented for Raymond, and while this was going on, Winstanley taught Lloyd magic.

After a few months, they were both sufficiently happy with Raymond to allow him to book a date in a club for a performance. Lloyd had a wig, plumpers to fill out her face, a body harness to give her the build of a young male, and a pair of glasses behind which to hide. Her hands were always kept out of sight, either behind her back, in her pockets or in gloves. Her voice was kept low and a class or two down from her normal patterns of speech. Raymond was a success – 'his show wasn't brilliant, but they liked the boy'.[6] The public admired his skill, application and determination. For a year, Raymond toured London, burning five-pound notes and making them reappear, making fire extinguishers talk, and releasing monsters from a carpet bag. There were awkward moments, such as when Lloyd forgot momentarily who she was, spoke out of character and was threatened by two men in a club. She was saved by a bouncer, who said to the men, 'He's only a kid – pick on someone your own age.'[7]

As soon as they felt reasonably certain of success, Winstanley and Lloyd applied for Raymond's admission to the Magic Circle. A date was fixed for his examination at a venue in South London, in front of an audience of two hundred people and an examiner. It took Winstanley and Lloyd two hours to make up, for Winstanley was also playing a part, that of Raymond's agent, though she treated the lad like her own son. Despite one or two hitches, the examination was a success, the toughest part of the evening coming immediately afterwards, when both had to mix socially with other magicians. Raymond passed, and was admitted to the Magic Circle; badges and certificates were forwarded to him.

A few months later, the Magic Circle changed its rules, and declared that women were eligible for membership (so far, none have passed the examination). The wig and glasses were discarded, and Sophie Lloyd and Jenny Winstanley revealed their illusion and their hoax. The Magic Circle were not amused. They withdrew

Raymond's membership, which seems fair enough in that Raymond didn't exist, and threatened Lloyd with legal action for deception. Lloyd and Winstanley were furious. 'It's such hypocrisy . . . Some of them are so pompous they just can't take a joke.'[8] Some people have taken the hoax very seriously indeed. Winstanley and Lloyd have received one phone call, late at night, announcing: 'You will never work again in this business.' This doesn't seem to have been an idle threat. Since the hoax it has been extremely difficult for them to get bookings. Hoaxing can be a dangerous business for both victim and hoaxer.

In 1948, when he was an undergraduate at Cambridge, Humphry Berkeley invented his *doppelgänger*, H Rochester Sneath. Sneath was supposedly the Head of Selhurst School, Berkeley giving the institution a far more believable name than he chose for himself. If there isn't such an academy as Selhurst, there should be; it sounds the epitome of a minor public school. Berkeley spread the word about his creations by repeatedly asking people, 'Haven't you heard of Selhurst?' The question was so scathingly delivered and so clearly expected the answer 'Yes' that it usually got it. Berkeley then had some headed writing paper printed, always a powerful tool in a hoaxer's armoury: SELHURST SCHOOL NEAR PETWORTH, SUSSEX – FROM THE HEADMASTER, H ROCHESTER SNEATH, it read, and on this paper he sent letters to the headmasters of the most famous public schools in the country – Marlborough, Stowe, Sherborne, The Oratory, Oundle, Ampleforth, Harrow, Malvern, Tonbridge, Rugby, Eton, among them – and to other people prominent in their walks of life. He wrote to the Master of Marlborough for advice on arranging a Royal visit to Selhurst. He wrote to Sir Giles Gilbert Scott, then busily rebuilding the Houses of Parliament, offering him the opportunity to design a new House at Selhurst. He wrote a second letter to the Master of Marlborough, warning him about a French teacher named Robert Agincourt, whose morals left something to be desired, and then a third letter asking for the name of a discreet private detective and a good nursemaid. Too late, it would appear, he contacted the founding Headmaster of Stowe for guidance on the provision of sex education to his pupils. To the Headmaster of Rugby, he offered advice on the treatment of homosexuality among his pupils: 'Harmless, and you can afford to ignore what is in most cases a purely transitory phase.'⁹

Sneath invited the Head of Ampleforth to join him in arranging an art exhibition that was to go to South America; he suggested to the Headmaster of the Oratory that it was a good and lucrative wheeze to apply for Government compensation for wartime evacuation, and thanked the Head of Blundell's for a (non-existent) request to preach there. He invited Sir Adrian Boult to conduct the School Orchestra in the first performance of the 'Selhurst Symphony', and George Bernard Shaw to speak at the School on the theme of 'A Clarion Call to Youth'. Neither invitation was accepted.

H Rochester Sneath also bombarded the press with letters on the difficulty of establishing compulsory Russian at his school – at a time when the Cold War was not considered a suitable subject for humour. It was his letter on this topic to the *Daily Worker* that aroused suspicions and brought the hoax to light. Sneath's real identity was discovered, and Berkeley was sent down from Cambridge for two years, the University having no more humour than the Magic Circle.

More transient than Rees-Bunce, Raymond Lloyd or Rochester Sneath, but less innocent, was the appearance in 1906 of Wilhelm Voigt as the Captain of Kopenick. Voigt was born in 1849 and grew up during the clamorous years when Prussia was hammering out the unification of Germany. He was seventeen when the Austro-Prussian War began, and twenty-one on the outbreak of the Franco-Prussian War. To many of Voigt's generation, it must have seemed that the new nation state of Germany owed its existence almost entirely to the army. Voigt, however, was a cobbler by trade, hammering away on a last in Berlin rather than the anvil of Europe. He was also a petty criminal, and a remarkably unsuccessful one. According to some accounts, he spent twenty-seven of the first fifty-seven years of his life in prison. Apart from rampant recidivism, Voigt had absolutely no claims to fame.

But there must have burnt within him the ambition to strut and fret his hour upon the stage, and in 1906 he made his move. In a society that was still mightily proud of its army, it is hardly surprising that Voigt's hoax was of a military nature. He obtained the uniform of a captain of infantry and put it on. Then, dressed in glory but with his cap badge upside down, he paraded through the streets of the capital. Nobody laughed, nobody jeered. Like Colour-Sergeant Maxwell,

Voigt discovered that a military demeanour was taken at face value and respected. If it worked in Berlin, it should work even better in a provincial town. He came across a squad of ten soldiers under the aimless command of a corporal. Voigt took charge and marched his little platoon up the street. He then used his military powers to commandeer a bus, into which he shepherded his troops; they then drove out to Kopenick, now a suburb of south-east Berlin. And here the hoax moved up a gear. With his squad of loyal, if bemused, men, Voigt marched to the Town Hall and arrested the Burgomaster and the Town Treasurer, saying that he had been sent to investigate the town's finances. Not being one to miss an opportunity, he then conned 4,000 marks out of the Town Council, whom he also placed under arrest. To round off his afternoon, he commandeered a number of coaches from the citizens of Kopenick, in which the Council were packed off to Berlin.

Enough was enough. Whether Voigt lost interest or his nerve is not known, but he now resigned his brief commission, and returned to Berlin as a civilian. The Captain of Kopenick, as Voigt had styled himself, became an overnight sensation. Whether the German people saw his exploits as a satire on the pomposity of the military or the stupidity of local councils is not clear, but everyone wanted to know who the Captain was – which posed a problem. 'The only sad part of it for Voigt was that as long as he remained undetected he could not benefit from this wave of popularity and admiration. After ten days his frustration got the better of him to such an extent that he led the police to his own hiding place and allowed himself to be caught.'[10] Once again the hoaxer's greed for notoriety brought about his own downfall, but in this instance it served only to increase Voigt's popularity. He became a national hero, even the Kaiser was amused and is said to have referred to Voigt as 'the lovable scoundrel'.

The authorities were more concerned with the scoundrel side of Voigt than any lovable qualities he may have had. Four thousand marks had been taken and, though most of it was recovered Voigt was sentenced to four years' imprisonment. It was a heavy sentence, and perhaps Voigt was being punished more for his lack of respect towards the military than for the con trick, in much the same way that poor Toad received fifteen years for cheeking the police. Public opinion was still very much on Voigt's side, and he was released after serving two years. Unlike most hoaxers, he ended his days in relative comfort, having been granted a life pension by a wealthy admirer.

One of the most extraordinary cases concerning the adoption of a new identity has come to be known in book and film as 'The Return of Martin Guerre'. The setting for this hoax was the village of Artigat in southern France. In 1548 Martin Guerre abandoned his wife, Bertrande, and suddenly and unaccountably disappeared. Eight years later there arrived in the village a man who was shorter, stockier, heavier, with smaller feet, who claimed to be Guerre. In fact he was Arnaud de Tilh, a man who had spent his dissolute youth in Sajas, a few miles away, a man who was said to have been absorbed in every vice, but who was wonderfully fluent of tongue, and a man with a memory that an actor would envy. De Tilh was a restless romancer, a kind of delinquent d'Artagnan. 'He dreamed of something beyond the seigniory of Sajas, beyond the hills of the diocese of Lombez. There was always the possibility of the King's band of foot soldiers, those "adventurers" among whom the Gascons loomed so large.'[11]

There were those in the village, those who stood to lose financially by the return of Martin Guerre, who said that de Tilh was an impostor, but the loudest voice raised against them was the voice that mattered most, that of Bertrande, Guerre's wife. She was adamant that the real Martin Guerre had returned, and she took him in to her home and her bed. For four years they lived together, though there can be little doubt that Bertrande knew that this man was not her husband. 'What Bertrande had with the new Martin was her dream come true, a man she could live with in peace and friendship (to cite sixteenth-century values) and passion.'[12] Like so many victims, Bertrande was the last to admit that a hoax had been played, but what made her unique among victims is that she knew all along that this was the case. And once again the structure of society aided and abetted the hoax. Bertrande's marriage to the real Martin had been an arranged marriage – why shouldn't she, given the opportunity with de Tilh, arrange her own marriage?

This is one of the saddest of hoaxes, for the happy, though illicit, domesticity of Bertrande and de Tilh was short-lived. De Tilh was arrested, taken to Rieux and then to Toulouse, and tried before Jean de Coras, a leading judge and professor of law. Bertrande refused to take an oath that de Tilh was an impostor, and the Court had not yet reached a verdict, when the real Martin Guerre appeared. Arnaud de

Tilh was found guilty of taking on someone else's name and person with intention to defraud, and he was sentenced to be hanged, his body then to be burnt 'so that the memory of so miserable and abominable a person would disappear completely and be lost'.[13] Shortly before his execution, de Tilh confessed; on the steps up to the gibbet he asked Martin Guerre not to be harsh with Bertrande, and he died praying for God's mercy.

Despite the confession, a haze of doubt lay over the case for many years. Jean de Coras later wrote a book about this most unusual crime. He painted de Tilh as a magician, a man aided by an evil spirit, a traitor and a criminal for whose death there could be no regrets, both judicially and morally. In this he was doing little more than echoing some of the fears of the villagers. But de Tilh was neither sorcerer nor devil.

> He was a rural Iago, evilly turning people against one another. But as he became an upstanding householder and father in someone else's name, he could never acknowledge his lie and never give them a chance to pardon him. In this way a deep uneasiness, uncertainty, and wariness would inevitably grow in village and family relations. When people began to wonder publicly about his identity, they also began to suspect him . . . of magic.[14]

Coras may have been frightened because, had the real Martin Guerre not so dramatically returned, he had been on the point of deciding the case in favour of de Tilh. Maybe he, too, was seduced by the romance that surrounds a hoax, or maybe he recognized 'that there was something deeply fascinating about Arnaud de Tilh which spoke to his own conflicting feelings and to the situation of people in his own class – and that there was something not only profoundly wrong but also profoundly right about the invented marriage of the new Martin and Bertrande.'[15]

De Tilh played for high stakes when he claimed to be someone who existed. While he was believed he gained everything: a wife, a home, a business. Once he lost, everything was forfeit, including his life. Far commoner, and far safer, as a hoax is to invent a character. George Psalmanazar arrived in London from the Continent in 1703, under the sponsorship of an Army Chaplain, the Reverend William Innes. Psalmanazar didn't claim to be anyone in particular, simply a native of Formosa, an island about which there was massive ignorance in Britain at that time. Formosans, said Psalmanazar, looked much more like Westerners than Orientals, and they had a language that was conveniently unintelligible to European ears and indecipherable to European eyes. He said he had been converted to Christianity by missionaries, on the strength of which claim the Reverend Innes was invited to introduce him to the Bishop of London – whether Innes saw through Psalmanazar is not clear. The Bishop certainly didn't and became Psalmanazar's patron, obtaining a sinecure for him at Christ Church, Oxford. Here Psalmanazar translated the Church of England Catechism into his version of Formosan (he declined a request to translate the Bible) and trained missionaries for work in Formosa.

The language he produced strengthened his credibility. It looked and sounded right. It was regular and grammatical, and, best of all, it was so different from any other language known in Britain at the time. It met people's expectations, and every successful hoaxer has to meet people's expectations. It was no coincidence that Psalmanazar, like Maundy Gregory, Lustig, Trebitsch Lincoln and many other hoaxers, was a fluent linguist. He spoke six languages and could converse with ease in Latin.*

In 1704 Psalmanazar published *A Historical and Geographical Description of Formosa*, written in Latin, and dedicated to his patron, Henry Compton. It was an immediate success (a second edition followed in 1705), largely because of the mass of spicy misinformation it contained. Psalmanazar explained that most Formosans lived to be a hundred years old because they ate raw meat and drank snake's blood. Perhaps this sanguinary diet was responsible for the cruelty of the Formosans – each year eighteen thousand boys† under the age of nine were ritually slaughtered and their hearts burnt to appease the gods. This led to a great shortage of males on the island and polygamy was rife.

---

* We are almost at a point where we can build up a paradigm of the archetypal hoaxer: male, middle class, ambitious, with a retentive memory and considerable acting and linguistic ability.
† Some authorities say 'children'.

The husband sends for one of [his wives] whom he has a mind to lie with that Night; and in the Day-time he sometimes Visits one of them, sometimes another according to his fancy. This kind of life is sweet and pleasant enough, as long as every one of them is of an agreeable humour; but if the Husband begins to love one Wife more than another, then arises Envy and Emulation.[16]

George Candidus, a Dutch Jesuit missionary, who knew Formosa well, denounced Psalmanazar's book as rubbish. He painted a very different and far less titillating account of life on Formosa. Far from being a bloodthirsty society, the laws on the island were so lenient as to be almost non-existent. Robbery was barely punished at all, and a present of a few hogs was considered ample compensation for adultery, or, in some cases, murder. Candidus may have exaggerated slightly the other way, but it seems that Formosa was well and wisely ruled during the latter part of the seventeenth century by the Emperor Coxinga (Kok-Seng-Ya) and his son Cheng Ching, King of Tywan. Psalmanazar, however, countered by saying that robbers and murderers on Formosa were hanged head downwards and then shot to death with arrows. The punishments for other offences, according to Psalmanazar, including burying alive, cutting off legs and arms, tearing to pieces by dogs, or boring holes in the tongue with red-hot irons. On the brighter side, Psalmanazar said that there were several gold and silver mines on the island.

Candidus continued to deny all this, but the picture that Psalmanazar had painted of Formosa was of the stereotypical far-off land – savage, primitive, cruel, heathen and packed with precious metals. He told people what they wanted to hear, what they were predisposed to believe, and so his version was accepted as the truthful one. In all this there is not a very profound or revelatory moral. And there was another element in the public's eagerness to believe Psalmanazar and disbelieve Candidus. The Dutchman was a Jesuit, and the Jesuits were mightily out of favour at that time. It was a period of 'that unparalleled code of repression', the Penal Laws in Ireland, and much anti-Catholic feeling in England. Psalmanazar may have planned to make use of this, but it is more likely that this is another example of hoaxer's luck.

The hoax lasted for twenty-five years. Innes left Psalmanazar and went off to become Chaplain-General to the forces in Portugal. By

1710 Psalmanazar had lost much of his kudos and was increasingly seen as a figure of fun. He was forced to take humble employment, working as a clerk to an army regiment. In 1728 Psalmanazar, then in his fifties, became ill. Fearful that there is perhaps no room in Heaven for hoaxers, he repented and confessed that he had invented the entire saga to lead a life of 'shameless idleness, vanity and extravagance'. He then had the cheek to contribute the chapters on China and Japan to Bowen's *Complete System of Geography*, basing his contributions almost entirely on earlier writings of Candidus. In 1752 he wrote his memoirs, but they were not published until shortly after his death in 1766. He spent the last few years of his life writing books and reflecting on the deceit he had practised when he first came to Britain. It was as though he wished to erase all memory of this masquerade, for he refused to put his name to the books he wrote, and directed that his body should be buried in some obscure corner of the common burying ground, 'in a shell of the lowest value, without lid or other covering to hinder the natural earth from entirely surrounding it'. Though Psalmanazar was subsequently ashamed of himself, others maintained a higher opinion of him. Boswell records that 'once talking of George Psalmanazar, whom he reverenced for his piety, Doctor Johnson said, "I should as soon think of contradicting a bishop."'

Psalmanazar's Formosan masquerade lasted twenty-five years, but there have been those whose false identities have been of the nine days' wonder variety. In 1817 a young woman arrived in the village of Almondsbury in Gloucestershire. She spoke no English, gave no name, and was of a hunted and untrusting manner. The local magistrate, whose name was Samuel Worrall, sheltered her in his house, but she refused to eat food other than that she had prepared herself, and insisted on sleeping on the floor. From time to time, she performed a weird hopping dance on one leg. The villagers were both fascinated and mystified. Craniologists were called in to measure her head. And then a young man named Martin Eynesso turned up. He claimed that he came from Portugal and that he could understand the speech of the young woman. Through Eynesso, the woman told the villagers that her name was Caraboo, and that she came from the island of Javasu, near Sumatra. She had been captured by pirates, who had taken her from the island and sold her into slavery. She had been bought by the captain of a ship sailing to England via the Cape of Good Hope, and had jumped ship in Bristol and swum ashore. Finally, she had walked to Almondsbury, only a few miles from Bristol. She was able to draw a sketch map of her route to England.

Caraboo became nationally famous, but with fame came recognition. She was identified by a Bristol woman who had formerly been her landlady as Mary Willcocks (some authorities give her name as Mary Baker), a cobbler's daughter from Devon. Her real life had been less romantic than that of Caraboo, but scarcely any happier. Her father had been a harsh disciplinarian, and Mary had left home at the age of fifteen to become general maid to a local family. Unhappy in this situation, she had resolved to walk to London. She became ill and spent time in hospital. Then she passed from one employer to another. In 1813 she mistook a brothel for a convent, and spent what must have been a confusing stay therein. A man who had travelled in the Far East gave her enough information for the basis to Caraboo's story.

More successful, from the point of view of longevity of deceit, was the Reverend Wilfred Ellis, who was Rector of Wetheringsett Manor in Suffolk from 1858 to 1883. Like Psalmanazar, Ellis lived his hoax to the full, caring for his parishioners, taking the Sunday service, officiating at marriages, baptisms and funerals. Unlike Psalmanazar, he didn't repent, and showed no sense of shame when it was revealed that he was not a Minister of the Church, but a pork butcher by trade. It is said that when this became known, a Bill was rushed through Parliament to legitimize the marriages that he had conducted and the offspring thereof.

Ellis's hoax succeeded because it was simple. He had only to dress and act as a clergyman to become a clergyman in the eyes of his parishioners. G K Chesterton appreciated the efficacy of such a disguise in more than one of his Father Brown Stories. Other hoaxers, such as Psalmanazar and Eynesso, worked on a more subtle assumption – that a little knowledge is a potential goldmine. In the eighteenth century there were those who knew that Formosa existed, but knew nothing else about it. In the early nineteenth century, there were those who knew that slavery was still imposed in exotic, far-flung parts of the world, and who greedily swallowed up the romance of a young woman who had escaped from it. We are not immune from similar hoaxes today. With more knowledge, the hoaxer's seam of gold becomes all the richer. If the layperson knows more about Formosa today, there are hundreds of other subjects of which he or she possesses only a little learning: holograms, nuclear fission, corn circles, the atmosphere on Mars, the drawings of Piranesi, the Common Agricultural Policy, the motives of politicians . . . .

And so, as the nineteenth century brought Europe greater access to all other parts of the world, the public learnt of the existence of new places and new peoples. Always the knowledge was incomplete. Always the ground was prepared for a new hoaxer. So little is needed to step from ignorance to fantasy. What Daniel Defoe could do for Robinson Crusoe, others could do for themselves. There is nothing new about fake travellers. Sir John Mandeville earned the title 'The Greatest Liar of All Time', after publishing an account of his so-called *Travels* in 1371. Most of the work was pillaged from the writings of Odoric, a seventh-century friar; the rest was original and worthless, though not without a certain horrific invention. Here is what Mandeville had to say about the Andaman Islands:

> There are a great many people in these isles. In one, there is a race of great stature, like giants, foul and horrible to look at; they have one eye only, in the middle of their foreheads. They eat raw flesh and raw fish. In another part, there are ugly folk without heads, who have eyes in each shoulder; their mouths are round, like a horseshoe, in the middle of their chest. In yet another part there are headless men whose eyes and mouths are on their backs. And there are in another place folk with flat faces, without noses or eyes, and a flat lipless mouth. In another isle there are ugly fellows whose upper lip is so big that when they sleep in the sun they cover all their faces with it.

For a while, in the fourteenth century, such rubbish passed muster, but hoaxers have to move with the times, and when Louis de Rougemont sold his story of life with the Aborigines of Australia to *World Wide Magazine* in 1898, he concentrated on bizarre customs and events rather than weird physiognomies.

Like *Robinson Crusoe*, the story began with a shipwreck. Rougemont claimed that his vessel went down somewhere near the Australian mainland, between Melville and Bathurst Island, and that only he and the ship's dog survived, the dog dragging him through the waves. For over two years the two of them lived on an island one hundred yards long, ten yards wide and eight feet above sea level. It must have seemed quite crowded. Like Robinson Crusoe, Rougemont saved enough materials and food from the wreck to survive. Early in his stay on the sandpit, he dug in the sand and unearthed sixteen complete human skeletons. He made a bow and arrow (he had always been interested in archery) and shot sea birds. He made fire by striking a steel tomahawk against a stone one, and for two and a half years he never allowed the fire to go out. He built himself a house of pearlshells, seven feet high, and ten feet long. Finding a stock of seeds in the hulk of the wrecked ship, he planted them in soil made by mixing sand with turtle blood. He successfully raised corn, which provided him with more food, and stalks with which to thatch his house. He made a hammock out of shark's hide, and a boat which he launched on the wrong side of the island so that it floated in a land-locked lagoon. His only reading matter was the New Testament, and he almost went out of his mind worrying over theological arguments.

One bright day a man, a woman and two children were washed up on the same island. They were Aborigines from Australia, and the woman's name was Yamba. Together, Rougemont and the Aborigines built a second boat, which they launched on the right side and sailed to the mainland of North Australia, a distance of at least two hundred miles. Here Rougemont 'became' a native and married Yamba. According to Rougemont, she was devoted to him: 'Often has that heroic creature tramped on foot a hundred miles to get me a few sprays of saline herbs; she heard me say I wanted salt.' There are parallels here with the devotion shown by Foulata to Captain Good RN in Rider Haggard's *King Solomon's Mines*, which had been published some thirteen years earlier.

Rougemont's article went on to outline a typical day among the Aborigines – swimming in the lagoon, watching for a passing sail, eating roots and emu, snake and kangaroo, rat and flying wombat, fish and worms. More excitingly, cannibalism was practised. Rougemont described the process in detail. After a fight or battle with another tribe, the dead were placed in trenches in the sand, seven feet long and three feet deep. These trenches were then filled with stones and sand and a huge fire was built on top. The fire was maintained with great fierceness for two hours, at the end of which time, the ovens were opened. 'I looked in and saw that the bodies were very much burnt. The skin was cracked in places and liquid fat was issuing forth . . . But perhaps the less said about this horrible spectacle the better.' Rougemont knew instinctively how effective it was to make it appear that the hoax was being wrung, unwillingly, from him.

The day came when Rougemont decided to return to what he called 'the outer world'. He set off overland with Yamba, taking with him 'a native passport – a kind of masonic mystic stick, inscribed with certain cabalistic characters. Every chief carried one of these sticks, stuck through his nose. I, however, invariably carried the passport in my long luxuriant hair. This passport stick proved invaluable as a means of putting us on good terms with the different tribes we encountered.' Nobody at *World Wide Magazine* asked how.

Again, like Robinson Crusoe, Rougemont went down with fever. Yamba, ever devoted, nursed him back to health, but once he had recovered he noticed a change in her.

> I asked her if anything had occurred to her during my illness. I then learned something which will haunt me to my dying day . . . To my unspeakable horror, Yamba quietly told me that she had given birth to a child, *which she had killed and eaten*. It took me some time to realise a thing so ghastly and so horrible, and when I asked why she had done it, she pleaded: 'I was afraid that you were going to die – going to leave me; and besides you know that I could not have nursed both you and the baby, so I did what I considered best.'

Yamba bore a small packet round her neck, containing some of the baby's bones, 'which she was preserving out of love for its memory'.

As Rougemont warmed to his theme, his story became more fantastic, more sensational and more repellent. While still suffering from fever, he killed a large buffalo, for he had learnt of a bizarre native cure. What he needed was warmth, so . . .

> scarce had the life left the body before I ripped the buffalo open between the fore and hind legs, and then crawled into the interior, fairly burying myself in a deluge of warm blood and intestines. My head, however, was protruding from the animal's

chest... next morning, to my amazement, I found I was a prisoner, the carcass having got cold and frigid, so that I had literally to be dug out. As I emerged I presented a most ghastly and horrifying spectacle. My body was covered in congealed blood, and even my long hair was all matted and stiffened with it. But never can I forget the feeling of exhilaration and strength that took possession of me as I stood there looking at my faithful companion. *I was absolutely cured* – a new man, a giant of strength.

For a moment *Robinson Crusoe* and *King Solomon's Mines* are swept aside, and we are in the land of *Siegfried*.

The article ended with Rougemont's return to England, sadly and significantly, without the devoted Yamba. Despite the article's success, there were those who didn't believe. The *Daily Chronicle* challenged Rougemont to prove the truth of his statements, to appear before the public. The latter at least he could manage – an elderly man, slight, tanned, with a wrinkled face and a cultured voice. He didn't look like a slayer of buffalo or a wrestler with alligators, and the truth emerged. His mother was brought from Switzerland, his wife from Sydney – claiming that he owed her a pound a week maintenance for some twenty years. Rougemont was really Henri Louis Grien, the son of an irritable and slovenly Swiss peasant. At the age of sixteen he had run away from home and into the arms of the actress, Fanny Kemble, then past her prime. She employed him as her footman, and for seven years he accompanied her on her theatrical tours. In 1870 he left Fanny, sailed to Australia and became butler to Sir William Cleaver Robinson, Governor of Western Australia. It was not a life that suited Henri Grien, and he drifted, becoming cook on a pearling vessel (he was shipwrecked), hotel dishwasher, street photographer, landscape artist, salesman of dodgy mining shares, and waiter in a Sydney restaurant. One of his customers in the restaurant was an explorer whose diaries Henri borrowed and copied.

In the spring of 1898, Grien arrived in England, with a letter from a Conservative MP which said: 'This man has a story which, if true, will stagger the world', but the article was a complete fabrication, most of the background information having been obtained from the borrowed diaries and the Reading Room of the British Museum. For a short while Grien was famous, dubbed the Baron Munchausen of

Australia, but his career as travel writer and amateur anthropologist was over. Henri Grien became a music hall turn, riding turtles in a huge tank on the stage of the London Hippodrome. The act was not a success, owing to the drowsiness of the turtles. Grien lapsed into obscurity and died a pauper, spending the last few years of his life selling matches in Piccadilly and Shaftesbury Avenue. There is one last description of him, by Edith Sitwell: 'This ghost of the streets was dressed in an old ragged overcoat, over the top of which the thin hair fell, and showed above it a calm, philosophical and curiously intelligent face.' Sitwell, for one, was sorry that Grien had been hounded and exposed.

Voigt, de Tilh, Caraboo and Rougemont adopted their temporary identities without conviction – they were not the products of childhood dreams and ambitions. Archibald Belaney was different. He was born in England in 1888 and was brought up by a pair of maiden aunts in Hastings, where he attended the local grammar school. As a boy he was passionately interested in animals and plants, and his great wish was to be a North American Indian. At the age of eighteen he left Hastings, sailed to Toronto, and went off into the Canadian forests to join the Ojibway tribe. He fell in love with the country, the Indian way of life and a young girl named Angele, whom he married.

He spent the next few years in the tribe of his adoption, but turned up in Flanders in 1915 as a private in the Canadian Army. He was wounded, sent back to England, and convalesced in Hastings Military Hospital. Here he renewed a friendship with a girl he had known in his childhood. Her name was Florence Holmes, and the pair married. The marriage lasted a couple of years, before Belaney returned to Canada and the Ojibways. He was shocked to discover that much of the old way of life had been destroyed in just a few years. His old hunting grounds were infested with mines, railroads and timbermills. He pushed westwards, trying to keep ahead of what passed for progress, and reached the land of the Iroquois. Here he married again. This time his bride was Gertrude Bernard, who adopted the Iroquois name of Anahareo. Under her influence, Belaney began to see that even the traditional ways of man were out of step with nature, that hunting and trapping posed a threat to wildlife survival.

Belaney began to write. He sent an article called 'The Fall of Silence' to a friend in England. The friend sent it on to *Country Life*, and the article was published. Belaney next wrote a book, *Pilgrims of the Wild*, and changed his name to Grey Owl. In Canada he gave public talks on nature, and discovered he could earn as much money that way as by hunting. In 1930 he was interviewed by another Canadian writer, Lloyd Roberts. By then Archibald Belaney had completely disappeared. Roberts described Grey Owl as 'The first Indian who really looked like an Indian – an Indian from those thrilling Wild West days of covered wagons, buffaloes and Sitting Bull. The stamp of his fierce Apache ancestors showed in his tall, gaunt physique, his angular features, his keen eyes, even in his two braids dangling down from his fringed buckskin shirt.'[17] Well, it made good copy and presumably Grey Owl wasn't wearing his Hastings Grammar School blazer.

He continued to write. He was furious when *Country Life* changed the title of one of his books from *The Vanishing Frontier* to *The Men of the Last Frontier*. White men were missing the point of what was happening – this was not a story of heroes, but of destruction. He wrote children's stories and a self-conscious semi-autobiographical work, *Tales of an Empty Cabin*. He was photographed by Karsh, and invited to visit England. He even lectured in Hastings, saying that if there were any Belaneys in the audience he would be happy to meet them. He was booked to speak on BBC Radio's *Children's Hour*, but the talk was cancelled. Grey Owl refused to delete a passage from his talk in which he urged children never to take part in blood sports. The BBC considered this was too contentious a statement. He appeared by command at Buckingham Palace.

But the call of the wild was as strong for Grey Owl in middle age as it had been for Archibald Belaney as a boy. He went back to Canada and died in Manitoba in April 1938. His was a gentle masquerade, and one of the most honourable. He was no Indian brave, but a man who cared about his planet at a time when the Earth had few friends. Bigamy aside, Archibald Belaney was an exceptional man, a noble hoaxer.

Jack Bilbo was a very different kettle of fish. His real name was Hugo Baruch and he was born in 1907. These are perhaps the only facts that we can be sure of in his life, for Bilbo was a line-shooter, a braggart and an absurd egotist. As a child he and his gang terrorized the inhabitants of Scheveningen in Holland, and Bilbo was sent away to boarding school. Here, he claimed, he bullied his way through the school, threatening the headteacher that if he weren't promoted each year his father would remove him and the school would lose valuable fees.

Bilbo left school and went to the United States, a visit that provided him with little beyond background for his later and most famous hoax. He sailed back to Germany and became an assistant director with UFA, the German film production company. He was sent to London as a correspondent for *Film Buhne*, a daily film paper, but was soon back in Germany, producing a theatrical show called *American Express Revue*. As with many other hoaxers, Bilbo's link with the theatre didn't last long. His leading lady attempted to poison him, being jealous of the attention he was paying to another woman. He went on tour with a circus revue called 'The Theatre of the Five Thousand'. Wherever he went, whoever he met, Bilbo came out on top. The difficult he could do in seconds, the impossible took a little longer. His glorious opinion of himself was unshakeable – he would have made a successful politician. By his early twenties he had worked out his philosophy of life: 'It's stupid to try and work against the law. It doesn't pay. It's much better to bring off criminal transactions *with* the consent of the law . . . to be a banker and spread about false news, to corrupt the Press, and under cover of false information to put inflated dividends in one's pocket. That's merely called intelligent speculation.'[18]

In the days of the Weimar republic, it was a philosophy to which many subscribed, but Bilbo himself went beyond it. After conspicuous lack of success in showbusiness, he toured Germany, repeatedly performing his magic carpet trick. He had two genuine hand-made Persian carpets, of quality and value, worth at least 400 marks each. These were the carpets he displayed, his bankers, his *bona fides*. Having convinced pawnbroker after pawnbroker that he possessed a store of expensive carpets, he then pawned cheap imitations of which he had an endless supply. He would buy a carpet for 100 marks and pawn it for 200 marks against a supposed value of 400 marks. All over Germany pawnbrokers were left with rolls of unwanted, cheap carpet.

Eventually the law caught up with Bilbo and he was thrown into gaol. He was appalled by the conditions in prison, and, to show his disgust, started a fight with the warders. 'I rather like fighting six people; every time one punches or kicks, one is sure to hit something, and even if one is overpowered eventually, one can do a hell of a lot of damage.'[19] It's a typical Bilbo boast, and it's followed by many more. He was more than a match for the 'hard' regime. The warders ended up giving him preferential treatment because he wrote their letters for them. Even when he was transferred to a lunatic asylum, he bounced back, lecturing the staff on 'The Place of Psychology in the Modern Prison System'. 'When I left they shook hands with me, clicking their heels and bowing: I in my prison uniform too!'[20] We are back in the land of *The Wind in the Willows*, and Mr Toad is treating Mole and Ratty to swollen accounts of his escapades; even the language is similar: 'Humbugged everybody – made 'em all do exactly what I wanted!'

Bilbo was released after eleven weeks in prison when the case against him collapsed and when they probably couldn't stand him any longer. He became a taxi driver and was one day hailed by his long-lost father, whom he hadn't seen for twelve years and who was a boaster in his own right – he claimed that he had sold the Crown Jewels of Tsar Ferdinand of Bulgaria for 100,000 marks. Bilbo gave up being a taxi driver after he met the editor of the *Müenchener Illustrierte Presse* and persuaded him to commission a book. 'What I really wanted was to be a writer, but all my books, sent to publishers under pseudonyms, were returned. Now, with a juicy murder on every page, fifteen different publishers in fifteen different countries were rushing to get their filthy hands on it.' For this was the book that made Bilbo famous, *Carrying a Gun for Al Capone*. It was a sensational work, purportedly written by one of Capone's own mob.

> 'Writing this in Europe, I am far from Chicago. Conversation goes on around me, about film stars, horse races, fashion. Often in the crowd, in the midst of the noisy chatter, I grow suddenly silent. People look at me and think me strange. But I stare at the far horizon and think of Chicago, of friends of mine who have probably died as I saw the gangsters die. I should like to die like that. I probably shall. I am 24 years old!'[21]

The book received favourable notices; the *Sunday Times* said it contained dramatic glimpses into a sinister underworld, and an excellent pen portrait of Al Capone – though how the *Sunday Times* was in a position to evaluate portraits of Al Capone isn't clear. Bilbo painted Capone as the Napoleon Bonaparte of the world of bootleggers and mobsters, with dialogue subsequently drawn on by Warner Brothers.

The book was still being published in the 1940s, though Baruch admitted the hoax in 1934. He kept his new identity, however, and continued to live the life of Jack Bilbo. The book made a lot of money, which Bilbo used to buy a car in which to drive to Holland. Here he renewed his friendship with one of his childhood gang, a young man whose slogan was 'Everything is mortal except human gullibility', and who made his living selling fake Rembrandts. Bilbo left Scheveningen and drove to Monte Carlo, where he came across a Russian named Gorguloff who told Bilbo he was going to assassinate the French President and invited Bilbo to join him in the venture.

Bilbo refused and returned to Berlin. A few days later, Wolfgang Krüger, a publisher, phoned Bilbo to ask about a letter that the German Universities Publishing Company had received from Gorguloff:

Honoured Herr Direktor,
While you are reading this letter I shall have assassinated the President of the French Republic, Daumier, today at twelve o'clock midday...

It was then 9.15 am. Bilbo claimed that he warned the police in France, but his warning went unheeded. After the assassination, the French press described Gorguloff as a Bolshevik agent. The French President of Police, Chiappe, was a right-wing politician. There are times when, every way you look, there is distortion. Bilbo received visits from the Nazis, telling him not to divulge what he knew of Gorguloff and the letter. He claimed that attempts were made on his life. There is no way of checking, but Nazi Germany was probably no place for a line-shooter of Bilbo's calibre. He fled to Paris.

His story doesn't end here. He lived life to the full and wrote several more books; hoaxers love to get into print. Wherever he went, whatever he did, his conceit saw to it that he still came out on top. He was a heavily built man. If he hit you physically, you were physically hurt. If he hit you psychologically, you were psychologically damaged. He had no need to carry a gun for Al Capone or anyone else.

It is tempting to see Central Europe as a hoaxers' paradise during the 1920s and 1930s. In the politically reeling aftermath of the Treaty of Versailles, impostors strutted from Paris to Berlin to Budapest to the Bosphorus. Some wore spurious uniforms, bedecked with false medals; some wore bowler hats and carried briefcases bunged with phoney share certificates and false credentials. Stephane Otto was a uniform and medals man, dubbed 'The King of the Impostors', a title he deserved more than the one he claimed, which was King of the Belgians. Otto was born in 1899. He had a distinguished look about him according to contemporary reports, spoke five languages with ease and drank only champagne. He enlisted in the Belgian Army, at the age of fifteen, on the outbreak of the First World War. He fought bravely and received a number of decorations, including the Croix de Guerre. He also became a drug addict during the War, and, in the words of the *Daily Express* 'to assuage his thirst for glory (and his need for money) he resorted to a number of impudent masquerades – a son of M Maeterlinck, a nephew of Cardinal Mercier, and so on.'[22]

Otto liked to present medals as well as receive them. On one occasion, in 1919, posing as a member of the Belgian General Staff, he visited the Headquarters of the United States Army of Occupation in Koblenz, held a review and, in the name of the King of the Belgians, pinned the Grand Cross of the Order of Leopold on the proud chest of Major-General H T Allen, commanding the United States forces. It was perhaps better to give than to receive, for a few months later Otto was in prison, convicted of wearing a uniform without authority. On his release he joined the Foreign Legion, which he deserted 'in order to pay court to an actress in Paris'.[23]

From then on it was all downhill. He visited Perpignan, where he posed as 'Lord Ashton', the representative of the Prince of Wales. He was recognized and sentenced to fifty days' imprisonment on a variety of petty swindling charges. He drifted to England, and had the book thrown at him in Crewe in 1927, being charged with giving false information to a hotel-keeper, landing in England while subject to a deportation order, and obtaining 12s 6d by fraud from a clergyman. He appeared in dock in the full dress uniform of an officer in the

French Navy, replete with medals, and made a touching plea for clemency. He was sentenced to nine months. Just over a year later he committed suicide, leaping to his death from the third floor of a small lodging house in Brussels. He was thirty years old.

It is one thing to change rank (Voigt, Ellis), or nationality (Otto, Psalmanazar, Caraboo), or even race (Belaney), but there are hoaxers who are prepared to change sex, not for temporary reasons, as Sophie Lloyd did, but on a more permanent basis. Karoly Hadju, another mittel-European hoaxer, was born in Hungary in 1920. He was the son of a tailor. After the Second World War, he came to England, as Baron Carl Hadju (it does seem such a wonderful name for a hoaxer). The title, he declared, was Hungarian, but the English press were suspicious. He married, set up an accommodation agency, and in 1956 raised money to send 'freedom fighters' from Britain to support the nationalist uprising in Hungary. The money never reached Hungary and Hadju was accused of embezzlement. The following year he was declared bankrupt. Like all good hoaxers, he decided that the way out of his difficulties was to adopt a new personality, and he became Michael Karoly, author, hypnotherapist and man-about-town. He dined with the rich and titled, rented an office in Mayfair, and had an affair with a marchioness. In 1965 Karoly's wife and mistress both died, and life took another downward plunge. He was bound over for a year after being found in women's clothes in Hertford. In 1966 he was gaoled for two months for obtaining credit while an undischarged bankrupt.

Two years later, Hadju or Karoly was reborn as Dr Charlotte Bach, a widow who had formerly been a lecturer in philosophy and psychology at Budapest University. For thirteen years he maintained this personality, though he did double as Daphne Lyell-Manson, whose less academic pursuits included a spanking service to those in the know. One of Madam Lyell-Manson's satisfied customers gave the following glowing testimonial: 'You were most generous and kind to spend so much energy on my ugly male backside.'[24] As Charlotte Bach, Hadju wrote a lengthy book expounding his theories that transvestites held the clue to human evolution. This was hailed by Colin Wilson as 'one of the greatest intellectual advances of the twentieth century'.[25] Hadju died in 1981, a lady to the end, or at least until the post mortem examination.

Adopting another personality is no easy thing. It took Sophie Lloyd and Jenny Winstanley months to prepare for brief appearances in false guises. It took all of Jack Bilbo's overwhelming personality to support the identity he assumed. Poor Louis de Rougemont was unable to sustain in real life the pretence he had so imaginatively produced in print. Mary Willcocks lived for only a short while as Princess Caraboo. The gains are not always commensurate with the risks and the trouble taken. There are those, however, who have tricked, fooled or at least puzzled the world for years, as we shall see.

5

Not What They Seemed

> 'I recognize that I am made up of several persons and that the person that at the moment has the upper hand will inevitably give place to another. But which is the real one? All of them or none?'
> W Somerset Maugham, *A Writer's Notebook*, 1896

Francis Percy Toplis was only twenty-three when he was shot by police in the cemetery at High Hesket. He never professed to be anyone in particular, but he has come to be known in recent times as The Monocled Mutineer. At the time of his death, he was described as an 'outlaw', 'a gunman', and 'daredevil Toplis'. The *News of the World* of 20 June 1920 devoted several columns to his death, and included a brief biography:

> Born in 1896 in the village of Shirlands near Alfreton, Percy Toplis, a promising, quick-witted, blue-eyed lad, attended a local school. Here by studious attention to his lessons he imbibed that knowledge which in later years enabled him with complete success to adapt himself to any and every situation in life. Very early he showed that he was glib-tongued and very ready to take advantage of any opportunity that presented itself, and once played the name part in a piece entitled *Poor Little Johnny* at a local theatre. . . .

It is not an unfair opening paragraph. Toplis was handsome, debonair, a natural actor, a fine pianist, and always possessed of a wild sense of humour. He was a tearaway delinquent as a boy, and his headteacher predicted that he would end his days on the gallows. By the time he was twelve, Toplis had been birched for larceny, had pulled off several neat swindles, had constantly disrupted his school (by such wheezes as passing a bottle of laudanum round the class), and had proved too much for parents, guardians, teachers and police alike. From the age of twelve until he enlisted in the RAMC in 1915, Toplis was regularly in trouble, though always for petty misdemeanours. For Toplis, as for so many others, the War brought opportunities to perform on a bigger stage. Order breaks down in war, people disappear, reappear; spare uniforms are there for the stripping and taking; medals can be stolen, ranks assumed. Toplis got hold of a captain's uniform and the Distinguished Conduct Medal. He returned to Mansfield and the colliery where he had briefly worked, and enjoyed himself reviewing and drilling the Local Defence Volunteers. He had his photo taken in the captain's uniform, a photograph that was later used on 'Wanted' posters across the country.

'In the West End of London he masqueraded as an Army officer with a distinguished record and was well known in some of the fashionable restaurants, claiming to be possessed of means and, when in mufti, sporting a gold monocle.'[1] He was a mixture of Burlington Bertie and The Man Who Broke the Bank at Monte Carlo, a man who 'made assignations with many young girls', and who instinctively knew when to change rank, regiment and residence. By 1917 he was back in France, a leading figure in The Sanctuary, an underground society of deserters and freebooters who lived in holes dug out of the sand hills near the British Army base at Étaples. The army of deserters nicknamed Toplis 'The General', and, when the Camp at Étaples flared into violent mutiny, it was Toplis who dictated terms to Brigadier-General Andrew Thomson and negotiated a settlement with Horatio Bottomley, 'The Tommies' Ambassador'.

From that time, Toplis became a marked man. He knew too much. Officially there had been no mutiny at Étaples; all evidence relating to it was suppressed until 1978. Officially there had been no such place as The Sanctuary. Bottomley, arch-hoaxer and politican, played the game the way the Establishment wished it to be played: 'I have asked the boys to jot down the main matters of complaint. . . .' Toplis never played the game that way – at school he had kicked a teacher who was about to cane him, and had then run off. Toplis had no protectors, no standing, no contacts. Toplis was a man the authorities could never trust to keep his mouth quiet. He was on the run for the rest of his short life.

After the Armistice, he stole the uniform of a captain in the RASC, a chequebook of the London County and Westminster Bank, a revolver and twelve cartridges. Dressed as an officer, he wrote dud cheques for whatever he wanted, always adding half a crown to the amount he was charged, as 'the mark of a gentleman'. He escaped from military and civilian prisons with apparent ease, and even had the effrontery to re-enlist in the RASC under his real and 'wanted' name. He ran blackmarket deals in Army petrol and food, using the money he obtained to spend long weekends (Thursday to Tuesday) in the West End, dining at the Savoy and trotting off to Ascot. He was arrested yet again, and escaped by picking his guards' pockets while he played cards with them, thereby gaining the keys with which he locked his guards in his cell. In January 1920 he joined the RAF, still as Francis Percy Toplis, but a few months later he became the prime, and convenient, suspect in a murder case. He fled to Wales, to Scotland, to the Lake District, and here the mad masquerade came to an end.

Accounts vary as to what happened in the last couple of hours of Toplis's life. His biographers, William Allinson and John Fairley, are certain that the police fired first, after a chase that owed a lot to Mack Sennett and the Keystone Kops, and after some not very bright police work. Contemporary newspaper reports give a totally different picture; Toplis fired first, there was no farcical chase, the police always knew what they were doing. Allinson and Fairley state that PC Alfred Fulton, who first came across Toplis on that midsummer evening, had no idea whom he had stumbled across. It was his wife who suggested that the young man trudging the roads might be the man all Britain was looking for. In the *News of the World* account, Fulton knew his man from the beginning:

> 'I said "Let me look in your kitbag." To my astonishment he threw it on the ground and stepped back a few paces. I then felt certain of my man, but knowing what a dangerous ruffian he was and as we were quite alone, I remarked, jokingly, "You might be the likes of Toplis." He smiled grimly and replied: "I am not that fellow." By that time I had made up my mind that

THE MAN BEFORE ME WAS TOPLIS

'But desiring to make sure I bade him a hasty adieu and made for home. Over my tea, I studied a description of the wanted man, and after hurriedly mending a puncture in my bicycle, I pedalled after him.'[2]

This *News of the World* Special reads like a pastiche of bygone reportage. Fulton returned to Toplis. '"Hallo, old boy," I said. In the twinkling the man was on his feet and I found myself looking down the barrel of a big revolver . . .' Toplis replied: '"If there is any hanky-panky, you go. Up with your hands."' We are in the world of the *Boys' Own Paper*; Toplis has become a cardboard villain, this is a good yarn, and truth is at a premium. 'When overtaken, Toplis realized the game was up but nevertheless attempted another desperate act. He levelled his revolver at the police and fired three times. The police returned the fire. Toplis fell dead.' In Allison and Fairley's account, however, Toplis was ambushed by the police: 'The two civilian-clad figures, Ritchie and Bertram, rushed out, guns blazing, followed by Fulton.'[3] Inspector Ritchie swore that the police never sought to kill Toplis, merely to 'bring him down or disarm him'. Allison and Fairley are certain that the order had gone out to silence Toplis permanently. Fleet Street points up the moral in an article headed 'DEAD MAN'S BLACK PAST':

> What a tragic fate for one so young, and what a lesson for youth of wayward habits. True he escaped the ignominy of the hangman's noose, but only because he was ignominiously slain when, with his back to the wall, as it were, he was doing his best to slay others.[4]

What makes Toplis different from other famous hoaxers is that he didn't seek fame. Most hoaxers puff themselves up into something greater than they are, like the frog in Aesop's fable. That was not Toplis's way, but history is perhaps doing it for him. From one perspective he was one of the ten-a-penny villains, wolves in officers' clothing, who conned their way into a world of privilege from which they had been excluded. From another perspective, Toplis was an agit-prop, working-class hero with such a reputation for lack of respect that, once he came into possession of dangerous information, the Establishment had to get rid of him. It is impossible to tell whether either of these is a true perspective.

Whereas Toplis may not have had an inflated opinion of himself, Ignacz Trebitsch Lincoln spent the first three-quarters of his life seeking ox-like stature. He was born in April 1879 in Paks, a small town on the banks of the Danube in central Hungary. His father was a prosperous Jewish merchant; his mother came from a wealthy family. Early in life Trebitsch (the 'Lincoln' came later) showed considerable skill as a linguist, and in 1895 he enrolled as a student at the Royal Hungarian Academy of Dramatic Art in Budapest. His acting career lasted less than a year, and by 1896 he was on the run from the police, accused of more than one theft. At this time he was a well-built young man, with black hair, a black moustache and piercing dark eyes. 'Superficially precocious and worldly in some ways, he remained naive, provincial and immature in others. Indeed, emotionally he probably never fully matured.'[5]

Trebitsch spent the next forty years in a state of physical, professional and emotional fidgeting. He went to England, back to Germany, to Canada, to Germany again, to Appledore-in-Ebory in Kent, to Hampton-on-Thames, to Brussels, Darlington, Budapest, Belgrade, New York. He was by turn clergyman, research worker, MP, venture capitalist, bankrupt, oil speculator, journalist and would-be spy. He failed in all capacities. He was an errant husband and a dreadful father. He had 'intimations of greatness, a desire to hobnob with the mighty, a taste for intrigue, a liking for public attention, a wish to boss other people around, fascination with the careers of Disraeli and Napoleon'.[6] His one talent was believing in himself, which he did to a mighty degree. His one achievement was to be a nuisance. His one ambition was to be on centre-stage, and from time to time he almost succeeded. He was a prominent figure in the attempted German *putsch* in March 1920, and a minor one in the White International. Hardly a year went by during the 1920s and 1930s without Trebitsch contacting some embassy (it didn't matter whose), somewhere (it didn't matter where) and offering a clutch of secrets to somebody (it didn't matter whom). He went through a string of aliases – Thomas Lamprecht, Thomas Lorincz, Thomas Longford, Leo Tandler. Sadly, he was limited to aliases with the initials 'TL' as his shirts and handkerchiefs were thus monogramed. By the late 1930s, he was *persona non grata* in most of Europe, and headed east, to China. He became depressed, introspective, the victim of massive self-delusion and fantasy. He turned to religion, his first legitimate employment as a young man, and popped up as the Buddhist Abbot of Shanghai after a spell as military adviser to one of the Chinese war lords. His death in 1943, when Shanghai was under Japanese occupation, remains something of a mystery.

As a hoaxer, Trebitsch Lincoln had few successes. He conned several hundred dollars out of the Presbyterian Church in Toronto, and a great deal more out of the philanthropic Seebohm Rowntree. He fleeced shareholders in such fly-by-night companies as the Oil and Drilling Trust of Roumania. He tried to convince the British that he was a British agent and the Germans that he was a double agent. But all the time there hung about him the aura of tatty failure. He was that sad case, the hoaxer who overestimates himself.

The most outrageous attempt to adopt a false identity, however, was that made by Arthur Orton, the Tichborne Claimant.

Orton is now regarded as a hoaxer and a conman, who claimed in the second half of the nineteenth century to be the long-lost heir to the wealthy Tichborne estate, and who brought an action for ejectment against Sir Henry Tichborne, the twelfth baronet. The action lasted 102 days, at which point Sergeant Ballantine, Orton's counsel, elected to be non-suited, a legal term which means 'threw in the towel'. Almost immediately, Orton was charged with perjury and arrested. There is an echo of the trials of Oscar Wilde here: from witness stand to dock in one swift move. Orton's criminal trial ran for 188 days, at the end of which he was sentenced to fourteen years' penal servitude. He served ten years, was released in 1884, and died in poverty eleven years later.

Against all the odds, the hoax almost worked. Orton had the support of thousands, and some of the phenomenally good luck that blesses many hoaxers. Strange personalities were involved. The whole affair was cloaked in mystery. There were conspiracies that worked for and against Orton. He made some inspired statements and connections, to the extent that, even today, it is possible at least to have doubts as to whether justice was done.

Assuming it was, the facts were these. Roger Tichborne (the man

Orton claimed to be) was the eldest son of Sir James Francis Doughty Tichborne, head of a very wealthy Roman Catholic family. Roger spent his early years in Paris, was educated at Stonyhurst, and then obtained a commission in the 6th Dragoon Guards. In 1852, he sold his commission and sailed to South America, seeking sport and travel. Two years later he embarked from Rio de Janeiro in a ship named the *Bella*. The ship was never seen again, though her longboat was discovered some time later, together with articles of wreckage. Roger was presumed dead, and his will was proved in July 1855. There the matter would have rested had not Lady Tichborne, Roger's mother, decided that her son was not dead. A photograph exists of her; she sits looking straight to camera, a dreamy, almost otherworldly look in her eyes, her hands clasped in her lap over what looks suspiciously like a reticule. She has a perfect oval face, crowned with a large black bonnet, and with a large black bow neatly tied under her chin. She looks gentle, fragile even, but she must have been a very determined woman. Alone among the family she persisted in the belief that Roger was not dead, and for ten years she placed advertisements for him in the English and colonial papers.

It took ten years to obtain the first and only positive response. In November 1865, Lady Tichborne learnt that a man said to be answering the description of her missing son had been found at Wagga Wagga in New South Wales. Letters were exchanged, 'but with an eagerness bordering on insanity', observes the *Dictionary of National Biography*, 'she had made up her mind, before seeing a line of his [Orton's] handwriting or learning a singular particular of his life, that her correspondent was her son'. She implored him to come home to Hampshire, and Orton duly arrived in Europe late in 1866, by which time fourteen years had elapsed since Lady Tichborne had last seen her missing son. Orton and Lady Tichborne first met in the darkened bedroom of a Paris hotel one grim January afternoon. She professed to recognize him, and from then on nothing that anyone else said could persuade her otherwise. Orton didn't look like the missing Roger: there was a weight problem. Roger had weighed ten or eleven stone, but when Lady Tichborne met Orton he already weighed twenty-one stone. Orton didn't recognize any members of Roger's family, who held that he was an impostor, but Lady Tichborne clung to her belief. Here was the luck that every hoaxer needs: the determination on the part of the victim to be tricked. She brought Orton to stay with her on the estate in Hampshire. She accepted his wife and children, and made him an allowance of £1,000 a year. Just over a year later, she died.

Without her support, Orton might have given up, but he now owed a great deal of money to many creditors from whom he had borrowed in anticipation of grabbing the Tichborne fortune; indeed, he had begun borrowing money long before he left Australia. However, Orton had made good use of the time that elapsed from the moment when he first came across one of Lady Tichborne's advertisements to the time when her protection came to an end. She had at least made it as easy as possible for him. An old black servant, named Bogle, had been sent to Australia to accompany him back to England. Bogle chatted readily to Orton, and Orton learnt a great deal about the Tichborne family from him. Lady Tichborne made all Roger's diaries and letters available to Orton. He was gifted with an extremely rententive memory, and he rapidly picked up a great deal of information. He gained allies in the old family solicitor, a Mr Hopkins, and in a well-known Winchester antiquary named Baigent. Both the villagers and the local gentry accepted Orton as Sir Roger. Fellow officers from the 6th Dragoon Guards were convinced he was Roger. Orton plied them with a number of details of the minutiae of regimental life. He 'recalled' incidents that took place at Stonyhurst. He 'remembered' where he had bought his clothes as a young man, and snatches of conversation that had passed between him and his tailor. He 'recollected' childhood aches and pains and illnesses. To finance what was clearly going to be a long and expensive campaign, he raised money by the sale of 'Tichborne Bonds', a standard hoaxer's ploy, borrowing money against some hoped-for future gain.

The trustees of the estate were unconvinced, as was Chief Justice Bovill and a special jury. Orton put up a considerable performance, however. His cross-examination at the hands of Sir John Coleridge lasted twenty-two days, and 'was remarkable alike for the colossal ignorance displayed by him [Orton], and for the acuteness and bulldog tenacity with which he faced the ordeal,' as the *DNB* put it: 'Did you ever see a more clever man, more ready, more astute, or with more ability in dealing with information and making use of the slightest hint dropped by cross-examining counsel?' However,

The first sixteen years of his life he had absolutely forgotten; the few facts he had told the jury were already proved, or would thereafter be shown to be absolutely false and fabricated. Of his college life he could recollect nothing.... About his amusements, his books, his music, his games, he could tell nothing. Not a word of his family, of the people with whom he lived, their habits, their persons, their very names.... When he reappears in 1865 he has undergone a physical and moral miracle: a slight, delicate, undersized youth has developed into an enormous mass of flesh.[7]

For Orton was now even larger than when he had first come to Europe – a massive twenty-four stone. Details of his background began to emerge. He had been an expert slaughterman at the age of seventeen, and had spent his time in Australia (1852–65) as a stockman, mail-rider, and, so it was rumoured, bushranger and horse-thief. When he came across Lady Tichborne's advertisement, he weighed only ten and a half stone, was working as a butcher and had just married an illiterate servant girl. He put on eight stone in as many months in Sydney, like some barrier between him and the outside world. Physically, it was an audacious claim to make, and yet it was on physical grounds that Orton was able to maintain the support of thousands of people long after he had been found guilty of perjury and had been sent to Dartmoor.

In the first place, once he was in prison he lost so much weight that the bone structure of his face was more clearly revealed and an apparent similarity to Roger Tichborne emerged. Secondly, much play was made at Orton's trial that his hair was naturally red and that he was dyeing it dark to resemble that of the original Roger Tichborne. On 12 September 1874, a few weeks after Orton's imprisonment, he was visited in Millbank Prison by his wife, Lord Rivers, Guildford Onslow and others, and Dr Edward Vaughan Hyde Kenealy, MP, QC, who had appeared as counsel for Orton at his trial. An eyewitness account claims that Dr Kenealy said to Orton: 'Sir Roger, the Jesuit and Whig parties are circulating far and wide that prison has unmasked one of your disguises, and that your hair is red, like Orton's. Permit me to request you to remove your cap, that I may judge for myself.' Orton is reported to have given a melancholy half-smile, and removed a dark coloured cap – it looked like brown paper – from his head. The red and carroty locks of Orton appeared not; but the dark hair of Roger Tichborne.'[8] Thirdly, evidence was produced *in camera* at the trial, and in support of Orton's claim, that he must be Roger Tichborne since he too possessed a retractable penis, a condition that had caused Roger much embarrassment at Stonyhurst and much worry when he came to consider marriage and parenthood.

The problem here is that Kenealy may be judged not too reliable a witness. He was himself, if not a hoaxer, at least a most odd man. He had been educated by the Jesuits in Ireland, but had then proceeded to Trinity College, Dublin, where he had proclaimed strong Protestant views. In 1850 he was sentenced to one month's imprisonment for cruelty to his natural son, following a prosecution by the Guardians of the West London Union. There is a strong suggestion that his mind became unsettled during his defence of Orton, for 'he made groundless imputations against witnesses and against various Roman Catholic bodies, insulted and trifled with the bench, and mercilessly protracted the case into the longest trial at *nisi prius* on record'.[9] The jury appended to their verdict a censure of the language he had employed. After Orton's conviction, Kenealy started a scurrilous paper, *The Englishman*, to plead the cause of Orton as Tichborne. It enjoyed a large circulation, partly because Kenealy threatened to reveal details of the private lives and morals of the Chief Justice, Sir Alexander Coburn, who had been one of the three judges at Orton's trial, and of the Solicitor-General, Sir John Holker. For these excesses, Kenealy was expelled from the mess of the Oxford Circuit, dispatented by the Lord Chancellor, and disbenched and disbarred by Gray's Inn.

Like Orton, Kenealy was not a man to be easily dissuaded from a course of action. He immediately founded the Magna Carta Association, ostensibly to continue to press Orton's claim, but partly to avenge himself. Kenealy perambulated the country, delivering a lecture in language always 'extravagant and abusive and often blasphemous'.[10] Such was the popular support for Orton, however, particularly among the poorer classes who saw his imprisonment as part of a conspiracy of the rich, that Kenealy was able to stand successfully for the Parliamentary seat of Stoke in February 1875. When he took his seat, no Members of the House were willing to introduce him, and on the motion of Disraeli, the ceremony was dispensed with. On 23 April 1875, Kenealy moved in the House of

Commons to refer the conduct of Orton's trial and the guilt or innocence of Orton to a Royal Commission. The motion in the House was rejected by 433 votes to 1.

Kenealy spent the last few years of his life visiting Orton and condemning the Jesuits, whom he accused of a conspiracy against his client. He was a strong supporter of *The Tichborne Almanack*, a journal which listed four hundred 'of the most important FACTS IN THE HISTORY OF THE CLAIMANT',[11] and urged that 'EVERYONE SHOULD READ *A Critical Review of the Tichborne Trial* - It proves indisputably from the sworn evidence before the Courts of Common Pleas and Queen's Bench that the Claimant is *not* Arthur Orton but is Roger Tichborne.'[12] One detects the hand of Kenealy behind many of the statements in *The Tichborne Almanack*, in which the Jesuits get an extremely bad press: '. . . they gave a small sample of their rascality during the Tichborne Trial by their lies and forgeries against the Claimant, and their polluting our Courts of Justice, as they have never been before polluted during this century, by the payment of a Bigamist, a Thief, and Prostitute for having committed perjury.'[13]

Kenealy again contested Stoke during the General Election of 1880, but this time finished bottom of the poll. A few weeks later he died of an abcess in the foot. Perhaps his best qualification for inclusion as a hoaxer on his own merit, is his claim that he wrote poetry which contained translations from Latin, Greek, German, Italian, Portuguese, Russian, Irish, Persian, Arabic, Hindustani and Bengali.

In all this, Orton had more of the fortune that seems to accompany many hoaxers: the support of people who are themselves obsessional. With such support, Orton refused to give up his claim. In prison, first at Millbank and then at Dartmoor, he conducted himself with great dignity on the few occasions he was permitted visitors. His supporters believed he was dying in prison: 'He is under the Doctor's hands, but his hours seem numbered: it is impossible that he can long survive.'[14] This was in Millbank, in September 1874. Dr Kenealy visited him at Dartmoor, eight months later. 'To a man like Tichborne, suffering from the hereditary asthma of his family, and racked with rheumatism, sleep in one of these cells must be about as pleasant as if he were slung in a hammock on the peak of a mountain.'[15] Orton's words to Kenealy during this visit are faithfully recorded:

I shall never leave this prison; I am destined to die in it . . . the Government have got the People down . . . and they mean to keep them down. If the whole of the working and industrial classes were to meet tomorrow in a public meeting . . . to declare that they thought I had been unfairly treated, the Government are so powerful that they would trample them beneath their feet. All the old English spirit is gone. There was a time when the feelings and opinions of Englishmen went for something; now they go for nothing. Therefore I shall live and die a prisoner in this place.[16]

In fact, as we shall see later, Orton lived another twenty-three years.

His claim, his hoax, lasted eight years. It was fuelled by his own greed, but supported by a most accomplished performance. It is hard to doubt that, by the time he had lost his case and was in prison, he really believed he was Tichborne, for the show had by then had a long run. The hoax came very near to success, and gained immense popular support. Believers and non-believers in Orton were divided along strict class lines. The poor believed him: the rich didn't. Those who sneered at Orton and rejected his claim, did so on the grounds that he looked coarse, that his hands were calloused, that he spoke with a common accent, and that he, therefore, couldn't be a gentleman. Shortly after his conviction, there appeared the *Tichborne Times* – 'A Journal for those Interested in the Great Tichborne Trial'. One of the contributions to this cynical little magazine was a poem: 'COPY OF LINES FOUND IN A RECENTLY OCCUPIED CELL IN NEWGATE' (where Orton was imprisoned during his trial).

> They say i can't spell Rodger, cause i spells it with a letter d,
> Such blessed rows on trifles, now i must confess i hate;
> What ere they did in Newgate, i don't mean to let this fetter me
> 'Cos folks should never grumble when i gives 'em over weight.
> A aitch-bone's better with H, although of course some drops it,
> A hatchet's better with it, and so is its handle too,
> But as they like the short way best, in future i will drop it,
> And make myself more pleasant to the stuck-up Doughty*
> crew.[17]

---

* In the previous century an ancestor of Sir Roger's had changed the family name to Doughty.

The poem was followed by a small ads column:

> TO BE SOLD – A quantity of Tichborne Bonds, at a little above waste paper price. For particulars, address U R Chisselled, at our office.
>
> TO BE SOLD – At considerably less than cost price, a quantity of Tichborne Stock. Address, Done Brown, Esq., Hanwell (NOTE, slightly past *Ealing*!)
>
> TO BE SOLD – A bargain, a quantity of green spectacles, which the jury who tried Roger refused to wear. Apply Barnacle, Turnham Green.
>
> WANTED – Anyone (not being at present an inmate of any lunatic asylum) who will attempt to prove successfully that Sir Roger Tichborne is alive.

The humour is ponderous. The impression is that a great many people were very relieved when Arthur Orton was adjudged not to be Roger Tichborne, for in his own ponderous way, he challenged the system just as much as the gadabout Trebitsch Lincoln, and the maverick Percy Toplis.

6

The Fairy Tales of Science

> 'Science is nothing but trained and organized common sense.'
> T H Huxley, 'The Method of Zadig' *Collected Essays*

> 'How often have I said to you, Watson, that when you have eliminated the impossible, whatever remains, *however improbable*, must be the truth?'
> Sir Arthur Conan Doyle, *The Sign of Four*

There are two types of scientific hoax: that played by the scientist and that played on the scientist. The former are rarer, the latter are sadder. Just occasionally, a kind of crossbred species emerges – that played by one scientist on another – and these become the most famous.

Any scientist who becomes involved in a hoax plays a key role. If he or she is the perpetrator, then the hoax starts off with a distinct advantage. Just as we tend to believe what we are told by newspapers and television, we tend to believe what scientists say: we may not like it, but we believe it. Similarly, if the hoax is fed to a scientist, and the scientist swallows it, then again the hoax gains considerable credence. If a scientist gives it his or her seal of approval, then the hoax has a certain authority. And, as science progresses and makes new discoveries, the apparent hoax of today may become the truth of tomorrow. This is how science works and this is what makes it vulnerable to the hoaxer. Six hundred years ago anyone who claimed that the world was round or that it revolved around the sun, would have been lucky to be regarded simply as a practical joker. Those dear old ignorant people who lived in the past knew nothing of transplant surgery, lasers, heavier-than-air flying machines, space walks, microwave ovens, or cordless telephones. The shaky knowledge we already have of these and a thousand other phenomena, makes us wary of crying 'hoax' when a man or woman in a white coat solemnly tells us something that seems incredible.

In 1835, a journalist on the New York *Sun* made use of a world authority in a simple if sensational hoax. The journalist's name was Locke, and the scientist whose authority he borrowed was Sir John Herschel. Locke prepared his ground in a series of articles in the paper. He reported that Herschel, who was conveniently out of the way in Capetown, had built a colossal twenty-four-foot, six-and-a-half-ton telescope with a magnifying power of 42,000X. The telescope was unique also in that the final image it produced could be transferred by artificial light to a giant screen, fifty feet wide. This, wrote Locke, enabled Herschel to study the surface of the moon as though from a distance of only a hundred yards.

The *Sun* was a popular illustrated paper, and Locke crammed his first article with diagrams and technical language, on the well established principle that if people couldn't understand what they were reading, they would believe it was true. On 26 August 1835 Locke published his second article. Herschel, he reported, had discovered an inland sea on the surface of the moon, and white beaches, hills covered in red flowers, forests of tall evergreens, deserts, volcanoes and pyramids of amethysts. Like God in the Book of Genesis, Locke created an unpopulated planet to begin with. The following day came the third article. Locke told his increasingly excited readers that Herschel had identified brown quadrupeds, like small bison, on the surface of the moon, as well as moose, reindeer, beavers that walked on their hind legs and lived in lodges with chimneys, and unicorns.

By then the paper had achieved a circulation of almost twenty thousand, making it the most successful in the world. By comparison, *The Times* in London had a circulation of only seventeen thousand. On 28 August came the fourth article. As in the Book of Genesis, man was saved till last. Locke now claimed that Herschel had discovered *vespertilio homo* – man bats! They were four foot high, and covered, save for their faces, with short and glossy copper-coloured hair, which grew from their shoulders right down to the calves of their legs.

It is, of course, impossible to tell how many people believed all this, and we are back at the old question of whom can we trust among reporters and recorders of hoaxes. There are those who say that 90 per cent of the *Sun*'s readership believed Locke's articles, but no one has produced any evidence to support this claim. Locke himself blew the hoax by alleging that Sir John Herschel had forty pages of scientific calculations based on his moon studies. It's one thing to say you've found the Missing Link or that there are fairies at the bottom of your garden. It's quite another to claim you have calculations. Calculations can be checked, simply to see whether they work as calculations. The ubiquitous two Yale professors arrived at the *Sun*'s office wishing to see these calculations, and Locke sent them on a wild-goose chase. However, when the New York *Journal of Commerce*, a respected rival paper, asked, in print, for the calculations, Locke admitted the hoax.

Edward Simpson was a much more down-to-earth hoaxer. He was born in 1815 in the village of Sleights, on the River Esk in Yorkshire, a few miles inland from the port of Whitby. His father was a sailor and his mother died soon after his birth, so Simpson was brought up by foster parents. He received little formal education but was reckoned a lively and intelligent lad. The countryside around Sleights was rich in Stone Age material, and a local historian and archaeologist introduced Edward to the study of fossils, and more particularly flint weapons and tools. In the next few years, Simpson acquired a reputation as an expert on such matters, and dealers came to him asking him to find arrowheads, spearheads, axeheads and hammers. It wasn't long before Flint Jack, as Simpson had become known, decided that it was easier and quicker to make prehistoric arrowheads than to trudge the moors looking for them. And, once he had discovered how easy it was to fool the experts with these, he looked around for other artefacts. Near Bridlington he set up a pottery specializing in Roman and prehistoric urns. The copies he produced were poor and crude, but the experts were taken in, and Flint Jack became more ambitious. He is said to have beaten a tin tray into the shape of a Roman breastplate and sold that 'for a handsome price'.

Flint Jack's audacity was matched by his buyers' gullibility. He sold a piece of stone on which he had scratched the words *IMP CONSTANT EBVR* – 'Emperor Constantine, York' – and a wooden ring inscribed with the name of the thirteenth-century Abbot of Croyland. He travelled across England, taking in experts and scientists whever he went. He sold many fakes to the British

Museum, was employed as fossil collector by the Museum at York, and carved amber necklaces in the Lake District. He came to London a third time in 1862 and was at last confronted by a geologist named Professor Tennant. Flint Jack admitted the hoax but stressed that he had never tried to pass off his work as genuine. He was a simple peasant traveller, offering his 'odds and ends' to anyone who fancied buying them.

Tennant appreciated Flint Jack's skill. He arranged for Simpson to give a lecture to a gathering of geologists and archaeologists at the headquarters of the Geologists' Association in Cavendish Square. He was introduced as a man who 'with the aid of only a small piece of iron rod, bent at the end' could produce almost any form of flint weapon head. The lecture was a great success, but Flint Jack's career was almost over. He had become a heavy drinker and needed money to quench his thirst. For a while he stumbled along, but in the late 1860s he was imprisoned for a year in Bedford, after breaking into a house and stealing a clock and a barometer.

Other scientific hoaxers, from more middle-class backgrounds, have fared better after exposure, especially if more sinned against than sinning. A scientist can afford to appear stupid at least once, it would seem, without too much harm being done to his or her subsequent career. This is especially so where the poor scientist has become the victim of what might be termed The Lab Assistant's Revenge.

Professor René Blondlot worked in the University of Nancy in eastern France at the beginning of the twentieth century. He was the creative force behind a theory that all living matter emits individual and specific rays. Rays were very popular at the time – it was only eight years since the discovery of the X-ray. Blondlot conducted a whole series of experiments on the rays he believed he had discovered, using a giant prism with which the rays could be focused and amplified so that the frequency of their emission could be electrically registered. Blondlot christened them N-rays. As each living object was passed into a box containing the prism, the charge of N-rays specific to the object was recorded on a dial.

Blondlot also discovered that malfunctioning organisms emitted deficient N-rays, and that the giant prism could therefore be used as a diagnostic tool. He published his findings and the University of Nancy gained world-wide fame. Blondlot received many visitors, among them an American scientist named R W Wood – not from Yale. During a demonstration of the N-rays, Wood secretly removed the giant prism from the box. It made no difference to the registration of the impulses. Wood confronted Blondlot. The professor was baffled, worried and apprehensive. A few enquiries revealed that his lab assistant had simply turned up the electrical current quite randomly each time an object was passed into the box, and had been doing so ever since Blondlot had started his experiments.

It was a cruel hoax. Blondlot had believed that not only was his discovery of great scientific importance, but that it would also prove beneficial to his fellow creatures. He may, however, have found some consolation the following year (1904) when he was awarded the Leconte Prize for 'outstanding advances in French science', and also the Grand Prize of the College of Science, the runner-up for this award being Pierre Curie. Blondlot's reputation as a scientist was by no means destroyed, and N-rays were not entirely discredited. It is said that the theory lives on and that there are still some French towns where N-rays are used, though no evidence of this is cited.

Little boxes have been the cause of much scientific trouble. The advance of science a hundred years ago seems to have depended greatly on mystery packages. There was still thought to be much magic in science and it wouldn't have been too surprising if someone like Uncle Abanazar had won the Nobel Prize for Science in the early days.

Dr Albert Abrams was an American and another scientist who invented his own box. He was born in San Francisco, but gained his medical qualifications in Heidelberg and Berlin. He pursued his studies in London, Vienna and Paris, before returning to San Francisco and practising at the Cooper Medical College. He lectured on spondylotherapy, the spondyl being a poetic-sounding part of the spine, but around 1910 this was no way to make a good living. So along came the box which Abrams claimed could diagnose a patient's disease from a drop of his or her blood on blotting paper. All the patient had to do was mail the blotting paper to Abrams, who would arrange for a stooge, *in loco patientis*, to stand in front of the box holding the sample. The principle behind the box's diagnostic skill was that every disease has a different vibratory rate, that the blood-soaked blotting paper would contain a trace of this disease, and that the box would register which disease it was.

From here it was but a small step for a hoaxer to move to the box's second and greater capability. About 1920 Abrams modestly announced the discovery of ERA (Electronic Reaction of Abrams). Since every disease had a different vibratory rate, it followed that so did every cure, and the wonderful box, which Abrams now called an occilloclast (try looking that up in your Funk and Wagnell), was able to identify the vibratory pattern needed for these cures. For example, malaria had a unique vibratory rate, as did its cure, quinine. The machine could now treat as well as diagnose. Abrams went into production.

He was undoubtedly helped by the fact that his box appeared at about the same time as the wireless. If a wooden box with a few old bulbs in it could receive and decode sound waves, bringing voices speaking from hundreds of miles away into your own home, why couldn't another, more expensive box decode the waves that diseases made inside your body? The public, and other doctors, ordered their occilloclasts.

Abrams was an astute businessman. The occilloclasts were only for hire, not for sale. A deposit of $250 was required and a further $200 for a course of instruction in how to use the box. Lessees of the boxes were said to take between $1,000 and $2,000 a week. Abrams was said to have amassed a fortune of at least $2 million. The sealed boxes were on no account to be opened. And the boxes were now even more efficient. No drop of blood was needed, the diagnosis could be made from the patient's handwriting. Abrams examined the handwriting of famous literary figures and announced that Dr Johnson, Samuel Pepys and Edgar Allan Poe all died from syphilis. The hoax was blown when he was sent a drop of rooster blood and the box diagnosed diabetes, malaria, and cancer, as well as the seemingly omnipresent syphilis. It was time to open the box. Inside the one selected was a condenser, a rheostat, an ohmeter and a magnetic interrupter, impressively but meaninglessly wired together. Abrams caught pneumonia and died. His obituary in the journal of the American Medical association bestowed on him the title of 'Dean of all Twentieth Century Charlatans'.

Britain, too, had its little boxes. In 1916 Sergeant James Shearer of the Royal Army Medical Corps produced his box which he called 'Shearer's Delineator'. Shearer had been trained as an auxiliary nurse in the First World War, and, though competent in this capacity, he had little medical knowledge beyond that needed to provide immediate aid to wounded troops. Nevertheless, he convinced Army medical officers, up to an including the Director-General of Medical Services in France, that his Delineator could provide instant information on the internal well-being, or otherwise, of anyone who stood in front of it. The Delineator resembled a cross between an X-ray machine, a Polaroid camera and a punch-card dispenser. It was a brass-bound box in front of which the wounded paraded. The box made clicking noises while in operation and produced a strip of waxed paper, rather as a telex machine does, with an impression of the patient's internal organs sketched on it.

The *British Medical Journal* devoted three pages to Shearer's Delineator, and it was hailed as a potentially life-saving device. The praise went to Shearer's head. Like Abrams and so many others, he took another step and made another claim. He said that the box also had military uses, that it could detect enemy aircraft as they approached the Allied lines – some kind of precursor of radar. The British Security Services became involved, a hard body of men without the blind faith of medical science. The Delineator was opened. Alas, it had no healing properties. All it contained was the clockwork mechanism of a pianola that tunelessly revolved and disgorged the strip of waxed paper. Shearer was arrested, court-martialled and shot, a mad end to a mad hoax.

The years leading up to the First World War were years of intense competition between the nations of Europe in technology, in weaponry, in trade and industry, and in science. The white heat of this rivalry forged many hoaxes, for such times are good times in which to practise deceit. Truth may be the first casualty of war, it is also often among the first casualties in any period of international antagonism and competition. This was the background to perhaps the most famous hoax of all, the Piltdown Hoax of 1912.

In 1856 the leg bone and skull of what has come to be known as Neanderthal Man were discovered in a small quarry in a cave near Düsseldorf in Germany. In 1868 the skulls and skeleton of Cro-Magnon Man were discovered in the Dordogne. In the decades that followed, more and more fossil bones turned up in mainland Europe. There were a huge number of French finds at the beginning of the twentieth century, and Heildelberg Man was unearthed in Germany in 1907. This produced intense pressure on British anthropologists and palaeontologists, much of it patriotically self-imposed, to turn up some similar or superior find in Britain. There was also clear hope and expectation as to what sort of find it should be, and even of where it should be made. There were those scientists who had long talked of the possibility of finding a late Pliocene deposit in the Kentish Weald or on the Kentish plateau. Arthur Keith later wrote of this period: 'That we should discover such a race as Piltdown, sooner or later, has been an article of faith in the anthropologist's creed ever since Darwin's time.'[1] The ground was prepared, literally as we now know, for the discovery in Britain of Darwin's missing link.

The discoverer was Charles Dawson, a Hastings solicitor and amateur fossil hunter. In 1912 he was forty-eight years old, described by a neighbour as 'an insignificant little fellow who wore spectacles and a bowler hat. Certainly not the sort who put over a false one.' Arthur Smith Woodward, Keeper of Geology at the South Kensington Museum, and a friend of Dawson, had a more flattering opinion of him: 'He had a restless mind, ever alert to note anything unusual; and he was never satisfied until he had exhausted all means to solve and understand any problem which presented itself. He was a delightful colleague in scientific research, always cheerful, hopeful and overflowing with enthusiasm.'[2] But Woodward wrote this as part of Dawson's obituary. It does not do to speak ill of the dead, and Woodward never knew how Dawson had duped him.

Dawson was a strange and ambitious man, desperate to become a Fellow of the Royal Society, who spent much of his leisure time looking for missing links, or what he called transitional objects. In 1894 he discovered a transitional boat, half coracle and half canoe. In 1909 he identified a transitional fish, a cross between a goldfish and a carp. He also believed he had discovered a thirteenth dorsal vertebra in certain races – the Arawak Indian, the Inuit and the Ancient Egyptian – caused, said Dawson, by manipulation of the hips to maintain equilibrium in a canoe or kayak. Certainly, late in the nineteenth century, Dawson had discovered natural gas at Heathfield in Sussex. In 1901 he presented what has come to be known as the Toad-in-the-Hole to Brighton Museum, a fossilized toad in a nodule of flint. The toad supposedly climbed into the hole in the flint when little and ate insects until too large to get out again. Dawson's story predates by twenty-five years that of Winnie the Pooh getting stuck in

Rabbit's burrow through eating too much honey.

When the First World War broke out, Dawson, known to some as The Wizard of Sussex, began work on phosphorescent anti-Zeppelin bullets, and towards the end of his life he was investigating the development of an incipient horn in a cart horse, a kind of transitional unicorn. The only clear evidence of skulduggery on Dawson's part, however, is to be found in his *History of Hastings Castle*, a work that brought accusations of plagiarism from other historians. He was also unpopular among other Sussex archaeologists.

The first step towards the Piltdown Hoax began in March 1909 when Dawson wrote to Woodward saying that he was 'waiting for the big discovery which never seems to come'. How far the hoax was planned by then, it is impossible to say. When the hoax came to light in 1953, a local Sussex paper offered some circumstantial evidence. 'Mrs Florence Padgham, now of Cross-in-Hand, remembers that in 1906, aged 13, when living at Victoria Cross, Nutley, her father gave Charles Dawson a skull, brown with age, no lower jaw bone, and only one tooth in the upper jaw, with a mark resembling a bruise on the forehead. Dawson is supposed to have said, "You'll hear more about this, Mr Burley." '[3]

On 14 February 1912, Dawson wrote to Woodward: 'I have come across a very old Pleistocene bed overlying the Hastings beds between Uckfield and Crowborough which I think is going to be interesting.' Gravel was being removed at this time for road making. There is an apocryphal story that a couple of workmen first came across the skull and took it to be a coconut shell. A few days later Dawson wrote again to Woodward to say that he had found part of a human skull which would rival *Homo heidelbergensis*, and at the end of the month he invited Woodward to come down to the Piltdown site. Their visit excited local curiosity. 'The Piltdown police constable appeared at Dawson's office on the following Monday and reported to him as Clerk to the Magistrates that "three toffs, two of them from London, had been digging like mad in the gravel . . . and nobody could make out what they were up to".'[4] A chemical examination of the skull was carried out by the Public Analyst at Uckfield.

The hoax was a clever and complicated one, for the site had been salted with more than just the skull. All sorts of other fossil pieces were included to provide an authentic background to the hoax. The timing also was good – there was a strong desire on the part of men of science to find further proof of the Theory of Evolution. Woodward was a wonderful victim, learned, serious and guileless. In the spring of 1912 he and Dawson began systematic excavations at Piltdown. The first day's hunting was recorded in Woodward's diary. 'On a warm evening after an afternoon's vain search, Mr Dawson was exploring some untouched gravel at the bottom of the pit when we both saw half of the human lower jaw fly out in front of the pick-shaped end of the hammer which he was using.'[5] In the light of subsequent knowledge we could be forgiven for thinking that Dawson knew just where to let fly with his hammer. They also found fossilized animal bones and stone tools. There was now enough evidence for Woodward to reconstruct the head of *Eoanthropus dawsoni*, Dawson's Dawn Man, with an ape-like jaw but a human braincase. Although the back teeth on the lower jaw were very flat and worn, Woodward modelled them as having been large and pointed.

This led to the first row about Piltdown Man. Arthur Keith, Conservator of the Hunterian Museum of the Royal College of Surgeons, argued that the teeth should be smaller, more of a match for the skull, and that Piltdown Man was of the earlier Pliocene, rather than the Pleistocene, period. In December 1912 an anonymous article appeared in the *British Medical Journal* which showed considerable knowledge of the Piltdown collection and which tended to back Keith's views. Woodward wondered who had written the article and who could have such knowledge, for he had jealously guarded his finds. Keith himself had been allowed only twenty minutes' superintended examination of them. The controversy and the argument became more heated, but nobody doubted the integrity of Dawson or Woodward or the authenticity of their finds. News of the discoveries were leaked to the *Manchester Guardian* in December 1912, and a few days later Woodward officially revealed Piltdown Man to a packed meeting of the Geological Society in London.

A few months later, in 1913, a tooth was found at Piltdown which matched Woodward's model. The finder was a young Jesuit priest and amateur palaeontologist named Teilhard de Chardin. Woodward was there to see him find it at the end of what had been a long and disappointing day. Woodward 'jumped on the piece with the enthusiasm of a youth and all the fire that his apparent coldness covered came out'.[6] All the professionals now threw in their weight with Dawson and Woodward: biologists, anatomists, geologists and palaeontologists. Only a few amateurs still doubted, foremost among them a bank clerk named Harry Morris. Morris considered that he had been ripped off by Dawson, who had swapped counterfeit flints stained with permanganate of potash for Morris's most valued and genuine specimens. Morris challenged the South Kensington Museum authorities to test the Piltdown collection with hydrochloric acid. He claimed that the brown stain of age would be removed by the acid and the fossils would be seen to be false. It was simple enough to buy jaw bones and other fossils from taxidermists or from Gerrard's in Camden Town. Few people listened to him: it was the luck of the hoaxer.

Famous names began to appear among the visitors to Piltdown. Sir Arthur Conan Doyle visited several times in 1912. Dawson sent a letter to Woodward: 'Conan Doyle has written and seems excited about the skull. He has kindly offered to drive me in his motor anywhere."[7] Conan Doyle was a keen amateur dabbler in most sciences and has even been suspected of being the Piltdown hoaxer. He almost certainly wasn't. On 12 July 1913 sixty members of the Geological Society made their way to the site. The local pub changed its name from The Lamb Inn to The Piltdown Man. Local shops sold penny postcards of the gravel beds with inset heads of Woodward and Dawson.

Woodward made subsequent finds at Piltdown which he kept secret for a couple of years, but Dawson died of septicaemia in 1916. When Woodward announced his later finds most of the doubters became believers. The place of Piltdown Man seemed assured in the history of early evolution. On 22 July 1938, Arthur Keith unveiled a small memorial to Piltdown Man and to Charles Dawson at the Piltdown site. He told a crowd of about thirty who had gathered that Dawson had given them . . .

> the entrance to a long past world of humanity such as had never been dreamed of, and assembled evidence which carried the history of Sussex back to a period to which geologists assigned a duration from half a million to a million years. . . . Professional men took their hats off to the amateur, Mr Charles Dawson, solicitor and antiquarian. They did well to permanently link Mr Dawson's name with this picturesque corner of Sussex and the scene of the discovery.[8]

That it was a hoax was not discovered until 1953, when modern dating and identification methods proved beyond all doubt that the skull and jaw were incompatible, since the jaw was that of a young orang-utan. The hoax was revealed in an article by Dr J S Weiner, Dr K P Oakley and Professor W E Le Gros Clark.

> From the evidence which we have obtained, it is clear that the distinguished palaeontologists and archaeologists who took part in the excavations at Piltdown were victims of the most elaborate and carefully prepared hoax. Let it be said, however, in exoneration of those who have assumed the Piltdown fragments to belong to a single individual, or who, having examined the original specimen, either regarded the mandible and canine as those of a fossil ape, or else assumed (tacitly or explicitly) that the problem was not capable of solution on the existing evidence, that the faking of the mandible and canine is so extraordinarily skilful, and the perpetration of the hoax appears to have been so entirely unscrupulous and inexplicable, as to find no parallel in the history of palaeontological discovery.[9]

Scientists were making sure that fellow scientists didn't lose face. *The Times* was prepared to identify the crime if not the criminal. The paper described how Dawson had found the lower jaw on the warm June evening with Woodward.

> In the same way in the next year, an eminent French scholar, Father Teilhard de Chardin, then a young priest staying at Hastings, was induced to examine some rain-washed gravel where he found the canine tooth – now shown to be that of a modern ape. Thus two witnesses of the highest character either found or helped to find the bones now known to be spurious, and it is hard to resist the conclusion that the jaw and tooth had been put there, by some third person, in order that they might be so unimpeachably discovered.[10]

Dawson, the amateur, got off less lightly. The finger was pointed at him as being the 'third person' referred to above. This provoked an angry letter from Dawson's stepson.

To suggest that he had the knowledge and the skill to break an ape's jawbone in exactly the right place, to pare the teeth to ensure a perfect fit to the upper skull and to disguise the whole in such a manner as to deceive his partner, a scientist of international repute, would surely be absurd. . . . No – Charles Dawson was at all times far too honest and faithful to his research to have been accessory to any faking whatsoever. He was himself duped, and from statements appearing in the Press such is evidently the opinion of those who knew him well, some of whom are scientists of repute.[11]

On the day that this letter appeared in *The Times* a Commons motion was tabled by six MPs: 'That this House has no confidence in the trustees of the British Museum (other than the Speaker of the House of Commons) because of the tardiness of their discovery that the skull of the Piltdown Man is partially a fake.' At that time, the three principal trustees of the Museum were the Archbishop of Canterbury, the Lord Chancellor and the Speaker of the House of Commons. It was a good-humoured motion and there was much laughter in the debate that took place on the following day.

THE SPEAKER: My attention has been drawn to the matter and I'm not sure how serious the motion is (laughter). I shall have to consider it, but speaking for my co-statutory trustees, I am sure that they, like myself, have many other things to do besides examining the authenticity of a lot of old bones (loud laughter).

One wag wrote to *The Times* suggesting that the Piltdown Man could now be considered the first human being to have had false teeth. For others it was not a laughing matter. The meeting of the Geological Society on 25 November was decidedly lively. A certain Dr Marston was very angry, both with *The Times* and the BBC. 'He asked how they could accuse a dead man's memory and besmirch his name. . . . The charges had been made to hide own ineptitude. The sycophantic humility of the Museum tradition had for the past forty years been playing a hoax on public opinion. Now they made a scapegoat out of Mr Dawson who could not answer back.'[12] There were reports in American papers that the meeting broke up in a series of fist fights and that the fracas resulted in the expulsion of several members. Father Teilhard de Chardin, then working in the Wenner-Gren Foundation for Anthropological Research in New York, said that, from his acquaintance with Woodward and Charles Dawson, it was virtually impossible to believe that Dawson, and still less Woodward, could have been guilty of a hoax.

Once it was known that Piltdown was a hoax, there were many suspects. Prime among them was Dawson, but it was always thought that he must have had an accomplice. Woodward, Teilhard de Chardin, Conan Doyle, almost anyone who had been near Piltdown or the Piltdown collection has been accused at one time or another. Arthur Keith's comment, when he was informed of the hoax, was: 'I think you are probably right, but it will take me some time to adjust myself to the new view.'[13] The new view in 1990 was that Keith was the brains behind the skull, and that Dawson was his accomplice. We shall return to Arthur Keith in a later chapter.

Piltdown is that rare thing among hoaxes, the hoax which nobody will plead guilty to having committed. Dr J S Weiner, one of the three scientists who revealed the hoax in 1953, saw that this distinguished it from what he called the 'Horace Cole School'. Piltdown was no prank. Had it been a mere piece of mischief, its perpetrators would have owned up the moment the British Museum had been hoodwinked. There was no money, no profit to be made out of the hoax. The conclusion that most authorities come to is that the hoaxers were after glory and lasting fame. Therefore, they had to keep quiet and hope that their deceit would never be discovered.

Flint Jack and Charles Dawson were by no means the first hoaxers to use fossils as the tools of their trickery. In 1725 two scientists at the University of Würzburg decided to play a hoax on the Dean of the Faculty of Medicine. The hoaxers were Ignatz Roderick (Professor of Algebra and Geography) and Georg von Elkhart (Head Librarian), and they were assisted by three students, Christian Zaenger, and Niklaus and Valentin Hehn, The victim was Dr Johann Beringer.

At the time there was much speculation as to the origin of fossils, although they had long been objects of study. Beringer was a fanatical fossil hunter, the perfect victim for a hoax. In a quarry where Beringer often hunted for fossils, Roderick and Elkhart planted 'fossilized' birds, beetles and lizards. As Beringer swallowed the bait, they became more ambitious and outrageous, and planted 'fossilized' comets, stars and moons. They also planted tablets of stone with the word 'God' inscribed in Latin, Arabic and Hebrew. Beringer found a way of accounting for them all. He devised the *lusus naturae* theory, that some stones mysteriously imitated the forms of other bodies. He attributed all the fossils to the work of the Divine Creator.

He wrote a learned book in Latin on his finds, the *Lithographiae Wirceburgensis*, with a lengthy preface, fourteen chapters and twenty-one pages of engraved plates. Roderick and Elkhart, whose motives we can only guess at, then felt enough was enough and confessed to Beringer that they had planted the fake fossils. Beringer, like so many hoax victims, refused to believe those who had tricked him. He accused them of professional scientific jealousy and of attempting to rob him of his glory. Roderick and Elkhart countered by planting fossils that had Beringer's own name on them. By March 1726 Beringer had had enough. He spent the rest of his life trying to buy up and destroy all copies of his great book. Sadly, it thus became a collectors' item, and a second edition was published in 1767, which is said to have outsold the original edition by several thousand copies.

The student involvement in the hoax was minimal. Zaenger and the two Hehns served merely as minions whose job it was to salt the quarry where Beringer worked. The idea was that of Roderick and Elkhart, and maybe time hung heavy on their academic hands.

So often hoaxers come from unlikely backgrounds, occupations, nationalities even. Had Sherlock Holmes investigated hoaxes, he would have told Watson that once he had eliminated all the probable perpetrators, whoever remained, however improbable, must be the hoaxer. To the war-weary world of 1917, the most improbable hoaxers would have been two sweet little Yorkshire lasses, Frances Wright and Elsie Griffiths, creators of the Cottingley Fairies.

In May 1917 *Punch* published the famous and much-lampooned poem by Rose Fyleman, 'There Are Fairies at the Bottom of My Garden'. Years later, Elsie admitted that *Punch* was taken at her house but insisted that she had not read the relevant copy before the photographs were taken. In June 1917, Frances borrowed her father's camera and trotted down to the bottom of their garden with her friend Elsie. Here she took five photographs of Elsie with attendant fairies. Two months later she again borrowed the camera and photographed

Elsie with a gnome. Frances's parents were not prepared to let her borrow the camera a third time, but for almost eighteen months the Cottingley Fairies remained a family affair. Then, in 1919, Anne Griffiths and Polly Wright, the girls' mothers, began to take an interest in theosophy and started attending meetings of the Theosophical Society at Unity Hall, Rawson Square, Bradford.

The photographs came into the possession of Edward L Gardner, a member of the Society, who was charmed and intrigued. He took the best of the pictures to a photographic expert, Harold Snelling, saying 'What Snelling doesn't know about faked photography isn't worth knowing.' Snelling examined the photo and reported that it was a single exposure, that the dancing figures were not made of paper or fabric, nor were they painted on a photographic background, 'but what gets me most is that all these figures have *moved* during exposure'.[14] He was convinced of the authenticity of the pictures, though to modern eyes the spirits in them seem woefully typical of the early-twentieth-century book illustrator's notion of fairies – slim female figures with ballerina's legs and dragonfly wings.

More people came to hear of the photographs. In the grim days after the First World War, when Britain was still counting dead and wounded and many had not recovered from the shock of the carnage, the Cottingley Fairies appeared as something clean, pure, enchanting, invulnerable and everlasting. Few may have believed in Tinkerbell and Never-Never Land, but many wished they could, including Sir Arthur Conan Doyle.

When news of the Cottingley Fairies first reached him, Conan Doyle was staying in Exeter, at the Rougemont Hotel (in view of what was to come and what we know of Louis de Rougemont, it was a significantly named temporary residence). He hastened to get in touch with the girls' families. He was interested, he was hopeful, but he was not yet convinced. He called in another photographic expert, Kenneth Styles. Styles reported to Doyle that the pictures were fakes: 'one at least is a most patent fraud and I can almost tell you the studio it comes from'.[15] Styles was way off course – no studio had touched them. The more he thought of it, the less Doyle liked it. It was a little too good to be true, for Conan Doyle was a passionate seeker after the supernatural and the spirit world. What counted against the girls was that they both refused to swear on the Bible that the photos were genuine. What counted in their favour was that they were prepared to take more photos.

The famous articles about the Cottingley Fairies appeared in *Strand Magazine* in November 1920 and March 1921, over three years after the original photographs had been taken. The story was enormously popular and excited great interest. Conan Doyle still wouldn't commit himself one way or the other. In the article in March 1921 he wrote: 'It is at the lowest an interesting speculation which gives an added charm to the silence of the woods and the wilderness of the moorland.'[16] The *Manchester City News* was similarly undecided: 'We must either believe in the almost incredible mystery of the fairies, or in the almost incredible wonder of faked photographs.'[17] Maurice Hewlett, in *John O'London's Weekly*, was blunter: 'It is easier to believe in faked photographs than fairies.'[18]

Truth Magazine appropriately provided the wisest comment: 'For a true explanation of the fairy photographs what is wanted is not a knowledge of occult phenomena but a knowledge of children.'[19] This is the crucial point in any hoax. It is not what Alfred Hitchcock used to call 'the McGubbin' – the object around which a film or, in this case, a hoax revolves – that matters. It is the initiator, the instigator, the hoaxer, on whom we should concentrate. Woodward should have looked harder at Dawson. McGraw-Hill, who sought to publish the authorized Howard Hughes biography, should have worried less about Hughes himself and kept a closer and more suspicious eye on Clifford Irving. Never mind the rabbit that the conjuror pulls out of the hat, watch his hands, especially the one that is supposed to be idle and empty.

More photographs were taken. The results were disappointing, but by now time and money had been invested in Cottingley and the hoax, and more and more people were gradually committing themselves to having to believe in it. Conan Doyle wrote: 'If I am myself asked whether the case is to be absolutely and finally proved, I should answer that in order to remove the last faint shadow of doubt I should wish to see the result repeated before a disinterested witness.'[20] He never got his wish. The debate stumbled on, the children had their critics and their champions. In 1925 Edward Gardner published his account of the events: *A Book of Real Fairies, The Cottingley Photographs and Their Sequel*. Five years later, Conan Doyle referred to them in a book called *At the Edge of the Unknown*. Slowly and steadily, the Cottingley Fairies became less and less important, though as late as 1965 Frances Wright remarked with pride: 'I've heard it said that every hour, somewhere in the world, somebody makes a reference to the Cottingley Fairies.'[21] It is perhaps every hoaxer's dream, the immortality that follows the perpetration of some well-staged and well-publicized piece of hocus-pocus.

Frances and Elsie finally admitted the hoax publicly in 1976 on a Yorkshire Television programme called *Calendar*. 'As for the photographs,' said Elsie, 'let's say they are figments of our imagination, Frances's and mine, and leave it at that.'[22] Faking the photographs had been simplicity itself. The fairies were cut out of the *Princess Mary Gift Book*, a work so popular and so well known that it seems amazing that no one identified them as soon as the photographs were published – or perhaps people believed that this was a case of life imitating art. Frances and Elsie stuck the cut-out fairy figures on leaves and twigs with hat pins. It is thought that Conan Doyle mistook the handle of a hatpin for an elf's navel. In 1981 Frances said, 'How on earth anyone could be so gullible as to believe that they were real was always a mystery to me.'[23]

In the 1970s Elsie worked as Matron at Epsom College, the setting some twenty or thirty years earlier for what was reported to me as the Harris Hoax. The story, passed on from generation to generation of little public-schoolboys, was that an eighteen-year-old pupil developed a loathing for the School Bursar, a man named Major Gifford. The pupil decided that he would wait until he had left school before playing his hoax. He obtained (I suppose 'swiped' is a better word) some schoolheaded paper, picked a dozen or more names out of the telephone directory (by the time I heard the story it was a hundred names), and wrote to each of the people he had selected. The gist of the letters was that the recipient had been included as beneficiary in the will of the late Benjamin Harris (I am guessing at the forename), that the will would be read in the Bursar's Office at Epsom College on a certain afternoon in August, and that the recipient was invited to attend.

It was a generous hoax, for the perpetrator denied himself the opportunity of enjoying the fruits of his creativity. He had fixed on August, the school holidays, a time when he was less likely to be connected with the hoax and when the Major would be more off his guard. He had also scheduled the meeting for after lunch, when the

Major would be at his most sleepy and his least welcoming. The hoax worked, we are told, for one delighted member of the teaching staff witnessed the arrival of at least some of the would-be beneficiaries, and greeted the perpetrator at the next Old Boys' Day with enthusiasm and appreciation.

But it is time to return to weightier matters and to the Theory of Evolution. Jean Baptiste Lamarck was a French biologist of the late eighteenth and early nineteenth centuries. His explanation for evolution was that new organs are brought into being by the needs of the organism in adapting to its environment. New characteristics acquired during the lifetime of one member of a species can be passed on to offspring through heredity, and this results in evolutionary change. Darwin's theories swept these aside, but even in the twentieth century there remained a few scientists who believed acquired characteristics could be inherited. One such was Paul Kammerer.

Kammerer felt that Darwin's theory was degrading and refused to believe that all progress came about through chance mutations. He worked in the Institute for Experimental Biology in the University of Vienna, and in 1924 he published a book called *The Inheritance of Acquired Characteristics*. For some scientists it was an exciting work. Dr Thornley Garden, Professor of Zoology at Cambridge University, reckoned that Kammerer had made the greatest biological discovery of the century. Kammerer had been working with reptiles, primarily toads and yellow-spotted salamanders. What his results showed was that the salamanders lost their spots when kept in the dark, shedding that which made them more easily visible; and that the toads, who had lost the suckers or nuptial pads from their feet, regrew them when kept in a temperature so warm that they had to spend all day in water to keep cool.

It was all a hoax, possibly another case of The Lab Assistant's Revenge. One account says that, once Kammerer's book was published, his assistant explained that he had painted Indian ink on the salamanders, to disguise their bright spots, and on the toads, to suggest incipient pads forming. Other accounts tell different stories – even that Kammerer's findings were genuine. The problem for poor Kammerer was that he could not possibly hope to repeat his experiments. He was regarded as a hero in the Soviet Union – where

Lamarckian theories were still accepted, and where hoaxing was given official status under such scientists as Lysenko – but was ridiculed in most of the rest of Europe.

The one scientist who may be said to have taken revenge on his assistants was Sir Cyril Burt, in that he dispensed with real assistants and invented totally false ones. Burt was a pioneer in educational psychology, a man much revered by many, but a slave to the theory that ability is primarily an hereditary quality. In the Nature–Nurture conflict, Burt came heavily down on the side of nature, to such a degree that he was prepared to cook his research results in support of his beliefs. After working for the LCC for many years, Burt took up an appointment at University College, London. After the Second World War, he founded his own statistical journal, to which he sent fake 'readers' letters', and for which he ruthlessly edited contributions from other scientists, desperate that their findings should be compatible with his.

His most famous studies were those relating to twins, but in 1972 doubt was cast on the validity of his findings, on the grounds that the statistical correlations he accorded his work were just too good to be true. More of Burt's research was examined. He was found to have made false claims as to the number of children in his samples, testing a hundred but giving figures relating to a thousand. In some cases he had even claimed to have made tests where none were possible. And in 1976, the *Sunday Times* revealed that J Conway and Margaret Howard, Burt's senior research assistants, simply didn't exist. They were figments of Burt's imagination, invented to give more credibility to his findings. His is a sad hoax, for many of the postwar structures and developments in education were based on his writings and theories.

Every hoax that succeeds does so because it is attractive, because it makes some claim that people want to believe is true, and this is particularly so with scientific hoaxes. The scientific hoaxer has it both ways: he can make false claims about both the past and the future. We are hungry for details of what science will do next, and just as hungry for news of the past, and if science can re-create the past, so much the better. It doesn't matter which branch of science is involved, and the more outrageous the hoax, the more attractive it is. It may even owe more to magic than science. Conan Doyle and hundreds of thousands of others wanted to believe that fairies had manifested themselves to Frances Wright and Elsie Griffiths. British archaeologists and palaeontologists longed for home-grown evidence of Early Man. Kammerer's entire career was staked on proving that Lamarck was right and Darwin was wrong. All the hoaxer has to do in such circumstances is spread the right ground-bait and invite his victims to feed upon it. The more popular the science, the easier it is for the hoaxer. If it's popular enough for television, there may be a minimum of risk. Television crews tend to shoot first and ask questions afterwards.

In 1971 the *National Geographic* magazine ran an article about the Tasaday tribe, the last people to be living a Stone Age existence. The Tasaday lived on Mindanao, one of the largest islands in the Philippines and some five hundred miles south-east of Manila. They were a forest tribe of hunter-gatherers, living a simple, almost child-like existence – the stuff of which dreams and television programmes are made. The *National Geographic* article pulled out all the stops. The Tasaday 'huddled deep in caves by fires where roots bake . . . leaf-skirted, bare-breasted young women knelt shyly beside us . . . a child clings to its mother, reflecting the affection that permeates all Tasaday life.'[24] The media came, saw and exposed, and then the Tasaday were sealed off from the rest of the world for a further three years.

The man who had opened the door on the past, and closed it again, was Manda Elizalde, Presidential Assistant for the Tribal Minorities to President Marcos of the Philippines. He claimed that he had discovered the Tasaday. He also claimed that they called him God. It was his private helicopter that had ferried journalists, camera crews and anthropologists to Mindanao, at a price. NBC paid a million pesos for the privilege of filming on the island. For Elizalde was a hard-headed businessman who had been educated at Harvard and whose family had considerable interests in mining, timber, guns and gold. He had money and, as a member of Marcos's government, he had power.

The hoax was more primitive than the Tasaday. Elizalde bribed and bullied two tribes living on Mindanao to act the parts of Stone Age people. They were made to put aside their clothes, leave their huts and farms, and act out their 'innocent' existence in the rain forest. An area on the island was sealed off by Elizalde's private army, and the Western world was invited in to film and record the lost tribe. The first journalist to visit the Tasaday came straight from Vietnam. The innocence of their existence contrasted appealingly with the horrors he had just left, for the Tasaday were said to have no words in their language for 'war' or 'enemy'. He must have wanted to accept the Tasaday at face value, as did the *National Geographic*, as did NBC. But stories subsequently began to emerge from Mindanao suggesting that all had not been what it seemed. Local missionaries reported that the native tribes were being used and abused. In February 1986 the Marcos Government fell from power, and Elizalde fled from the Philippines with an estimated $55 million. Unlike Louis de Rougemont, there is not the slightest chance that he will end his days selling matches in the street.

When a British television crew returned to the island in 1987, they discovered that the Tasaday had disappeared as an anthropological entity, but that members of the tribe were now to be seen wearing T-shirts and jeans, indistinguishable from millions of other peasant farmers in the Philippines. In 1988 *Scandal*, a Central TV programme, produced by John Edwards, revealed the truth about the Tasaday and Manda Elizalde. 'The essence of a good conman,' said Edwards, 'is having an audience that wants to believe it wasn't a hoax. The people were utter pawns, the real victims. The anthropologists wanted to believe in them and it just escalated.'[25]

In the 1830s it was man-bats on the moon: in the 1980s it was Stone Age tribes in the Pacific. Some time in the future, when we will not be expecting it but when we will be delighted to hear of it, it will be something else.

7

True Colours, False Canvases

'Art for art's sake, but money for God's sake.'
Ancient Hollywood Saying

Perhaps the first hoax that each of us comes across is in the Hans Christian Andersen story, *The Emperor's New Clothes*. It's an important story in the study of hoaxes, because it emphasizes the part played in any successful hoax by the sheep-like tendency of the masses. In Andersen's story, no one wanted to be the first to point out that the Emperor had no clothes. It took the innocence, and perhaps the egotism, of a young child to burst the bubble and show that nothing lay inside it but a lot of air. We live in an age when art and music are especially over-respected. Because some of the works of Beethoven or Stravinsky were booed at the first performances, nobody nowadays dares to boo the première of any piece of music, no matter how awful it sounds, just in case it turns out to be the work of a genius. Similarly, because Picasso was underrated in his early days, every contemporary artist, or charlatan, is free to paint, weld, glue or build anything at all and is guaranteed a sympathetic if not respectful reception. Thus, when it comes to hoaxes perpetrated in the world of art and literature, most of us are sheep, and those that aren't are wolves.

In the art world too many people are playing for money for the humorous side of any hoax to be uppermost. It is a strange world. Nobody needs art, but men and women have drawn and painted and sculpted for thousands of years, and a thriving industry has sat on its back like the Old Man of the Sea in one of the stories of Sinbad the Sailor. There are art historians, and art experts. There are valuers and dealers and agents and collectors. There are museums and galleries locked in intense rivalry. Great works of art are like diamonds, scarce and almost priceless. But, unlike diamonds, we cannot have a regular and controlled supply of new Michelangelos or Van Goghs or Titians or Vermeers. So, when all the great works of art are safely displayed in museums and galleries, or locked away from view in private collections, what is to happen to the dealers and the valuers and the agents and the experts? There is a limit to the number of Old Masters lying neglected in attics. Most of us are on to that game, and there can't be many attics left unexplored, *The Antiques Road Show* has seen to that. A new supply of old works has to come from somewhere, and this is where the hoaxer steps in.

Some 'fake' artists have played only for fun. In 1929 Evelyn Waugh and Tom Mitford invented a painter called Bruno Hat and held an exhibition of his work in London on Midsummer's Eve. The paintings were of the Modern Eclectic School, some surrealist, some Cubist, and some merely bits of wood and cork stuck on canvas. The pretentious text in the catalogue was written by Waugh, Mitford supplied the pictures. Most of the visitors were taken in by the hoax. Lady Diana Mosley was said to have thought the paintings 'lovely', and Lytton Strachey went so far as to buy one. Waugh and Mitford admitted the hoax the following day.

In the 1920s Paul Jordan Smith was the literary critic of the *Los Angeles Times*. He invented not just an artist, but a whole school of art – the Disumbrationist School – of which the founder was one Pavel Jordanovitch, a Russian artist. The first picture that Smith produced was entitled *Exaltation,* and depicted a woman holding up a peeled banana. The picture received some cautiously good reviews, and the art world wanted to see more of the works of Jordanovitch. Smith kept the pictures coming and the hoax running for three years. In 1927 one critic wrote of Jordanovitch: 'This artist has a distinctly individual manner and uses his brush to symbolize the sentiments: he explores the heights and does not hesitate to peer into the abysses.'[1] The time had come to call it a day. Smith exposed the hoax himself in the *Los Angeles Times* in August 1927.

One of the few prepared to declare the real state of the Emperor is Muriel Gray, who presented a series of programes on Channel Four TV in the summer of 1991 called *ART IS DEAD – Long Live TV*. The inspiration for the programme was the belief that too much attention was being paid to mediocre art. Indeed, the original name for the programme was *ENC* (*Emperor's New Clothes*), but it was feared that some bright spark might identify what the initials stood for, as the series was prepared in secret. The victim of the hoax was to be the Art Establishment, and the series was filmed in Edinburgh – another safeguard against discovery. Zad Rogers, Gray's co-producer, says that one of the reasons why no one became suspicious of a hoax while they were making the series, was because people were treating the same subject seriously so often.

The series consisted of five programmes, the first four of which highlighted the work of four 'artists'; a sculptor (Kenneth Hutchinson), a novelist (Laura Mason), an art-film maker (Richard Bradley-Hudd), and an architect (Hannah Patrizzio). Hutchinson specialized in works of art made from rotting carcasses. Mason's novels were constructed from transcripts of telephone chat-lines. Bradley-Hudd's films included his fridge's eye-view of New York 'simply because we fancied going to New York while we were making the series'.[2] Patrizzio had designed bio-degradable houses for a woodland retreat in Bavaria (in fact a remote part of the Scottish Highlands).

These first four programmes were accepted at face value, by press, Art Establishment and public alike, and only in the fifth and final programme did Muriel Gray reveal that none of the artists were what they had seemed or what they had claimed to be. They were 'ordinary' people, and what they had said was basically a load of rubbish. Originally it had been planned to use actors as novelist, film maker, sculptor and architect, but Gray and Rogers found that actors were unable to carry the hoax through as convincingly as their friends. In the end, the entire series was 'real' enough to lead some critics and art experts to feign prior knowledge of the four artists covered in the programmes, claiming that they had already heard of Patrizzio, Bradley-Hudd, Hutchinson and Mason.

The fifth programme took the form of a discussion between Gray and the four artists. Tempers became frayed – the acting was brilliantly convincing – and the discussion was brought to a premature end when one of the 'artists' threw a glass of wine in Gray's face. Then came the revelation. It was all a hoax. The public, in general, was delighted, many feeling that Gray and Rogers had done what had long been needed. The press pounced on the hoax, and many papers that would not normally cover any matter artistic devoted articles to the series. The art world, however, was not amused. It never is. Zad Rogers offered some belated advice on how to avoid becoming the victim of such a hoax: 'Rely on your own judgement, believe what you believe, and you won't be fooled.'[3]

A line finer than one in a Dürer etching has to be drawn between the various forms of art hoax. There is the legitimate copy, where an artist produces a duplicate of, say, Whistler's *Mother* or Constable's *The Hay Wain*, but labels or marks the back of the canvas in such a way that it is obvious that it is not the work of the original artist. There is the conscious and fradulent fake, where the artist passes his or her work as that of another, more famous and more expensive artist – say, Whistler's *Father*. As yet there are no known instances of Rembrandt or Hockney or El Greco passing off their works as those of lesser-known artists, though that would be a wonderful hoax. And there is the painting or drawing by a lesser-known artist, in the style of a master but not declared by the artist to be the work of that master. It is this last category that has produced the most controversy though not the most famous art hoaxes.

Until Tom Keating became notorious in the 1970s and 1980s, the most famous art hoaxer was Han van Meegeren. He was born in 1889 in the small town of Deventer in the Netherlands, about fifty miles east of Amsterdam. He was the second son of the family and the middle of five children, a position of almost the least importance in any family. His father was a stern, unimaginative schoolteacher who married a little later in life than most. His mother was delicate and sensitive, and fifteen years younger than her husband. Van Meegeren began to draw in a businesslike way when he was eight or nine years old. In his drawings, he said, 'I invented a world where I was king and my subjects were lions.'[4] His father habitually tore up his son's drawings. As van Meegeren grew up he showed signs of rebelliousness against both the State and the Church, but he succeeded brilliantly as a student at the Institute of Technology in Delft, where he studied architecture. A lot was expected of him.

In 1912 van Meegeren married Anna de Voogt. Anna was the only child of the marriage between a Dutch government official, serving in the East Indies, and a Sumatran woman. The marriage lasted only five years, and Anna was then sent back to Rijswijk to live with her grandmother. By the end of 1912 van Meegeren was running around in ever-decreasing circles, studying for his final exams, attending to his heavily pregnant wife, and working hard at a watercolour which he hoped would win him the gold medal awarded every five years by the Institute for the best painting submitted by a student. Van Meegeren failed his exams but won the medal. The painting was subsequently sold for £100, a considerable amount of money before the First World War.

In the summer of 1914 shortly before war broke out, the van Meegerens moved to Scheveningen, now a suburb of The Hague, but then a respectable little seaside town terrorized by the seven-year-old Jack Bilbo. It is pleasant to imagine that Bilbo may well have played 'knock-down ginger' on van Meegeren's front door. It was here the van Meegeren produced his first fake – a copy of his own watercolour that had won the Delft gold medal. Anna refused to let him pass it off as the original, and the two of them rowed fiercely about it. Already the marriage was splitting at the seams. Van Meegeren took on the first of many mistresses, and in 1923 he and Anna were divorced.

The next dozen or so years were unsatisfactory ones for van Meegeren. He did not live up to his promise as a student, his paintings were considered poor efforts, at best run-of-the-mill portrait work. Van Meegeren bagan to show signs of paranoia, of a belief that the entire world was conspiring against him. In an attempt to prove the world wrong, he became technically the best forger of Old Masters that the world has known. His fakes were brilliant in their conception, their timing, their subject matter, their execution. Helped by the very people whom he was later to hoax, van Meegeren taught himself how to prepare canvases, mix paints, and artificially age paintings so that he was a match for the combined wisdom of the experts. Between 1937 and 1943 he sold eight paintings to dealers, museums, and Field-Marshal Hermann Goering, for a total sum of about £2 million pounds. (It is almost impossible to translate this figure into modern terms. In 1967 it might have been around £6 million. In 1992 perhaps ten times as much.) By the time a confession was wrung from van Meegeren, he owned fifty houses, several hotels and night-clubs and many genuine works of art. To explain his wealth, he said that he had won the *gros lot* on the National Lottery twice.

The first, and to many the greatest, van Meegeren top-class forgery was a fake Vermeer, the *Christ at Emmaeus*. It has been said that his original intention was legitimate. He simply wished to produce a painting that would be indistinguishable from a seventeenth-century materpiece. Once it had been accepted as the work of Vermeer, van Meegeren said he planned to admit that it was a fake. This may well have been true, for van Meegeren wanted above all to show that he was a great painter in his own right, and it would also enable him to expose the ignorance of the critics, gallery owners, art historians and all the other so-called experts. Once the painting had been pounced upon by the experts, however, and once van Meegeren had been paid £50,000 for it, it became impossible for him to carry out his original intention. In some ways it was all too easy. There was a lot of ignorance and imprecision about Vermeer and his works. The acknowledged expert was Dr Abraham Bredius, who had always said that there were more Vermeers hidden away, and that one of them would be a great religious painting. When van Meegeren turned up with a Vermeer on a religious subject, Bredius was overjoyed to see his theories proved right. It was too much of a temptation for van Meegeren. He had to repeat the hoax.

In the next six years he produced five more Vermeers and two de Hooghs. Three paintings were bought by D G van Beuningen and two by W van der Vorm (both wealthy collectors); one was bought by the Netherlands State, to prevent it falling into the hands of the Nazis; and one was taken by Goering in exchange for eight other (genuine) paintings that the Nazis had already taken. It is ironic that van Meegeren, who had duped Goering into parting with these paintings and had therefore saved them for his country, was later accused of trading with the enemy.

Eventually he went too far, cut a few corners, was exposed, arrested, charged and found guilty. He was sentenced to a year's imprisonment, the lightest sentence possible, but died within two months of his trial. He took no secrets with him, explained all that he had done and how, and left the world the discovery of the use of phenol and formaldehyde to produce bakelite. To some, he had come to epitomize 'that heroic figure, the victorious underdog; a little man, a forgotten failure and outcast, who had accumulated by guile a vast fortune and fame at the precise expense of those who had refused him recognition'.[5] To others, he was a criminal who had exposed the perennial difficulty for the art expert – that there is no way, other than having been present in the studio during its execution, of knowing who painted a picture. And the older the picture, the more this is true. The experts can only give opinions, and 'the very continuance of the market depends on such decisions being generally respected'.[6] The honest expert does all he or she can to establish the provenance of a painting, the rest is guesswork. The dishonest expert does all he or she can to avoid being caught. It is fertile ground for the hoaxer and for those painters who wish for revenge on a system that gives them a very small slice of a very large cake.

Van Meegeren's was a seminal hoax, and since his death the faking of paintings and drawings has become a growth industry. Doubtless it had gone on before, but van Meegeren was the first to show that very large sums of money could be made this way. As the industry grew, the marketing of fakes became official business. Paintings were sold to and through galleries, and high values were placed on works that were known to be fakes. There are clearly many ways of placing a value on a work of art. 'Goodness,' as Mae West said, 'has nothing to do with it.' Once it became known that van Meegeren's Vermeers were forgeries, the pictures themselves were considered to have almost no value. By the 1960s, however, fake paintings and drawings were considered eminently saleworthy, and to have a value in their own right.

David Stein was an art forger who started in a small way with a 'Cocteau' sketch which he sold for about 600 francs. Throughout his career as a faker, Stein preferred sketches, drawings, watercolours and gouaches, as they could be produced faster than oil paintings, and their basic materials were not so expensive. Every art forger has his or her method of prematurely ageing the product. Stein employed a mixture of Lipton's tea and a sun lamp.

After a period touring Europe, faking paintings as he went along to pay for food and lodging, Stein went to New York in the mid-1960s, where he is said to have dashed off forty 'Cocteaus' and a 'Chagall' gouache in a couple of days, making approximately $8,000 from their sale. He is also said to have forged pictures by 'dozens' of artists, though the list usually stops after three or four names: Cocteau, Picasso, Modigliani, Chagall. (Chagall would seem to be the art forger's favourite artist – so many people fake Chagalls that you wonder whether there are any genuine ones.)

The system Stein used was very straightforward. He painted a Picasso, signed it as Picasso, passed it as a Picasso, ad added a fake Certificate of Authenticity to prove it was a Picasso. For a while all went well. Stein made an estimated $1 million, and opened an art gallery where his fakes were hung alongside genuine paintings. Eventually, however, a New York dealer began to get suspicious and identified several of Stein's paintings as fakes. Questions were asked as to the provenance of the paintings. The Certificates of Authenticity were examined and found to be worthless. Stein fled to San Francisco, a hotbed of hoaxers, but the New York dealer followed him. The art world does not take kindly to *proven* illicit Old or New Masters. Stein was arrested and tried on ninety-seven counts of forgery. He spent eighteen months in gaol in the United States and a further two years in France.

Once he had been released, however, Stein's career recovered. Many of his fake paintings were put on sale at Sotheby's. In fifteen minutes seventy of his pictures were sold for a total of $11,000. On the principle that if you can't trick 'em, join 'em, and that fakers make the best art-keepers, Stein established himself as a highly successful lecturer on how to identify art forgeries.

The 1960s saw a great boom in the art world, a huge increase in the demands for 'great' works, and a corresponding rise in prices. Any period that isn't calm and settled is good for a hoaxer, and Stein was only one of several operating at this time. One of the best-known, thanks to the biography of him by a fellow hoaxer, was Elmyr de Hory. De Hory was born in 1911, the son of wealthy Hungarian parents. He studied art in Budapest and then in Munich, and made his way to Paris. Here he had reasonable success as an artist, earning enough to support himself. During the Second World War he survived the horrors of a Nazi concentration camp, but fell on hard times after the war. He struggled to further his career as an artist, but had little success and began producing fakes for money. He went to the United States and worked there for ten years, leaving hurriedly for Mexico once the authorities were after him.

In the late 1950s he returned to Europe and settled on the isle of Ibiza. Here he produced more fakes, which were sold into the art world by his partner, Fernand Legros. In six years they made some $60 million from oils, watercolours and drawings – fake Dufys,

Modiglianis, Bonnards and, of course, Chagalls. The pressure of work which Legros placed on de Hory began to tell. De Hory started taking short cuts in the production process, and just before it was due to be auctioned, the paint began to peel from a 'Vlaminck'. The painting was traced through Legros to de Hory, and he was gaoled in Ibiza. De Hory protested that he had never faked a painting. He had merely produced works as other, more famous artists, would have done them. The authorities were not impressed. In 1976 moves began to have de Hory extradited from Ibiza to face charges in France. For the moment, we shall leave de Hory in the pleasant Ibizan gaol.

More famous, more successful, and perhaps more a genuine hoaxer, was Tom Keating. He was born in Forest Hill, London, in 1917. He left home at the age of fourteen to become a housepainter, following his father's trade. His mother was a charwoman. He attended evening classes in signwriting and commercial art, first at Croydon and then at Camberwell School of Art. During the Second World War he was a stoker in the Royal Navy, serving in the Far East, where he was almost captured by the Japanese following the fall of Singapore, and where he was later torpedoed. He was invalided out of the Navy, and his health was never subsequently strong. After the war, he was given a grant to study at Goldsmiths College, but failed to gain a Diploma in Art.

As a struggling painter, Keating was enraged at the lack of respect shown to artists and the shoddy treatment meted out to them. Paintings that he sold to dealers for a fiver were sold on for a hundred times as much. He always insisted that it was the anger that such practices generated within him that made him determined to beat the system, to ridicule the experts, and to paint forgeries. For a quarter of a century from the mid-1950s, Keating produced and fed into the system two and a half thousand fakes. The technical skill and knowledge that he had gained as an art restorer enabled him to 'create' Rembrandts, Goyas, Constables, Turners, Gainsboroughs and Renoirs. Towards the end of his life, when he had turned legitimate, Keating made a series of TV programmes to show how it was done.

His speciality was Samuel Palmer, an artist whom Keating admired and who he claimed was guiding his hand. There were some who doubted that Keating's Palmers were genuine, but for years nobody took the trouble to check. With a constant need for new pictures by dead artists, the art world isn't always (or even often) fussy about whence they come. And, once Keating's business was up and running, once a Samuel Palmer market had been created, it became increasingly distasteful to galleries and experts to listen to the few doubters. So, although collectors and museums and valuers must have realized that what David Stein had done in the United States, *someone* could well be doing in Britain, nobody checked Keating's paintings.

The gullibility or dishonesty within the system was exposed after Keating's death in 1984. A sale of his pictures was organized by Christie's in London, and in September 1984, *The Times* carried a report on preparations for the sale. Originally it had been expected that many of the paintings would fetch between £100 and £200, but public interest in Keating, 'staggering' acording to David Collins, one of Christie's directors, made them revise their estimates. Collins told *The Times*: 'It now looks extremely unlikely that any of the works will go for £200 or less. . . . There has been a lot of public interest in the man – and public interest is what pushes up prices.'[7]

Next day *The Times* reported that the two hundred and four works of Keating had fetched well over a quarter of a million pounds, four times the amount they were fetching less than a year earlier, when he was alive. Top prices went for a 'Monet' and a 'Van Gogh', which sold for £16,000 each. A self-portrait, a 'Keating' by Keating, fetched £7,500. 'Private buyers,' said *The Times*, 'dominated last night's sale – those that paid the top prices preferred to stay anonymous.'[8]*

Keating had been brought to trial for forging paintings, but had escaped sentence through ill health. This, and the fact that he had made a lot of people appear very foolish, prompted some luminaries in the art world to foam with anger. One gallery director wrote to *The Times* asserting that, far from being duped by Keating, it was the art cognoscenti who had exposed him, and suggesting that Keating had been let off the hook simply because his mother had been a charwoman. The writer went on to say how much van Meegeren must have wished that he'd been born in Britain, where, she implied, the

---

* In February 1992, the wheel came full circle. A London pawnbroker bought what he believed to be a genuine 'fake' by Tom Keating, only to find that it was a fake 'fake'.

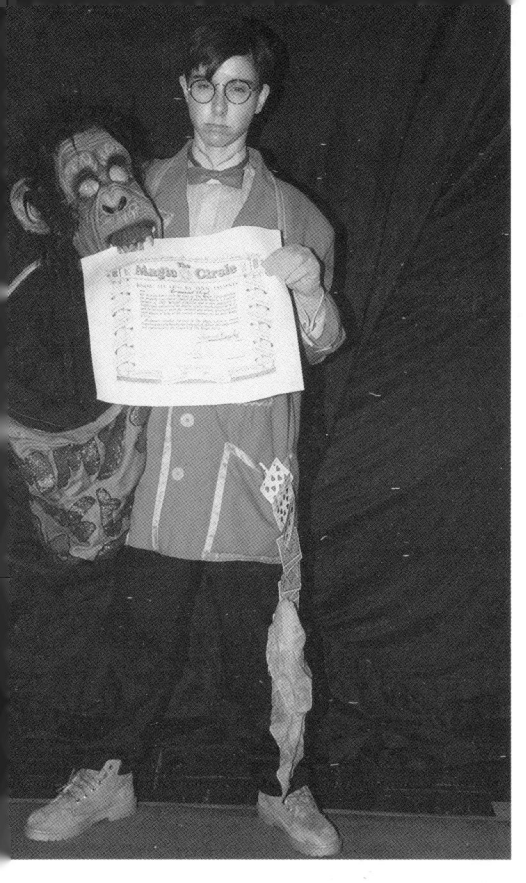

Sophie Lloyd as Raymond, as 'he' appeared for the Magic Circle entrance examination. Note the gloves: Lloyd never appeared as Raymond without them. *(Sophie Lloyd)*

Sophie Lloyd (far right) as herself, with Jenny Winstanley, her agent, and the certificate that was subsequently withdrawn. *(Sophie Lloyd)*

Victor Lewis-Smith, master of the telephone hoax. His victims have included The Vatican, The White House, television evangelists and fellow members of the media.
(E Beer)

As part of her *Art is Dead* series, Muriel Gray interviews Hannah Patrizzio, supposedly the designer of the bio-degradable log cabin in the Bavarian forests – in reality Loch Treig in the north-west Highlands.
(Ross Murray)

George Psalmanazar (right), author of *An Historical and Geographical Description of Formosa* and an illogical illustration from this entirely spurious work (below).
(Hulton Deutsch Collection)

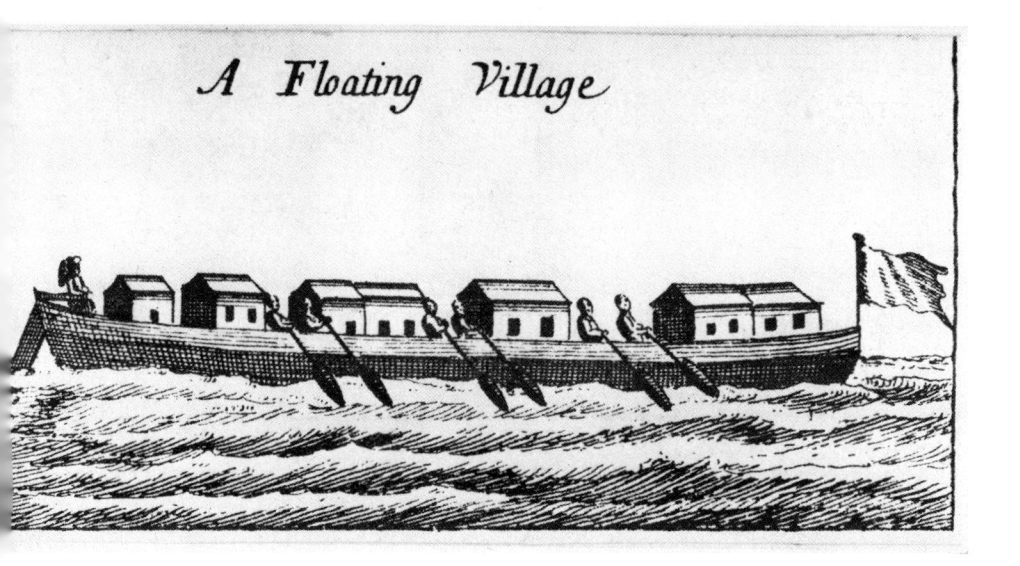

A Floating Village

A fresh fillip was given to the world-shaking comedy of Koepenick last week, when the bogus captain of Footguards was captured. The clever rogue proved to be a squat-nosed, horny-handed, unwashed cobbler, who had already spent twenty-seven years in penal servitude. Voigt was quietly arrested while he was breakfasting in his lodgings in the Langestrasse, in the eastern district of Berlin. At his examination he kept the officials, gendarmes and detectives in roars of laughter as he related, with obvious relish, how he carried out his famous coup.

PORTRAITS OF VOIGT, TAKEN BY THE BERLIN POLICE ON THE DAY OF HIS ARREST

In the middle of the room is seen the trunk where the bogus captain kept his uniform.

THE ROOM IN WHICH VOIGT WAS CAPTURED BY THE POLICE

THE MAN WHO CONVULSED EUROPE : THE COBBLER CAPTAIN OF KOEPENICK

Wilhelm Voigt, who in three hours as a captain in the German Army brought chaos to Kopenick and much enjoyment to the Kaiser.
(Hulton-Deutsch Collection)

Jabez Spencer Balfour, 'The Napoleon of Finance', coming home to face his creditors. *(Hulton-Deutsch Collection)*

Arthur Orton, the Tichborne Claimant, whose weight went up and down faster than his fortunes. *(Hulton-Deutsch Collection)*

Trebitsch Lincoln (left) in his later career as a Buddhist Abbot. As usual, his footsteps appear to be dogged by authority. *(Hulton-Deutsch Collection)*

Henri Grien, alias Louis de Rougemont, as seen by *Punch* following his exposure. *(Mary Evans Picture Library)*

MONS. ROBINSON DE CRUSOE SECUNDUS (LIMITED).

HIS MOST THRILLING ADVENTURE.

After his escape from appalling dangers, Mons. Crusoe (*Secundus*) is attacked by some queer fish of the "Critic" species; who, finding him bound (in magazine form), squirt ink at him and try to destroy his tale.

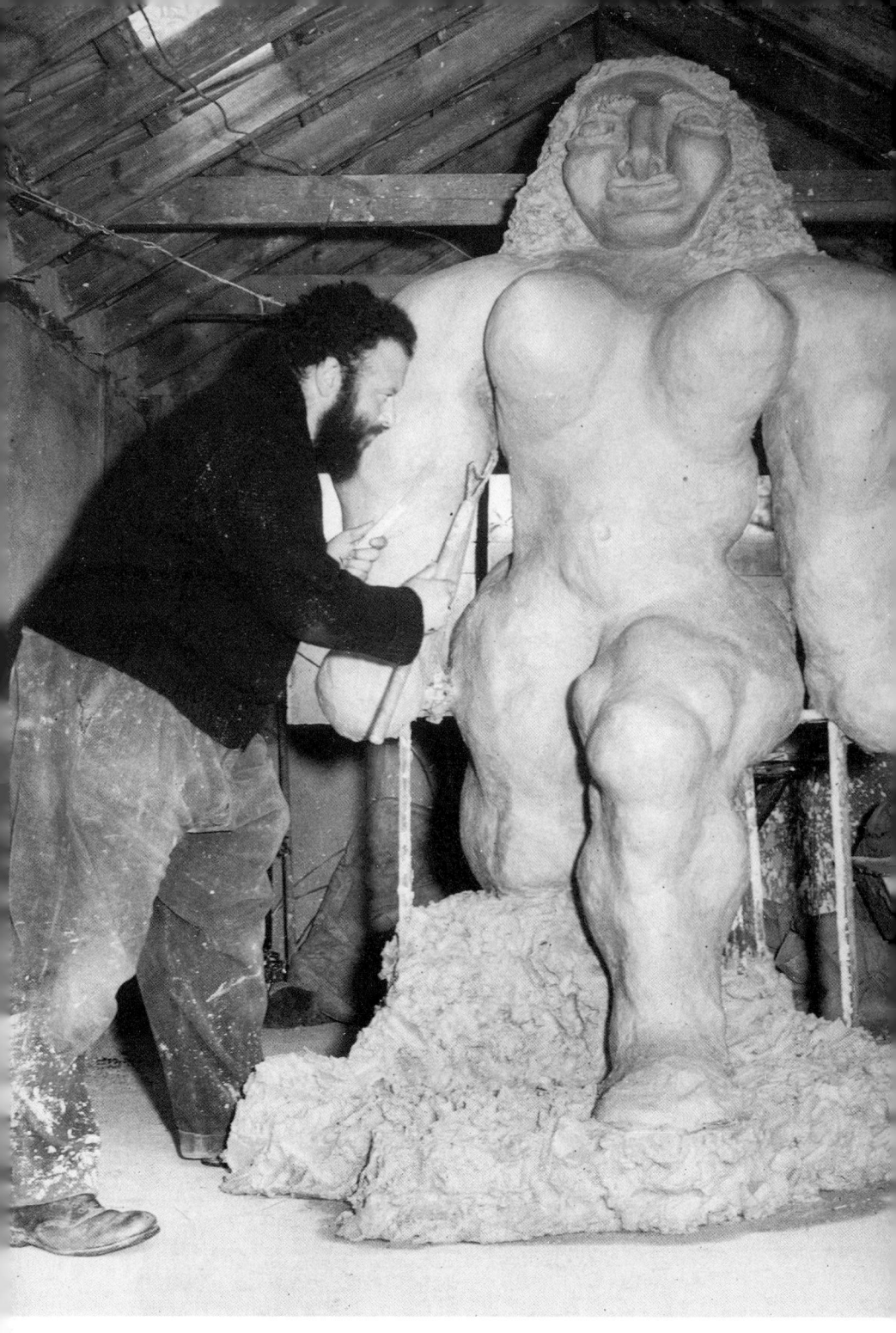

Jack Bilbo, Chicago gangster, bartender, gun-runner, midwife, author and sculptor, working on his clay model of 'Life'. Allegedly, the whole 6000 pounds of clay was mixed by Mrs Bilbo, on her own. *(Hulton-Deutsch Collection)*

Fairies and gnomes at the bottom of a Cottingley garden, photographed by cousins Frances Wright (left) and Elsie Griffiths (right). *(The Brotherton Collection, Leeds University Library)*

The Piltdown Gang. Seated with skull, Arthur Keith (probably a hoaxer); standing behind, near right, Charles Dawson (definitely a hoaxer); and standing next to him, Smith Woodward, the innocent victim. *(Geological Society)*

General view of the Court of Justice in Amsterdam, October 1947. In the dock on the left is Hans van Meegeren. A number of his fake paintings hang around the walls. *(Hulton-Deutsch Collection)*

Thomas Keating, in front of one of his fakes, enjoying his hoax a great deal more than the art experts did. *(Hulton-Deutsch Collection)*

law didn't have the sense to hammer such wickedness. Had Keating still been alive, he would probably have laughed, for there was much humour in him as well as much anger. Before starting on one of his Sexton Blakes, he often daubed 'Keating' or 'fake' (or some other four-letter word) on the canvas. In his fake Impressionist pictures he often included tiny portraits of the artist whose work he was forging. The hoax was there for all to see, if they wished to look.

It is a complicated game. There are 'forgers' and 'copiers' and 'artists' at work here. *The Times* took care to describe Keating as an 'artist and imitator of other painters',[9] for many of Keating's pictures were not strictly forgeries. It isn't simply a question of whether the faker 'signs' the painting or not. There are many artists who have made legitimate careers by copying famous paintings. They style themselves 'master copiers', and they include the signature of the artist they are copying because it is a part of the picture and because the buyer wants as exact a copy as possible of the orginal. The hoax painter operates in a different way. He 'creates' paintings or drawings which the art world is happy to attribute, innocently or otherwise, to a famous name. In the autumn of 1991, Eric Hebborn explained how he had worked this system.

Hebborn was born in 1934. His father was always out of work and found it hard to support the large family. His mother was an unhappy woman, who treated Hebborn badly – her way of exacting revenge for her own sadness. Hebborn was interested in drawing from a young age, and this got him into trouble at school. He had discovered that a 'dead' match, dipped in school ink, was a useful tool for drawing, but the headteacher at his school saw the match as evidence of potential arson, and caned him. Hebborn decided that, since he had already been punished for the crime, he might as well commit it, and set fire to the school cloakroom. He then reported the fire to the headteacher, and subsequently found himself in the Juvenile Court. He was found guilty and sent to Borstal.

In 1957 he began his studies at the Royal Academy and showed great talent as a draughtsman, winning all the prizes for drawing. 'There was a sort of gypsy look about him, and a myth that Eric had emerged from a caravan in Epping Forest as a fully formed artist.'[10] Here he discovered that he was colour blind, and that he couldn't distinguish certain greys from certain greens. 'I had to look at the tubes of colour and read the labels to make sure I didn't fall into the trap of using the wrong one.'[11] In 1964 he left Britain and settled permanently in Italy, living first in Rome, and then moving to the small town of Anticoli Corrado, some twenty-five miles east of the capital. Here Hebborn established the Pannani Galleries, through which he fed into the art system drawings acknowledged as his own, and those that he allowed the experts to attribute to others. He bought a 'real' Brueghel drawing for £40, only to discover that it was almost certainly a copy. He made his own copy of the drawing, improving on it by giving it more vigorous movement. He then tore up the copy from which he had worked and flushed it down the lavatory. His own version he sold to a dealer, and it found its way through the art market to the Metropolitan Museum of Art in New York. The Museum has tested the paper and the ink,* and say they are happy with the drawing, although Hebborn has publicly admitted that it is his work. 'What sort of experts are they?' he asks.

In 1970 he produced a Van Dyck drawing, for which a dealer paid him £200. The drawing travelled to Colnaghi's, a leading New York auction house, and was eventually sold to the British Museum for an undisclosed sum. He has also supplied drawings to Sotheby's and Christie's, and claims to have fed at least a thousand drawings into the system. The mark-up in price on Hebborn's drawings has been high. A few years ago he produced thirty drawings for an Italian dealer who gave the pictures false attributions and provenances. One of the drawings was sold for £9,000: Hebborn was paid £750 for it. Hebborn told an interviewer: 'I don't think you'll find an honest man who is also a dealer.'[12] He has a poor opinion of most branches of the art world. 'The dealer is not interested in art, he's interested in money. The art historian is more interested in his career, and whether he can get a knighthood. Art is neglected – nobody is studying it with the kind of honesty that is necessary.'[13]

It may seem wrong for a hoaxer to be laying down rules about how his victims should behave, but Hebborn sees himself as more honest than most of the people he comes across in his work. 'I'm not a crook. I'm just doing what people have always done. . . . The real criminal is

---

* Hebborn makes his own ink from oak apples, rainwater, gum arabic and iron sulphide. The paper he obtains from the flyleaves of old volumes bought in antiquarian bookshops.

the person who makes the false description.'[14] In much of what he says, he echoes Tom Keating – there is a well-thumbed copy of Keating's autobiography *The Fake's Progress* among Hebborn's jars and brushes. Like Keating, Hebborn works in a variety of styles. He had produced drawings from the Dutch, Flemish, German, Swiss, Italian and English schools. His works are in many leading collections and museums, wrongly attributed to Renaissance masters. The National Gallery of Denmark paid £14,000 for a 'Piranesi' in 1969. The drawing is still there, as is the Brueghel in New York. Hebborn's victims stubbornly hold onto the hoax, proving his point, and giving him satisfaction. 'Only the experts are worth fooling, and the greater the expert, the greater the satisfaction.'[15] 'It is the so-called experts who fool themselves. If I write Rembrandt's signature on a piece of lavatory paper, there are Bond Street dealers who will claim that Rembrandt used it.'[15]

What makes Hebborn unique among art hoaxers is that he has never attempted a Chagall.

8

There Must Be a Man Behind the Book

'All the great story lines are practical jokes that people fall for over again and again.'
Kurt Vonnegut, *Palm Sunday*

As in the world of Art, so in the world of Literature, there has been a great variety of hoaxes, from the pure prank to the straightforward fraud. Business first, fun later.

The commonest form of literary hoax is the production of a book that isn't what it says it is, whether the claim is that it's the Hitler Diary or the biography of Stalin by his nephew or the Howard Hughes autobiography. There have been dozens of such hoaxes and we hear only of the ones that succeeded, or came near enough to succeeding to be embarrassing to publishers. The motives behind such hoaxes also vary. Some hoaxers want money, some want fame, some have deluded themselves into believing that what they are writing is true though it stems from a fantasy world entirely of their creating.

Norman Moss in *The Pleasures of Deception* outlines the story of Pierre Dupont (not the hoaxer's real name). Dupont was a French Canadian and lay preacher who discovered that any sermon, address or lecture packed a far greater punch to its audience if it included details of allegedly real-life struggles that he had had to overcome adversity. As he repeated these stories, they grew in detail and began to take on an increasingly powerful existence. Dupont started to believe the fictions he had built around himself. In the late 1940s, the *Reader's Digest* became interested, and invited Dupont to tell his story to Quentin Reynolds, an ex-war correspondent who had written for the magazine.

The story was exciting. Dupont said he had been transferred from the Canadian Air Force to Intelligence during the Second World War, and had been parachuted into German-occupied Normandy. Here he had posed as a garage mechanic while smuggling Allied airmen out of France and working for the Resistance. The Gestapo had caught him, and had tortured him to make him betray others in the group. Dupont showed scars on his hand (which he said had been crushed in a vice) and on his throat (he said the Gestapo had made him swallow boiling water). Reynolds was impressed by Dupont. 'He had a remarkable knack for describing people. I soon felt I knew them all – the priest, the doctor, the blacksmith, and the brave young girls who carried messages in the handlebars of their bicycles.'[1] The book, entitled *The Man Who Wouldn't Talk*, was written and published. Almost immediately it went into a second printing. The *Reader's Digest* published an abridged version. A former colleague of Dupont then appeared and announced that he had served with Dupont all through the war, and that the entire Normandy saga was a fantasy. Dupont admitted it was all a hoax. The scars on his body were from childhood accidents. He had been carried away by the power of his own imagination and oratory. It was a sad end to a sad hoax, for both Dupont and his wife were ashamed of what he had done.

A few years later, in 1956, Dr Kuan arrived at the publishers Secker & Warburg with a manuscript. The book was called *The Third Eye* and was written by a Tibetan, Lobsang Rampa (some versions of the hoax substitute 'Lobsany' for 'Lobsang'). Dr Kuan modestly admitted that he had written the book and that Lobsang Rampa was his pseudonym. Like *The Man Who Wouldn't Talk*, *The Third Eye* was a story of suffering, struggle, capture and torture (this time at the hands of the Japanese), but was set in Tibet. Dr Kuan, alias Lobsang Rampa, claimed that he was the son of an important Tibetan family, and that he had been ordered by astrologers to become a monk at the age of seven. He had studied medicine, helped by memory-training sessions under hypnosis. After his training, he had travelled extensively in the Far East, and had fled from the Communists in China. He also claimed that he had had a hole bored in his skull, which had given him a 'third eye' with which he was able to see into a further dimension and identify among other things, evil aura. He gave a graphic description of the operation involved:

> The instrument penetrated the bone. A very hard, clean sliver of wood which had been treated by fire and herbs . . . just entered the hole in my head. I felt a stinging, tickling sensation apparently in the bridge of my nose. It subsided and I became aware of subtle scents which I could not identify. For a moment, the pain was intense. It diminished, died, and was replaced by spirals of colour.[2]

The pain subsequently proved worthwhile, as Lobsang Rampa was able to read other people's minds, levitate his own body, and travel through time and space.

Secker & Warburg saw no immediate evil aura, but arranged for the manuscript to be examined by two experts. One said the book was genuine, or at least that it was written by someone who had been brought up in Lhasa. The other reckoned that it was a load of rubbish. An American publisher doubted its authenticity. The *Reader's Digest*, perhaps still licking its wounds from *The Man Who Wouldn't Talk*, was not interested in the serial rights. But the book was published, sold over 40,000 copies, and brought Lobsang Rampa a certain amount of fame, as well as £20,000. John Irwin, a television producer, arranged to meet Dr Kuan, but was not impressed. He described the Tibetan as an obviously Occidental man who talked with a West Country accent and wore a saffron robe. Television ofen seems to have the third eye, for, when a private detective was hired to follow the Tibetan, the trail led to Plymouth and to the home of Cyril Hoskins, alias Dr Kuan, alias Lobsang Rampa. Hoskins was the son of a plumber from Plympton in Devon, who had left home in 1939, at the age of twenty-eight, and moved to Surrey. Here he had shaved his head and persuaded his neighbours that he was an ex-instructor from the Chinese airforce, who had endured privation and torture at the hands of the Japanese. Hoskins tried to ride out the storm by explaining that he was both Lobsang Rampa and Cyril Hoskins, the former having entered the body of the latter. This had happened at Thames Ditton, when Hoskins had fallen from a tree while attempting to photograph an owl. Hoskins had been concussed, but had recovered consciousness in time to see Lobsang Rampa, clad in saffron robes, entering his body. 'The lama severed Hoskins's astral cord and watched the now spent astral corpse float off. Lobsang Rampa then cut his own cord (which stretched all the way to Tibet), tied the loose end to the end protruding from his host's physical body, and took possession.'[3] It was this lama who had used Hoskins's mind to write *The Third Eye*. Hoskins, or Lobsang Rampa, went on to write several more books, each one explaining more and more unlikely adventures.

It may seem that Secker & Warburg, and other publishers, have been naive in their approach to such works, but perhaps publishers who are tricked by fake manuscripts deserve more sympathy than art experts who are tricked by fake paintings. In general, the hoaxer who arrives with a manuscript does not pretend that it was written by Thomas Hardy or Jane Austen. He or she simply hands over something that he or she has written. In this respect the manuscript is at least partially genuine, and if the author says that it's an account of adventures in wartime France or of Tibet in the 1920s, it would be expecting a great deal from a publisher to try to check it. On the other hand, all publishers want to make money, and this may well influence how suspiciously or trustingly they look at certain manuscripts.

In 1966 Mike McGrady, an American reporter on the Long Island *Newsday*, and twenty-four journalist colleagues, decided to write a steamy novel. McGrady was angry at the success of such books as Jacqueline Susann's *The Valley of the Dolls* and Harold Robbins's *The Adventurers*. It seemed to McGrady that the *genre* of the sex novel was only one step up from outright pornography, so he and his colleagues set to work to write the outrageous story of one Gillian Blake, a radio talk-show hostess who took revenge on her philandering husband by seducing all the married men she knew on King's Neck, Long Island. McGrady sent out strict guidelines to the other writers: 'There will be unremitting emphasis on sex. Also, true excellence in writing will be blue-pencilled into oblivion.'[4]

The book was called *Naked Came the Stranger*, and it took only two weeks for the team of writers to complete the first draft. The book was bought by Lyle Stuart, an astute publisher and a man who had managed to publish two of the only three biographies of Howard Huges that escaped the legal restrictions imposed by Hughes and his lawyers. Stuart knew what he was buying, and realized that all was not what it seemed about *Naked Came the Stranger*. Ostensibly, it was written by a Long Island housewife named Penelope Ashe, in reality Mike McGrady's sister-in-law. Stuart discovered what was going on but entered into the spirit of the hoax and spent over $50,000 on a promotion campaign. The book was a great success, selling 20,000 in the first month after publication. Once knowledge of the hoax became public, it sold even better – it is said that 9,000 copies were sold in the first hour following exposure. In all, over 100,000 hardback copies were sold; Dell bought the paperback rights for an undisclosed six-figure sum and one publisher offered McGrady half a million dollars for a sequel. The twenty-five contributors each received $5,000.

McGrady had mixed feelings about the outcome of his hoax. He had made his point and neither he nor his colleagues had any desire to write a sequel. He did, however, write a follow-up book, *Stranger Than Naked, Or How to Write Dirty Books for Fun*; on the whole he was appalled at the success of his hoax. 'It was all to easy; it went all too smoothly. America, you sit there, you plump beauty, still buying neckties from sidewalk sharpies, still guessing which walnut shell contains the pea, still praying along with Elmer Gantry. America, I sometimes worry about you.'[5] Harry Reichenbach would have been delighted.

The biggest and most famous literary hoax was that of Clifford Irving. At the time of the hoax, Irving was forty, a dangerous age so it is said, and may well have felt bitter about his lack of success as a writer. There are many parallels between Irving's reasons for faking the autobiography of Howard Hughes and van Meegeren's reasons for faking paintings of Vermeer. Irving knew all about art fakes, and was the biographer of Elmyr de Hory, who was a friend and neighbour on the island of Ibiza. In his book on de Hory, Irving had written: 'All the world loves to see the experts and the establishment made a fool of, and everyone likes to feel that those who set themselves up as experts are really just as gullible as anyone else.'

Even so, the task that Irving set himself was a tough one. He went to McGraw-Hill, his own publisher, and convinced them that he was in touch with the billionaire aeroplane designer, film producer and hermit, Howard Hughes. Hughes had disappeared from the real world some sixteen years earlier and was the subject of enormous speculation and surmise. He was guarded by the tightest possible security, a select group of Mormon guards who made sure that no one had access to him at any time. Hughes wrote no letters, made no phone calls, save to a few top people in his business empire. His past life, however, had been one of excitement and achievement. His story, his own version of his life, would be a bestseller, a publisher's dream.

Irving forged letters from Hughes, purporting to give him permission to write such a book and saying that he would permit Irving to record a series of interviews with him, at locations to be fixed by Hughes. The more secretive Irving became, the more McGraw-Hill were convinced that the deal was genuine. They gave him an enormous advance and promised all possible co-operation. *Time-Life* were persuaded to buy the serial rights, and they gave Irving access to all their information on Hughes. Irving later claimed that in so doing they had provided most of the material with which they were hoaxed, but he also had the luck of the hoaxer. While working on the book he was asked by an acquaintance, Stanley Meyer, to rewrite another biography of Hughes, written by Noah Dietrich. Dietrich had been employed by Hughes and therefore had a great deal of inside information. Irving held onto the manuscript of Dietrich's biography just long enough to get it photocopied, but understandably turned down the request to re-write it.

Irving also had the daredevil spirit of the successful hoaxer. He invented and wrote up a meeting that he had with Howard Hughes and Spiro Agnew in a car park in Palm Springs at five in the morning. 'The wackier it is, the more they believe it,' Irving wrote later. 'The wilder the story, the deeper their need to believe it. And, of course, it's less checkable.'[6]

From conception to completion, the book took just one year. Irving pocketed three-quarters of a million dollars and almost got away with it. Some versions of the explosion of the hoax suggest that it failed simply because Irving misheard the name 'Meier' (an ecologist who had worked for Hughes in the late 1960s and was seeking election as Senator for New Mexico) as 'Meyer', and thought that McGraw-Hill and the rest of his victims were about to connect him with Stanley Meyer and the Noah Dietrich biography. Once people knew that Irving had had access to Dietrich's book then they would guess that that was where he had obtained much of his intimate knowledge of Howard Hughes. They would doubt that there had been a series of meetings in cars and motel rooms from Florida to the Caribbean to

Mexico. They would wonder whether Irving had ever been in contact with Hughes. They would want their money back.

Irving's hoax is in many ways the archetypal hoax. The hoaxer had nerves of steel, the luck of the devil, the power to convince, rampant self-deception, a greedy market, and contempt for his victim. Most hoaxes for financial gain are both illegal and unforgivable, but there are occasions when it is difficult not to feel that a victim has got what he deserved. In the words of Irving: 'A moment in time arrives when the victim's willingness may lead him, consciously or otherwise, across the thin dividing line between gullibility and culpability.'[7] In looking at the Hitler diary hoax of 1983, it is hard not to feel that the victims were either not very bright or a touch too greedy. For, sixteen years earlier, the *Sunday Times*, one of the Hitler Diary victims, had had its fingers burned when it spent a quarter of a million pounds on the fake Mussolini Diaries. Somebody, somewhere, it seems, should have had a feeling of here-we-go-again.

Diaries would appear to be seldom what they seem. In 1981 *The Diary of a Good Neighbour* was rejected by several publishers until it turned up at Michael Joseph. There a senior editor thought the book had merit and that the author's style was reminiscent of the young Doris Lessing. According to the manuscript, the author was Jane Somer, but Michael Joseph soon discovered that Jane Somer was indeed Doris Lessing. The publisher colluded with the hoaxer, and the book was published as the work of Jane Somer. It sold only a couple of thousand copies, received few favourable notices and was rubbished by many reviewers. Three years later Doris Lessing revealed the hoax.

Stories of fake books abound. In 1987 Futura published *A Soldier for Eden*, the story of an American teenager who became a Palestinian terrorist and a hitman for Colonel Gaddafi. The cover of the book carried a photograph of thirteen-year-old Christopher Rustom who had been left an orphan in Libya after his parents had been killed in a plane crash. The *fedayeen* trained him. He learnt to speak Arabic and to kill. In 1985 Rustom was sent by Gaddafi to Damascus, where he met James Congdon, aka Peter Ebel. Congdon wrote Rustom's story and took the book to a London agent. The agent accepted the book in good faith: 'You have to take people on trust,' he said. 'If somebody produces what seems like good documentary evidence, you tend to believe him.' And the book did seem to have a good pedigree. There was a foreword by a former Libyan Education Minister, Mr Ashem Muhammad Besada, hoping that Rustom's 'heroic efforts will inspire others'. The book was a success, and was featured prominently in various newspapers. The BBC bought the rights to make it into a film.

Too much success is a bad thing for any hoax. A researcher working for the BBC could find no evidence of Rustom's existence in the Middle East, and no evidence of his parents' existence back home in Vermont. The cover picture also was worrying – Rustom was standing in front of a sort of tree that doesn't grow in the Middle East, wearing false badges on his uniform. Further inquiries revealed that the boy in the picture wasn't Rustom. Congdon admitted he'd never met the boy and then hurried to the United States. The book was labelled a 'non-book' and was pulped.

In Britain the golden age of the literary hoax was the late eighteenth century, when at least a dozen forgers of manuscripts were in production at the same time. The more respectable side of this industry was represented by Horace Walpole. In 1764 he pretended that his first novel, *The Castle of Otranto*, was not his own original work, but his translation of an Italian composition, written some two hundred years earlier. Only when the second edition was published did Walpole admit to being the author, and asked pardon of his readers 'for having offered his work to them under the borrowed personage of a translator. As diffidence of his own abilities and the novelty of the attempt were the sole inducements to assume that disguise, he flatters himself that he shall appear excusable.'

It was a poor justification, and it's far more likely that Walpole was attempting to cash in on the vogue for things old that flourished at the time. As the Industrial Revolution accelerated, people began to look more and more admiringly back into the past. Whatever they saw, they liked: castles, the unspoilt countryside, Shakespeare, ballads, the heroes of old. As soon as the new factories appeared, the call of the wild was heard as never before. Dr Johnson went on his tour of Scotland, Wordsworth wrote his *Lyrical Ballads*, the Gothic Revival appeared from nowhere, landscape paintings became the rage.

And in 1760 a young Scotsman named James Macpherson published *Fragments of Ancient Poetry, Collected in the Highlands of Scotland, and Translated From the Gaelic or Erse Languages*. Two years later came *Fingal, an Ancient Epic Poem in Six Books, Composed by Ossian, son of Fingal*. The poems told the story of a third-century chief in heroic language:

> Oscur my son came down; the mighty in battle
> descended. His armour rattled in thunder; and the
> lightning of his eyes was terrible . . .

It was an unpropitious time for producing militant Scottish heroes, Bonnie Prince Charlie and the Jacobites were only a few frights away. William Hazlitt placed Ossian with Homer, Dante and the writers of the Bible. Goethe was impressed and wrote a monograph on *Ossian and the Poetry of the Ancient Races*, but the London literary establishment, at that time extremely strong, was highly prejudiced and highly critical. Macpherson came from the wrong background, he produced no evidence of original Gaelic texts – he couldn't really, for the epic of Fingal had been handed down in an oral tradition – the work was provincial, its main audience uncultured. Dr Johnson was at his most snooty and boorish: he cursed Macpherson, the Scots, their language 'the rude speech of a barbarous people who had few thoughts to express' and everything about them, and the epic poems in particular: 'Sir, a man might write such stuff for ever, if he would *abandon* his mind to it.'[8] Threats passed to and fro. Johnson was adamant that the work was a fake – he was still smarting from having been duped by one James Lauder, who had convinced the good Doctor that he had found Latin texts proving that Milton was a plagiarist. In 1797, a special committee was set up to examine Fingal, Ossian and Macpherson. Eight years later the committee reported their finding, that Macpherson had embroidered what was genuine. It was eight wasted years. Macpherson had admitted this in the Preface to the work.

Macpherson spent the rest of his life as a successful politician and Highland laird. When he died, he was laid to rest in Westminster Abbey next to Dr Johnson, an uneasy eternity for both of them. There is still controversy about Macpherson. His work was attacked by Hugh Trevor-Roper in 1983, a case of the bitten biting.

A totally different reception greeted the work of Bishop Thomas Percy, who was a contemporary of James Macpherson. Percy's real name was Piercy, and he was the son of a Bridgnorth grocer. He adopted the name Percy, however, as it had better connections, and he happily allowed people to believe that he was a member of a branch of the great family of that name. He became Chaplain to the Earl of Northamberland, and then to George III, Dean of Carlisle and finally Bishop of Dromore. At one time he had been tempted to expose George Psalmanazar, whose *Miscellaneous Pieces Relating to the Chinese* was republished in 1762. But Percy decided to remain silent: 'I had once thought of publishing a Pamphlet to correct the mistakes of that Volume but . . . I laid aside my Intention on account of the Age and Poverty of the Author.'[9] Johnson, a great admirer of Psalmanazar, was happy to see in Percy's work a counterblast to the awful Scots.

The work itself was the *Reliques of Ancient English Poetry*, published in 1765, an anthology of old English poems that had been handed down orally for four or five hundred years. Probably only a quarter of the poems were genuinely old, the rest were written by Percy himself, among them the famous 'Ballad of Chevy Chase'. There were those who guessed what was going on, but unlike *Fingal*, *Reliques* was warmly received by the establishment. These were English poems, and Percy was a bishop. And he had already published volumes of Chinese, Norse and Hebrew poetry. He was no upstart, and there was no reason why he should not be admitted to the London literary circle. The Johnson clique tended to regard Percy as a counterblast to Macpherson and other Scots, but, in his own way, Percy, too, was challenging the poetical status quo. The problem, for any aspiring poet then as now, was how to become accepted by the establishment, and if you couldn't make it on your own merits, one way was to produce long-lost gems from the past. Scholars and critics were keen collectors of old poems. There were missing chunks in the history of poetry, just as there were missing paintings in the story of Vermeer. It was simply a matter of finding, or forging, an acceptable chunk.

Thomas Chatterton was the 'boy wonder' who turned to forgery. He was born in 1752, the posthumous son of a writing master and lay clerk at Bristol Cathedral. His father had left him a chest of old documents relating to Bristol and to one Master Canynge, who had been Lord Mayor of Bristol before his death in 1474. Canynge had

had a friend named Thomas Rowley, and Chatterton adopted Rowley as his poetic persona. Such was Chatterton's talent that he taught himself to read and write Middle English, and at the age of twelve he produced *Elinoure and Juga*, which he passed to an antiquarian as the work of Rowley. Chatterton went on to produce other works attributed to Rowley, several of them extolling the virtues of Bristol and comparing it favourably with 'cowarde Londonne'. This was what the citizens of Bristol wished to hear. The poems became extremely popular, and Chatterton increased his output. His friend Edward Gardner later described how Chatterton had aged the manuscripts that he produced. Chatterton would 'rub a parchment in several places in streaks with yellow ochre, then rub it several times on the ground, which was dirty, and afterwards crumple it in his hand, saying "That was the way to antiquate it".[10]

Chatterton then sent Rowley's *A History of English Painters* and some of the poems to Horace Walpole, hoping that Walpole would become his patron. For a short while they exchanged an amicable correspondence, Walpole was intrigued to find that his theories on the origins of oil painting were backed up by Rowley's *History*, but Chatterton resented some of Walpole's advice regarding a future career, and it is said that Walpole discovered the true origin of the *History*. Chatterton turned on his would-be benefactor:

> Walpole! I thought not I should ever see
> So mean a heart as thine has proved to be.

Bristol held few delights for Chatterton, and he was frightened by the approaches of an admirer, Esther Saunders, who wrote to him in April 1770:

> Sir, to a Blage you I wright a few Lines to you but have not the weakness to Believe all you say of me for you may Say as much to other young Ladys for all I kno But I Cant go out of a Sunday with you for I ham afraid we Shall be Seen to go Sir if it agreeble to you I had Take a walk with you in the morning for I be Belive we Shant be Seen a bout 6 a Clock But we must wait with patient for ther is a Time for all Things.

Chatterton hastily wrote back: 'There is a time for all things – Except Marriage my dear.'

Two weeks later he left for London. It was an ill-advised step. He had no success in London as a poet, although his burlesque opera, *The Revenge*, was successfully produced. Exactly four months after his arrival in London, Chatterton poisoned himself with arsenic. He was seventeen years old.

The furore about the authenticity of the Rowley poems took place after Chatterton's death. In a way Chatterton was too good a poet. The language of the Rowley poems was ancient enough, but the form of the poems was too modern. Nobody in the fifteenth century wrote in heroic couplets. Nevertheless, there were many who held that the poems were genuine, among them Thomas Warton, who had been happy to include some of them in his *History of English Poetry*, where they conveniently plugged a gap that he had hitherto been unable to fill. Chatterton was subsequently reviled as a forger, but praised as a poet on his own merits. It is difficult not to feel that he was an unlucky hoaxer. Had his background been less humble, the establishment would almost certainly have taken more notice of him. Edward Rushton, a contemporary of Chatterton, was one of the few to defend him and to see how shabbily he was treated compared with Percy: 'A Common Observer would imagine, that both writers were in the same Predicament, but mark the Influence of Wealth and Situation; whilst the One is nothing more than the Innocent Artifice of an Honourable Author, the Other, is loudly reprobated as the vile Forgery of an obscure Charity Boy.'[11] It wasn't quite as simple as that. Some critics of Chatterton and admirers of Rowley had made life very difficult for themselves. They could not accept that the Rowley poems were forgeries without admitting that Chatterton himself had great talent.

Chatterton wrote only a handful of poems, Iolo Morganwg wrote hundreds, as well as books on agricultural practice, folk sayings and customs, the Welsh religion, and political reform. He was the son of a Glamorgan stonemason, proud of his humble origins and dangerously progressive in his thinking. Like Percy, Macpherson and Chatterton, Morganwg produced his own ancient poetry, and, like that of the others, it was work of a high quality. Like Macpherson, he was insulted by Dr Johnson. In the early 1770s, Morganwg came to London. He met Johnson in a bookshop, where Morganwg asked Johnson which of three English grammars would be most useful.

'*Either of them* will do for *you*, young man,' said Johnson, waspishly and ungrammatically. Like Percy and Macpherson, Morganwg produced a mixture of forgery, genuine ancient poems, and great original work. Also, like Machperson, Iolo Morganwg was seeking to establish the validity and tradition of non-English poetry. This had its difficulties, but also its advantages. 'Part of the reason why Iolo was never fully exposed as a forger in his lifetime was that he himself was the best Welsh scholar of his time.'[12]

He was an eccentric figure. Although a republican, he sought the patronage of the Prince of Wales, and composed alternative lyrics to *God Save the King*. He falsified his own lineage, making himself out to be descended from other Welsh poets. He was imprisoned for debt in Cardiff. He wrote pacifist poetry, 'Ode on Converting a Sword Into a Pruning Hook', while Britain was at war with Revolutionary France. He was considered a potential traitor, but invited the Prince of Wales to Druidical meetings on Primrose Hill. For a short time, he lived almost next door to the house in which Thomas Chatterton had committed suicide. Towards the end of his life he declared that he wished to form a Priestless Society, and wrote a manuscript entitled *No Priest, No Parson, Liberty, Peace and Truth*. And he had heard about Joanna Southcott, who in 1814 at the age of sixty-four declared she was pregnant with Shiloh, the child of the Lord, a hoax that stands unique to this day.

Morganwg died in 1826, but it took a hundred years to uncover his biggest hoax. In 1789, Morganwg published a modern edition of the works of Dafydd ap Gwilym, a fourteenth-century Welsh poet considered by Morganwg (and others) 'the Shakespeare of Welsh Lyric and Rural Poetry'. We now know that many of the poems included in this collection were by Morganwg himself, but such was the literary establishment's ignorance of the Welsh language while Morganwg was alive that his hoax and his forgeries went undiscovered.

What Percy, Macpherson, Morganwg and Chatterton tried to do for poetry, William Henry Ireland attempted for drama. He was born in 1777, met Chatterton's sister while in his early teens – showing considerable interest in the exploits of her brother – and received much of his education in post-Revolutionary France. As a young man, Ireland constantly sought to gain the admiration of his father, a man whose life was spent in the pursuit of Shakespeariana. By 1790 Shakespeare had become something of a national obsession, and this intensified during the war with France. Shakespeare became the symbol of England. It was, therefore, a propitious time for Ireland to produce and present to his father the title deed to a property near the site of the old Globe Theatre, with Shakespeare's signature on it. Ireland's father, Samuel, was delighted. He took the document to an expert who pronounced it genuine.

William Ireland told his father that he had an elderly contact who had more of these documents. The contact, said William, was prepared to allow him access to the papers as he had found a title deed proving the contact's right to a certain property. William produced more letters from Shakespeare, a love poem to Anne Hathaway, a letter from Elizabeth I to Shakespeare, the original manuscripts of *Hamlet* and *King Lear*. He must have had a great deal of spare time to do all this. He also produced what became known as Shakespeare's *Profession of Faith*, a document so moving that Boswell went on his knees before it and kissed 'the valuable relics of our bard to thank God I have lived to see them'.

In his own words, William Ireland then became 'fired with the idea of possessing genius to which I had never aspired'. He decided to write a new Shakespeare play. The inspiration, if that's not too bold a word, came from a picture that hung in his father's bookshop, of *Vortigern and Rowena*. William studied the story in Holinshed's *Chronicles*, and told his father of the existence of the play before he had written a single word. When the play was ready, William took it to Richard Sheridan who had his doubts about it. 'It is very odd; one would be led to think that Shakespeare must have been very very young when he wrote the play. As to the doubting whether it be really his or not, who can possibly look at the papers, and not believe them ancient?' He agreed to produce the play at Drury Lane. Nobody who saw the manuscript made any suspicious connection between the subject of the play and the painting in Samuel Ireland's shop: 'Every person . . . admired the strange coincidence of Mr Ireland's having so long possessed a drawing on the very subject of that drama.'[13]

Accounts vary as to the sequence of events that followed. Edmond Malone, a right-wing critic and writer, had been preparing a work for publication entitled *Inquiry into the Validity of the Papers Attributed to Shakespeare*. Malone was convinced the papers were fake, and was especially suspicious of their origin. 'It is to be observed that we are not told where the deed was first discovered; it is said in a mansion house, but where situated is not stated.'[14] He was also critical of Ireland's 'Shakespearian' spelling – 'ande' for 'and', and 'forre' for 'for'. The final straw for Malone was that the letter from Queen Elizabeth to Shakespeare referred to the Globe Theatre and the expected presence of the Earl of Leicester – who died six years before the theatre was opened. Most of all, Malone was appalled that anyone should dare to falsify anything to do with the divine Shakespeare. Some accounts suggest that Malone's work was published just before the first night of *Vortigern*, others say that it was published afterwards. It may not matter, for the play already had enough going against it. John Kemble, the play's director, was convinced that it was a fake, and wanted the play to open on April Fools' Day. Sheridan wouldn't allow this, and the play opened and closed on 2 April 1796. One line alone ('And when this solemn mockery is o'er') was enough to bring howls of derisive laughter from the audience and to wreck the performance. A second 'Shakespeare' play, *Henry II*, was never performed. 'Had the play of *Vortigern* succeeded with the public, and the manuscripts been acknowledged as genuine,' wrote William Ireland, many years later, 'it was my intention to have completed a series of plays from the reign of William the Conqueror to that of Queen Elizabeth; that is to say, I should have planned a drama on every reign the subject of which had not been treated by Shakespeare.' We have perhaps been spared a great deal.

William Ireland admitted the hoax. At first his father did not believe him, and thought his son was seeking undue fame and glory, but others believed and could not forgive. To have taken Shakespeare's name in vain was a crime, and to have forged a play which contained Jacobin sentiments was treachery. William rode out the storm, but later went to live in France.

In every category of hoax, there are those who are mainly out for a little fun, and there are plenty of literary hoaxes that display high spirits. Charles Julius Bertram wrote a topographical account of Roman Britain, ostensibly the work of a fourteenth-century monk named Richard of Cirencester. Bertram was Professor of English at the Royal Marine Academy in Copenhagen, one of a long line of academic hoaxers. It took two hundred years to bring the hoax to light.

William Beckford was a young man who became inspired by the strange names that his housekeeper rattled off while showing guests around his house at Fonthill Abbey. He had inherited a fortune at the age of nine, and it may be that this left him with too much time on his hands. At the age of twenty he wrote his *Biographical Memoirs of Extraordinary Painters*, a book of total rubbish which included such great artists as Og of Bason, Blunderbassian of Venice, Herr Sucrewasser of Vienna, and Watersouchy of Amsterdam. One reviewer praised the work as containing 'the results of already extensive observation and judgment of refined taste'.[15] The work was listed in *Encyclopaedia Britannica*.

In 1916 Walter Bynner, himself a poet, and others invented the Spectrist School of Poetry. It was the age of all the -ists and -isms – Imagism, Dadaism, Existentialism, Surrealism and Vorticism. Bynner's motive was to poke a little fun at the avant- and all the suivant-gardes. The poetry was awful, but its serious reception must have both delighted and horrified Bynner. Here is a sample:

>Cream is better than lemon
>In tea at breakfast
>I think of tigers as eating lemons.
>Thank God this tea comes from the greengrocer,
>Not from Ceylon.

The poems were so successful that they became the subject of parody by the Ultra-Violet School of Poetry, a unique example of a hoax on a hoax. Fortunately, that particular school was not treated seriously, or the hoax could have achieved a kind of permanent motion. When the original hoax was revealed, Bynner wrote about it in *Poetry* magazine: 'Our intent in publishing the book was not to question the use of free verse and not to bait the public, but to satirize fussy pretence.'

The 1920s saw a plethora of travel books published, many of them extolling the wonders of the Pacific, of palm-fringed islands and blue lagoons, of dazzling white sand and tropical nights, and every other cliché that now comes so readily to mind. Most of them were genuine, if sloppy, but there were those who felt that enough was enough and that a little satire wouldn't come amiss. One of the best of these hoaxes was a book called *The Cruise of the Kawa* by Walter E Traprock. The immediate inspiration was a series of newspaper articles about the South Seas and the discovery of a new group of islands in the Polynesias. The book was the brainchild of George S Chappell and George Palmer Putnam, the latter being that rare breed, a hoaxer among publishers.

Chappell and Putnam named their group of islands the Filbert Islands, because of the abundance of filbert nut trees, a faraway heaven where the natives spoke Filbertese, or nut-talk. To this paradise sailed the *Kawa*, with her crew of five – Reginald K Whinney ('scientific man, world wanderer, data-demon and a devil when roused'), Herman Swank ('Bohemian, artist, and vagabond, forever in search of new sensations'), Captain Ezra Triplett, and First Mate William Henry Thomas, and Traprock ('of Derby, Connecticut, editor, war correspondent and author, jack-of-all-trades, mostly literary and non-lucrative'). Traprock also claimed that he had written the book for a musical version of *Les Misérables* called *Jumping Jean*.

George Putnam thrust aside modesty in his introduction to the book:

> Uninfluenced by professional self-interest, unshaken by our genuine admiration for its predecessors, and despite our inherent inclination toward modest conservatism, we unhesitatingly record the conviction that *The Cruise of the Kawa* stands pre-eminent in the literature of modern exploration – a supreme, superlative epic of the South Seas.[16]

The book wasted no time in allowing the expedition to get under way. The first chapter opened thus:

> 'Is she tight?' asked Captain Ezra Triplett. (We were speaking of my yawl, the *Kawa*.)
> 'As tight as a corset,' was my reply.
> 'Good. I'll go.'

Once they reached the Filbert Islands, the crew of the *Kawa* discovered, and photographed, the ooza snake (which lived on coconut milk and was of a loving disposition), the fatu-liva bird (which laid cubic eggs with the pattern of dice on them), crabs big enough to tow a boat, pearls the size of onions, and the dew-fish:

> Just as the sun's rays flash across the horizon they rise to the surface of the water in vast numbers, turning the entire ocean to a pulsating mirror of silver. For five minutes they lie thus, then suddenly sink simultaneously. Their work for the day, so far as we know, is done. The natives fill their cheeks – which are very elastic – with hundreds of these tiny fish which they afterwards eject on shore.

The water round the Filbert islands was perfectly clear to a depth of 482 feet, and the natives could stay under water for hours at a time.

The Filbertese had never heard a word that ended in a consonant, but had a lively and attractive language. Traprock quoted some words from their vocabulary:

> oo-pa – a sort of vegetable cream puff
> alova – a flower with a bloom, one inhale of which contained the kick of three old fashioned mint juleps
> hoopa – a delicious 27 per cent proof milk.

Among the Filbertese were Baahaabaa (Durable Drinker), Abuluti (Big Wind Constantly Blowing), and Zambao-Zambino (Young-Man-Proud-of-His-Waist-Line).

Eventually, and with much sadness, the crew of the *Kawa* sailed away, leaving behind a sorrowing island. In true Rider Haggard tradition, Traprock wrote: 'They will forget. . . . We must remember they are a race of children. They have no written records of the past, no anticipations of the future.'[17] The book was a success on two levels. There were those who saw it for what it was, a hoax, and those who took it seriously. Traprock was invited to lecture by the editorial board of the *National Geographic* in Washington DC. Enough people took the book seriously for Traprock and company to produce a sequel, the authenticity of which was doubted more.

A very simple and delightful hoax was perpetrated by the doyen of writers on cricket, Neville Cardus. In 1929 he was the cricket correspondent for the *Manchester Guardian*. When England played

South Africa at Leeds, it seemed to Cardus, and to most people, that there would be very little play on the last day as England were in such a strong position. Cardus left Leeds and spent the day in Barnet. That evening, he was horrified to discover that South Africa had fought back heroically and that there had been a full day's play. So Cardus sat down and wrote 'a column of "eye-witness" descriptive writing' of a day's cricket that he had never seen. It amounted to over 1,500 words and gave a detailed account of all that had happened, from a vantage point two hundred miles away. It was good enough to earn the praise of the captain of the South African team: 'You must have had the glasses on [the game] all the time.' Cardus did not admit what he had done, and for many years secretly admired his own audacity. There was one particular sentence in the report of which he was proud: 'The South African kicked back from a position so hopeless that few of us even took the trouble to be present at Leeds until we scented battle from afar.'[18]

One conclusion emerges: hoaxers love getting into print. For some (Hoskins, Chatterton, Macpherson, Mike McGrady, Clifford Irving, Chappell and Putnam, Ireland, Psalmanazar, de Rougemont) this is the hoax itself. For others (Jack Bilbo, Keating, Hebborn, Adrian Stephen, Alan Abel, Reichenbach, Hugh Troy), this is the means by which their hoax hopefully achieves immortality. Very few hoaxers have shown a readiness to let their hoaxes die with them.

9

Growing Weary, Growing Wary

> Life is made up of sobs, sniffles and smiles, with sniffles predominating.
> O Henry, *The Gift of the Magi*

What subsequently happens to a hoaxer depends to a large extent on what happened to the victim. A prank may inspire a counter-prank, if the victim has a sense of humour. Few do, however – that is often why they become victims. Where a lot of money is involved, however, the victim usually seeks restitution, revenge or both. Sometimes this comes swiftly; at other times what follows is more of a saga, akin to the pursuit of Butch Cassidy and the Sundance Kid by E H Harriman and the Superposse. If we are to believe FBI Agent James F Johnson's account of his time spent following Count Victor Lustig, it can take years to bring a hoaxer to justice.

A few hoaxers grow old gracefully. The hoax for which they became famous turns out to be a one-off affair, a youthful escapade that made its point and served its purpose. Humphry Berkeley went back to Cambridge, took his degree, became an MP for a while and is now a TV producer. Save for a brief 'memoir' in 1974, no more was heard of Rochester Sneath or Selhurst School. Although Ken Campbell continues to write, act and direct, his hoax – the Royal Dickens Company – made its mark briefly, as we shall see, and then retired from the theatre. George Psalmanazar regretted and repented. Richard Dimbleby never again donned the cap and bells in public – the Panorama Spaghetti Hoax was a uniquely comic moment in his distinguished career. Frances Wright and Elsie Griffiths cut no more fairies from books.

There are those, of course, who were never in a position to continue hoaxing. James Shearer and Percy Toplis were both shot, the former by an Army firing squad, the latter by the police. Arnaud de Tilh paid for his false identity by being executed. Stephane Otto and Moses Shapira (of whom more in a later chapter) committed suicide. Elmyr de Hory took an overdose of sleeping pills in December 1976 while awaiting extradition to France. Charles Dawson died in mid-hoax. We still do not know for certain who was his accomplice. Currently, the favoured suspect is Keith, a man who lived the post-Piltdown part of his life in professional respectability, adjusting himself to the perceived new view of the story of evolution. Teilhard de Chardin and Sir Arthur Conan Doyle, both themselves suspects in the Piltdown Hoax at one time, never attempted any further hoaxes if they were hoaxers, though Conan Doyle became an accomplished victim. De Rougemont, Morris Newburger, Ralph Paine, Roderick and Elkhart ended their days in apparent obscurity. The Princess Caraboo (alias Mary Willcocks) sprang a second time on to centre-stage. Some time after 1815, the Governor of St Helena, at that time Napoleon's keeper, went down to the beach to watch a longboat pulling for shore. The rower turned out to be a woman. The story she told was that she had been on a ship passing the island, but had been seized by a determination to visit Napoleon. So she had borrowed the longboat and rowed to the island. Her 'fluent' Chinese convinced those on the island that she was indeed the Princess Caraboo, and she was introduced to the former French Emperor. Naploeon was enchanted by her, and is said to have written to the Pope, asking to have his marriage dissolved so that he could marry the Princess: 'Her manner is noble and fascinating in a wonderful degree'.[1]

Poor Stanley Weyman was shot in 1960 when working as the night manager at a motel in the United States. A gunman tried to rob the motel safe. Weyman resisted and was killed. Bottomley, Balfour, Orton, Hartzell, Irving, Abnagale, Arthur Furguson, Stein and others went to prison – Lustig and van Meegeren died in custody. Hebborn has risked criminal prosecution, Sophie Lloyd and Jenny Winstanley have been threatened with civil action. Hoaxing is clearly a high-risk occupation, not one to put on the form when applying for personal insurance.

But some managed to make a career out of pretence and foolery, disguise and deception. Horace Cole seems to have had nothing else to do. Alan Abel has a string of hoaxes to his credit (or discredit, depending on your point of view). He sent the *New York Times* his own obituary after arranging for his skis to be found in the form of a cross on a snow-covered mountain in Utah. In 1985 he staged a 'faint-in' among the audience of a TV chat show. Half a dozen friends of Abel collapsed, raising the spectre of an outbreak of Legionnaire's Disease. The ratings of the show improved as a result. He rented a suite at the Plaza Hotel in New York for an Idi Amin lookalike, and invited 150 reporters to cover Amin's wedding there. Reporters, FBI agents and representatives of the State Department all arrived, to find a drunken judge officiating, a reluctant bride and uniformed Pinkerton guards. Abel also produced a fake 'Deep Throat' at a press conference at the height of the Watergate Crisis, and appeared himself, swathed in bandages, as Howard Hughes at the St Regis Hotel in New York. He still has ambitions:

> I'd like to land a Martian; someday I'd like to have somebody dumped from a spaceship and discovered along a remote region of North Carolina . . . who'll speak a language no one will understand . . . who'll have no surgical scars. We were going to do it a few years ago, but we couldn't quite get enough money together to build the spaceship.[2]

Harry Reichenbach died young from cancer of the oesophagus.

> He still longed to keep his finger on the pulse of the world. And the last thing he clung to in the newspapers was the columns of comment and gossip. Almost to the end he cupped his ear to the voice of Walter Winchell. Then that too faded out into the fast gathering circle of darkness around him. . . . He clung only to his little cigars. He smoked them to the last. There was something in the feeble puffs of smoke that still symbolized the world of phantom fame to him. Then that too dropped from his pale, tired lips. Everything grew dark about him. On July 3rd 1943, at the age of 49, Harry Reichenbach passed away.[3]

The obituary seems so far over the top as to border on a hoax itself.

Hugh Troy spent years as a hoaxer, and then joined the CIA, the unkindest hoax of all. He died in 1967. Trebitsch Lincoln ended his days as a Buddhist monk in Shanghai during the Japanese occupation; still causing anxiety to the Special Branch and M15, and still threatening the world order – an odd way for a Buddhist to behave. Frank Abnagale, after years as a paediatrician, lawyer, sociology teacher and civil airline pilot, was imprisoned for twelve years. While in gaol he wrote *Catch Me If You Can*, his autobiography. He spent four years in gaol, after which, it is reported, he went into the crime prevention business and made a fortune.

The hoaxing careers of Hewitt and Demara (pages 59-61), who, like Stanley Weyman, never settled to one identity or one profession, merely ran out of steam as their various personae and qualifications were discovered one after the other to be phoney; quietly, they slipped into obscurity.

On his release from prison in 1933, Maundy Gregory left England for ever and settled in France. In 1938 he was living in Paris, drinking a bottle of either Johnnie Walker or White Horse whisky each day and smoking heavily. He still kept a bank account in England, unknown to the Official Receiver, for Gregory had been declared bankrupt in 1933. He moved to Dieppe on the outbreak of the Second World War, but was captured by the Germans and moved back to Drancy, a north-eastern suburb of Paris. We do not know why (though it is tempting to guess), but the Germans wished to return Gregory to England. He refused to go, saying: '*You* arrested me. *You* are going to keep me until the end of the war and *we* are going to win it.' He died on 28 September 1941.

Following the débâcle of the performance of *Vortigern* and the discovery of his hoax, William Ireland married, began a circulating library, and produced mock Elizabethan manuscripts which he sold as curios rather than the genuine article. His politics stuck out like a sore thumb in Britain during the Napoleonic Wars, and he moved to France. Here he became an educational administrator under the Emperor and wrote more than a dozen novels and plays. He died in 1835.

Perhaps the hoaxer with the most remarkable subsequent career was Jack Bilbo, the author of *Carrying a Gun for Al Capone*. Following the Gorguloff affair, when the French President was assassinated, and his own troubles with the Nazis in Germany, Bilbo fled to Paris. He worked for a short while as a journalist, and then decided, in his words, to 'quit the civilized world'. So he went to Cala Ratjada on the island of Majorca. He visited Algiers, returned to Cala Ratjada, where he went down with typhoid, and then, on his recovery, set up the Wikiki Bar. According to Bilbo, the bar was a huge success, but the Majorcan authorities were not keen to maintain Bilbo's presence on the island. With an English girl called Billi, he crossed to the Spanish mainland, and built a house and another bar in the village of Sitges on the Costa Brava, not far from Barcelona. Here he served Jack Bilbo's celebrated 'Knockout' – one quarter gin, one quarter absinthe, one quarter vodka and one quarter kümmel – and here he had, or claimed to have, many famous visitors: Douglas Fairbanks, Max Schmeling (the German heavyweight boxer), Leslie Woodgate (of the BBC), Anny Ondra, Ronald Colman, and G K Chesterton.

In his autobiography, Chesterton describes a visit to Bilbo's bar:

> ... outside Barcelona, where the proprietor was an authentic American gangster who had actually written a book of confessions about his own organized robbery and racketeering. Modest, like all great men, about the ability he had shown in making big business out of burglary and highway robbery, he was very proud of his literary experiment, and especially of his book; but, like some other literary men, he was dissatisfied with his publishers. He said that he had rushed across just in time to find that they had stolen nearly all his royalties. 'It was a shame,' I said sympathetically, 'Why, it was simple robbery.' 'I'll say it was,' he said with an indignant blow on the table. 'It was just plain robbery.'[4]

Another visitor was Bilbo's father, on the run from the Nazis, and a broken man. While still in Germany he had tried to poison himself. Yet another visitor was an old Chicago buddy with whom Bilbo went off to smuggle gold needed by the Abyssinians in their fight against the Italians. They reached Marseilles, where, according to Bilbo, his Chicago connections gained him access to the underworld. It was perhaps the one time in his life that Bilbo found himself living with characters almost as ridiculous as he was. He described the backstreets of the city, where naked girls from twelve years old upwards lounged in doorways, the drug dens, the hovels, the gambling dives. He came across Father Philip, the tramps' padre, a conman who staged regular road accidents in which he was always the victim, and from which he always extracted appreciable compensation.

In the company of a strange pilot, and a man called John Brook, Bilbo travelled on to Genoa (yet more brothels), Athens, Cairo and the Sudan, where the plane he was on made a forced landing in the desert. A typical Bilbo exchange followed. While the pilot was frantically repairing the machine, a horde of 'wild tribesmen' surrounded the plane, firing at Bilbo and company. 'Luckily, their shooting was not as good as ours,' wrote Bilbo afterwards, with characteristic modesty. The plane was repaired and took off once more. They landed at Aksum in northern Abyssinia, some fifty miles south of Asmara. Here Bilbo, Brook and the pilot were arrested by the Italian army and thrown into a guardhouse. Bilbo bribed a servant to bring him some Italian uniforms in which they escaped. They commandeered a plane and flew on to Addis Ababa, where they were given a wonderful reception by the King of Abyssinia (Bilbo never mentions Haile Selassie by name). Bilbo then discovered that the pilot had come to take over the Abyssinian Air Force, and that John Brook had come to take over the management of the National Bank. 'I suddenly stopped being astonished. Things like this are always happening to me. . . . Once a person starts living by his wits, he just can't escape adventure.'[5]

Bilbo returned to Sitges and opened a small shop next to his bar. By now, the Spanish Civil war was well under way, and Bilbo soon found himself in the thick of it. He set about arranging the evacuation of foreigners, among them Billi, with whom he was still living, and their daughter, whom he put on a British destroyer, HMS *Garland*. Bilbo himself was, of course, the last to leave. He went only as far as Monte Carlo, where he lost everything at the Casino, but soon returned to Spain with a lorryload of medicine and bandages for the Red Cross. He does not explain where he got them from, but outlines how he acted as a midwife *en route*, at the birth of a baby boy. Never on the fringe of things, Bilbo met up with a squadron of Moorish troops who told him that their officers had said they were fighting in Spain for Islam against Christianity, and that General Franco wished to reintroduce the Mohammedan religion into Spain.

Back to Sitges, where Bilbo shut up his bar; he then collected Billi and his daughter from Marseilles, and the three travelled to London. 'But I am not down. I am only just twenty-nine. The world stands open before me. I have strength. I have energy. And the harder fate hits me – the harder I'll hit back. Writing this book I am once again an author. And I laugh.'[5] Bilbo had many more books to write. Inasmuch as he ever settled down, he became an author, writing children's books and other fiction – much of it autobiographical. After the Second World War he gained a reputation as a sculptor and broadcaster. In 1949 he sailed round the world in a 30-foot motor launch, the *Bambula*. On his return, he set to work on a monumental sculpture, two and a half metres high, entitled *Life*, 'symbolizing the Women of England beaten to a kneeling position by the Blitz, but getting up more powerfully every time'. The piece weighed 6,642 pounds, and was executed for the World Fair. Everything that Bilbo did was larger than life. It is hard not to be attracted to the man. His boundless energy has its own kind of magnetic appeal. He is a cosmopolitan Billy Liar.

By becoming an author, Bilbo achieved what few hoaxers manage – he got what he wanted. By contrast, Arthur Orton, the failed Tichborne Claimant, had a miserable existence once his hoax was exposed. He was sent to Dartmoor, where he was allowed one twenty-minute visit every six months. Sad parties of his supporters made their way to the Moor, where they were greeted with a pathetic sight. 'The poor fellow made no complaint, except one. He said it was torture and cruelty to him to make him associate with felons and blackguards, and at times he felt an inward desire to make away with himself.'[7] Orton's words as reported by Dr Kenealy (see page 101) – 'I shall never leave this prison; I am destined to die in it. . . . I shall live and die a prisoner in this place' – sound more like Kenealy than Orton, more the words of a restless, dissatisfied politician and lawyer from Ireland than a slaughterman from Wagga Wagga.

Orton, however, lived for another twenty-four years. He served eleven years in prison and was then released on ticket of leave. He had lost almost fifteen stone in weight while in prison. For some time he toured the music halls as the ill-used baronet, and gave lectures on the justice of his cause in public houses. He still commanded some support, but interest in the matter waned, and in 1895 Orton brought the charade to an end by publishing his 'Confessions'. This was a series of articles in the *People*, in which Orton related with considerable detail how his attention had been called to Lady Tichborne's advertisement for her son, and how he had responded 'merely for a lark'. The initial aim had been to get enough money out of the pretence to go to Panama to join his brother. That had remained his aim until Bogle, and other representatives of Lady Tichborne, arrived in Australia. Then he had to go through with the hoax, to the very bitter end. He 'sucked people's brains' to obtain as much information as possible about Sir Roger, and so thoroughly worked himself into the part, that 'by degrees he began to believe that he really was the rightful owner of his estates'.

After a few years, his health began to fail as his cause died, and he gave up lecturing. He bought a small tobacconist's shop, but that venture also failed. In the last few months of his life, he made a living by 'showing' himself at various public houses in Kilburn, as much for his bulk as his fame, for he regained all the weight he had lost in prison. His funeral took place on 6 April 1898. *The Times* of 7 April reported:

> At the Paddington Cemetery . . . several thousands of persons had congregated, and a body of police had to be told off to clear the people away from the church doors. After the mourners had taken their places, the public were allowed to enter and the rush that followed quickly filled the edifice. The service was conducted by the Reverend Twisaday. The church having been cleared, after another struggle on the part of the curious to get out quickly, the coffin was borne to the grave through dense crowds that lined the way on either side. . . . The coffin, on which were many wreaths, bore the following inscription: Sir Charles Roger Doughty Tichborne, born 5th January 1829, died 1st April 1898.

A few days earlier, Messrs Knight, Frank and Rutley had held an auction of Tichborne memorabilia – briefs, letters, documents, complete files of the *Tichborne Gazette* over six years of publication, volumes of Dr Kenealy's *The Englishman*, photographs, and posters that Orton had taken around the country when drumming up support for his cause. The entire collection realized £7 17s 6d.

The *Dictionary of National Biography* is brusquely concise in its account of the subsequent career of Horatio Bottomley: 'Independent MP, South Hackney, 1918–22; new enterprises ended in imprisonment, 1922–7; died in want and obscurity.' There is a little more to it than that. Bottomley was released in 1927. He immediately set about trying to re-create some of his old careers. He founded a new magazine called *John Blunt*, a pale shadow of *John Bull*. It was a failure. He turned to writing books: *Songs of the Cell* and *Humours of Prison Life*. Not surprisingly, there were few buyers in the dark days of the Depression. In 1930 his loyal wife died, and with her Bottomley's hopes of a comeback. Towards the end, as *The Times* of 27 May 1933 reported, 'Bottomley fell on evil days, and it was stated that he had been obliged to apply for an old-age pension.' In May 1933 he was admitted to the Middlesex Hospital in London. Four days later, he died.

Jabez Balfour fared slightly better. On 12 December 1895, he arrived at Wormwood Scrubs, a prison he had often passed on his way from Paddington to his estate in Oxfordshire. For almost nine years he never saw himself in a looking-glass, and lived in a cell 'provided with a Bible, prayer-book, hymn book, and generally some specimen of goody-goody literature.'[8] Balfour had ten years in which to study the prison system from the inside. 'I had sedulously cultivated relations of respect and good-will with the great majority of the disciplinary staff, and I thus became familiar with the inner workings of the system.'[9] On his release in 1906, Balfour wrote *My Prison Life*, an account of his years in gaol, 'dedicated to the Right Honourable the Lord Northcliffe in Recognition of his Interest in Prison Reform and of the Sympathy, Encouragement and Help he has accorded to the Author'.

It is in many places a moving book. In the Introduction, Balfour was at pains to say that he didn't intend to plead his own case, though by page 4 he was attempting to disprove the rightness of his conviction. Nevertheless, his account of life in prison is a bold critique of existing practices. He deplored the soul-destroying routine, the inhuman living conditions, the lack of facilities and recreational equipment. He wrote: 'The deep sympathy which I feel for these unfortunate people . . . is heightened and accentuated by the fact that I myself shared to the full in their misfortune,' though he cannot help adding, 'there was no greater victim among the sufferers than I, no ruin more complete than mine.'

There are a few hoaxers who survive and prosper. Boris Vian, an existentialist jazz trumpeter who lived in Paris just after the Second World War, wrote two novels, *J'irai Cracher Sur Vos Tombes* and *Les*

Morts Ont Tout La Même Peau, both of which were published as the work of a black writer named Vernon Sullivan. The books were seriously reviewed, for they captured the French view of life in America – wild, violent, sexually rampant and shocking. Many guessed that the books were the work of Vian and few were surprised when he admitted this. From then on, he wrote in his own name and had a successful career as an author.

Fritz Kreisler survived the storm that blew up in the music world when it was known that he had written works that he had claimed were those of Pugnani, Couperin and Vivaldi. Orson Welles went from strength to strength after the famous Mercury Theatre production of *The War of the Worlds*. Cyril Hoskins, alias Lobsang Rampa, wrote and published several other books after *The Third Eye*. Humphry Berkeley has had at least two extremely successful careers.

But, on the whole, few hoaxers live happily ever after.

10

The Psychology of Hoaxers

'There's no art,
To find the mind's construction in the face.'

Shakespeare *Macbeth*, Act I sc.iv

For anyone examining a hoax, the greatest difficulty lies in seeing into the hoaxer's mind. Deceit is at the centre of a hoax; the bigger the hoax, the greater the cunning behind it. Help from the hoaxer is unlikely, for he is not likely to tell the truth. His career has been built on a strong and certain ability to lie. Whether languishing in a prison cell, standing in the dock awaiting sentence, or sunning himself on the beach in Ibiza, the hoaxer would rather appear a card than a cad, would rather be a joker than a knave.

Hoaxers are also masters of self-deception, which means that they are great self-justifiers too. Frank Abnagale, who spent the whole of his adult life hoaxing, said: 'I stole every nickel and blew most of it on gourmet food and luxurious living. I never felt I was a criminal. I was simply a poseur and swindler of astonishing ability'.[1] Clifford Irving had similar misconceptions about himself: 'After all, it was a hoax, not a crime'.[2] 'I would have to confess to more than a hoax and what apparently was a crime'.[3] 'I had never realized I was committing a crime – I thought of it as a hoax'.[4] In 1991, Eric Hebborn, who claimed to have passed over 500 fake drawings to various art experts, repeatedly said much the same thing in interviews: 'Maybe they will lock me up but I am not a criminal';[5] 'They are all trying to make out I'm some kind of criminal. I am not'.[6]

Strongly linked to this is the element of conceit. When asked, the successful hoaxer may well produce grand-sounding reasons for what he has done, and present himself as a champion of the people, a fine satirist, one who sees through the hypocrisy of the age in which he lives. This is especially true of the many modern American hoaxers, or pranksters as they usually call themselves.

When Joey Skaggs placed an advertisement in *Village Voice* in 1978

> CATHOUSE FOR DOGS
> featuring a savoury selection of hot bitches.
> From pedigree (Fifi, the French Poodle) to mutts
> (Lady the Tramp). Handler and vet on duty. Stud
> photo service available. No weirdos, please. Dogs
> only. By appointment. Call 254-7878

– the piece was taken as genuine and he had to establish a real cathouse for dogs. Business was brisk. The next step was to involve the media. 'Just doing the hoax is not the total performance. It's not the end of the piece; it's not the finale *or* the objective. What's more important, and more difficult to do, is to get the media to come back to allow me to say why and what it means'.[7] The ASPCA was appalled, and Skaggs was subpoenaed by the District Attorney for illegally running a cathouse for dogs.

A fellow American hoaxer, Jello Biafra, summed up the feelings of many of the satirical hoaxers by saying: 'When we're treated like mice, why not bite the elephants?'[8] In this spirit, Biafra cites the case of a disgruntled employee who sent a computer printout message to all his fellow shift workers announcing that they would be laid off. The workforce was shocked and spent a whole day in meetings and discussions before they realized the computer notes were fake. The point of the hoax, in Biafra's eyes, was that it cost the company thousands of dollars in lost work time. Hoaxing can be a political weapon, in more ways than one.

Many of the art hoaxers have adopted similarly assertive-defensive attitudes when explaining the reasons for hoaxing. Keating claimed that he tricked the art world for the sake of all those he was proud to call brother artists. Van Meegeren claimed that his forgeries took possession of him: 'I came to a condition in which I was no longer master of myself'.[9] Walter Bynner's only ambition in founding the Spectrist School of Poetry was 'to satirize fussy pretence'. Mike

McGrady seems to have had a genuinely satirical aim in conceiving and managing the composition of *Naked Came the Stranger*, and there can be no doubt that *The Cruise of the Kawa* was intended purely as a piece of fun. This is one of the few truly innocent 'book' hoaxes. Usually the victim of a book hoax is the publisher, but here Putnam collaborated in the hoax. The public may have been duped, but at least they had a chance to look at the book before they bought it. Usually, the victim is not so lucky.

There is at least one case of a hoax where the public has been invited to join in. Jean Shepherd was a New York radio disc jockey who worked the dead hours between one and five o'clock in the morning. He established a close bond with his night audience, whom he found to have less unquestioning acceptance of the world as it was. He suggested to them that together they whip up a demand for a book that didn't exist, and asked them to send in ideas for such a book. Shepherd and his listeners decided that the work should be a racy novel of the life of an eighteenth-century rake. It was to be called *I, Libertine*, and was supposedly written by one Frederick R Ewing. Shepherd and company not only invented the author, they also gave him a background. Ewing, they said, was a former officer in the British Royal Navy, and a man with a reputation as a student of eighteenth-century erotica.

The book was widely discussed on Shepherd's night-time radio show. Soon casual listeners, who were not aware of the hoax, began to ask questions about *I, Libertine*. The *New York Times* listed it as one of the forthcoming publications; magazines ran articles about Commander Ewing. A number of people phoned leading newspapers asking why they hadn't reviewed the book. It is said (by at least two writers of books on hoaxes) that a student at Columbia University wrote a dissertation on the novel and its historical background, and received 'a reasonable mark' – whatever that means. The demand for the book was sufficient for Shepherd and a colleague to write it. It was published by Ballantine Books but was not a success.

For all the talk of fun and satire, the reality may be that the most any hoaxer aspires to is money or revenge or both, and perhaps relief from boredom. Morris Newburger may have invented the Plainfield Teachers for no better reason than that he didn't have enough to do as a New York stockbroker. Joe Orton and Kenneth Halliwell occasionally livened a dull moment by writing spurious letters of complaint from 'Edna Wellthorpe' to commercial and social targets. As Edna, they wrote to Crosse and Blackwell, complaining that a tin of blackberry pie filling had almost poisoned Edna's Aunt Lydia: 'You say on the label, glucomates have been added. Yes, and one wonders what else you've added to bring about this extraordinary malaise'.[10] Crosse and Blackwell sent a letter of apology and a crate of tins of blackberry pie filling. Edna then wrote to her local vicar, asking for the loan of his church hall to stage a defence of homosexuality entitled *Nelson was a Nance*. The vicar was less accommodating than Crosse and Blackwell had been, so Edna's mother followed up with a letter advising the vicar of her daughter's recent death. The vicar replied: 'I was appalled to read of the death of your daughter. Alas, I did not see it in the local paper . . . but I am very sad to hear that she has passed on. On the other hand I can't help feeling that she had got in with the wrong set'.[11] Edna bounced back to life with a letter to the manager of the Ritz Hotel in Piccadilly, informing him that she had left her handbag in the hotel lounge: 'The bag contained a Boots folder of snaps of Mrs Sullivan and me in risqué poses. You will naturally appreciate that neither of us wish such things to fall into the wrong hands'. The manager replied: 'An exhaustive search by our staff has failed to uncover any moroccan leather handbag'.[12] Some of us take a long time to grow up; Humphry Berkeley noted that 'the frivolity of a boy of twenty-one would be unpardonable in a man of forty-seven'.[13]

The use of bogus letters is a favourite technique of the hoaxer, and has produced several books which illustrate how effective they can be as hoaxes. Berkeley sent letters to the headmasters of almost all the most famous schools in England. Henry Root sent letters to publishers, Chief Constables, politicians, media celebrities, the BBC, bankers, industrialists and the Royal Family. The letters were scantily clad in the garb of a supporter of the political right, but clearly sarcastic. The replies Root received showed how easy it is to draw even sophisticated victims into the hoaxer's mad world. Brian Bethell published *The Defence Diaries of W Morgan Petty* in 1984. This was an account of the unilateral stand on defence taken by Petty and his friend Roger at their home in Cherry Drive, Canterbury. Much of the material for the book came from correspondence between Bethell (as Petty) and MPs, the Ministry of Defence, the RAF, the USAF, ICI, ITV, etc., all on the subject of how Petty and

Roger could equip themselves to ward off a Soviet attack. Bethell sees hoaxing as having much in common with street trading. Words are very important. Little phrases such as 'I'm not sure I can get you this' and 'May I say how much I agree with you on . . .' are part of wooing victims into a state of mind where they help bring about their own downfall. 'Always make the victim do the work . . . make an itch that they've got to scratch. They'll believe the most outlandish thing if they're led by the hand.'[14] The weapon that the hoaxer uses is logic. If the premise of a hoax is logical, the victim can't take the risk of challenging that logic, and thus enters into a conspiracy with the hoaxer. The invitation to join this conspiracy has to be made subtly, gently, and it has to contain a grain of truth. The hoaxer has to pretend to be naive, to seek advice, to let the victims feel that they are making the running.

Victor Lustig was a master of this method. He had his own Nine Commandments for a hoaxer, which he rigidly adhered to all his life:

1 Be a good listener.
2 Never give political opinions until the mark (the victim) has expressed his, and then agree.
3 Wait for the mark to reveal his religion, and then become a member of the same church.
4 Hint at sex, but don't pursue it unless the mark is eager to explore the subject.
5 Never discuss personal ailments unless the mark shows an interest in the subject.
6 Never be untidy or drunk, yet always be ready for a party.
7 Never appear bored.
8 Never pry; let the mark volunteer information.
9 Never brag; let the mark sense your success.

All these commandments have the same aim: to make the victim feel superior to the hoaxer. Once the victim feels in charge of the situation, he or she will do most of the hoaxer's work for him. One of the maxims of British Military Intelligence in the Second World War was that 'an item of misinformation that someone has worked out for himself is worth ten that he has been told'.[15] Victims become totally unaware of the hoaxer's role, and believe that what is happening is what they have willed. Thus the hoaxer makes them his principal allies, and staunch defenders of the deception. All the hoaxer has to do is plan a simple programme of induction whereby the victim is hooked. In the case of the Piltdown Hoax, all that was needed was to provide evidence of a man-ape in unknown gravel-pits at Barkham Manor, surrounded by appropriate fauna and man-ape tools. For van Meegeren, the ground had already been prepared by the theories of Dr Bredius that there was, somewhere, a major work by Vermeer on a biblical subject. London was already eager for Shakespeariana when William Ireland 'found' the Bard's letters and plays. Locke produced his series of articles about man-bats on the moon at a time when there was much conjecture about life on other planets. Lady Tichborne did far more than Arthur Orton to smooth the Claimant's path.

There is no easy or satisfactory way to try to get into the mind of a hoaxer. The best we can hope for is informed supposition. Bernard Wasserstein, in his brilliant biography of Trebitsch Lincoln, picks upon a time when Lincoln was twenty-five and living in Hampton-on-Thames to describe the state of the young *émigré*'s mind. 'Intimations of greatness, a desire to hobnob with the mighty, a taste for intrigue, a liking for public attention, a wish to boss other people around, fascination with the careers of Disraeli and Napoleon – all these ruminations appear to have swilled around inside the ex-curate's head as he gazed out of his study window at suburban Hampton.'[16] Well, probably, but there is no way we can be sure. Perhaps Wasserstein is on more solid ground with a general description of Lincoln's character: 'Trebitsch Lincoln possessed in overflowing measure the first requirement of the successful conman; an absolute belief in himself'.[17]

This is an attribute we can discern in almost all hoaxers. Cole, Abel, Bilbo, Lustig, Bottomley, Balfour, Troy, Weyman, Reichenbach, Irving, Maundy Gregory, and dozens of others, never doubted their ability to get their own way, to sell their product, to make people believe in the false world that they created. What drove them to do this, we don't know. In Adlerian terms they may have been striving for achievement, and their hoaxes may be seen as the struggles of a developing infant to assert his personality against the environment. In Jungian terms, most hoaxers are out-and-out extroverts. In Freudian terms they may have been exercising aggression, or, as was true in the case of van Meegeren, since many were the offspring of unimaginative, stern and strict fathers, they may have been seeking revenge for their unhappy early lives. Sometimes a hoaxer appears to have been stung into action by a cruel remark from a relative or colleague. Anthony Blunt, a friend of Eric Hebborn, once told him: 'The trouble with you, Eric, is that you can't draw.' One thousand drawings later, Hebborn has proved the stupidity of that remark.

What hoaxers certainly share is cunning. Dawson made sure that each of his finds at Piltdown was witnessed by men of unimpeachable character (assuming that they weren't party to the hoax). Irving turned disadvantage to advantage when he faced the daunting task of forging Hughes's handwriting for the first time. He had only a small sample to work from, with only five capital letters – A, I, M, H, and R. 'I mulled that for a few minutes and then hit on the simplest solution. Hughes would be the supereme egotist. He would begin every possible sentence in his letters with the pronouns *I* and *My*'.[18] Lustig demanded, and received, a bribe from his victim to clinch the sale of the Eiffel Tower. When Harry Reichenbach's call to the President of the Anti-Vice League was ignored, he bribed children to leer at the picture, *September Morn*, in the Brooklyn shop window. This was enough evidence to convince the President that something had to be done. We have to remember that Reichenbach was a hoaxer smart enough to have made money exhibiting 'The Only Living Brazilian Invisible Fish'.

If we have to classify hoaxers by what motivated them, there would seen to be four main headings: Fun, Fame, Money and Revenge.

First the pranksters, those out for fun: Ken Campbell, Birault, Hans Keller, Malskat and Fey (more on all these later), Abel, Brian Bethell, Bynner, Berkeley, Waugh, Cole, Graham Greene, Hook, Hughes, Jordan Smith, McGrady, Mencken, Newburger, Joe Orton, Paine, the Panorama Team, Sophie Lloyd and Jenny Winstanley (though they had a second and more serious side to their hoax), Henry Root, Shepherd, Stone, Victor Lewis-Smith, Stroller White, Traprock, and Troy. This list encompasses a wide range of hoaxes, from the simple fun of Hughes and the alley cat that won a prize at the New York Cat Show, to the cynical satire of Mike McGrady and *Naked Came the Stranger*.

Secondly, those who sought fame: Abrams, Bilbo, Casadesus (more on him later), Chatterton, Sir Cyril Burt, Locke, Hoskins,

Irving, Watters, Ireland, Kreisler (more on him later), Macpherson, Morganwg, Dawson and his accomplice, Otto, Psalmanazar, de Rougemont, Shearer, Stein, Tetro, (another art forger specializing in Chagalls), Mary Tofts (see page 177), Trebitsch Lincoln, van Meegeren, Vian, Voigt and Percy. Several of these hoaxers appear to have had mixed motives – money and fame are often twin aims.

Thirdly, the greedy, Balfour, Bottomley, Dossena (more on him later), Furguson/Fergusson, Maundy Gregory, Hartzell, Kujau (of Hitler Diaries fame), de Villegas (he who claimed he could dowse for oil), Vrain-Lucas (more on him later), Lustig, Reichenbach and Shapira (more on him later), Stein, and Arthur Orton.

The list of those seeking revenge is much sorter: Blondlot and Kammerer's lab assistants (though we shall never know why), Hebborn, van Meegeren, Keating, Roderick and Elkhart (though this is pure assumption on my part – I imagine poor Dr Johann Beringer must have done something to annoy them), and Jonathan Swift. Swift greatly disliked an early eighteenth-century work called *Partridge's Almanac*, which was used to make prophecies suitably helpful to the Whig cause. In 1708, Swift published an alternative Almanac, reputedly the work of Dr Isaac Bickerstaffe, and gained considerable publicity for the work by roundly condemning it. One of the prophecies in *Bickerstaffe's Almanac* was that Partridge would die at 11pm on the night of 29 March 1709. Swift then spread the word that Bickerstaffe had been right and that Partridge had died. It took Partridge six years to recover the lost sales that resulted from this rumour.

There are also those who have spent their lives donning false identities: Abnagale, Belaney, Mary Willcocks, Demara, Ellis, Hewitt, Toplis and Weyman. There is an element of fun in a lot of what they did – more mischief than fun in Toplis's case – but Abnagale, Demara, Hewitt and Weyman were also in it for the money. We do not know why Mary Willcocks pretended to be the Princess Caraboo, or why Archibald Belaney became Grey Owl, or why Wilfrid Ellis, the butcher, pretended to be a vicar for twenty-five years. It may be that he sought a position of greater power in his community, for all hoaxers want power* of one sort or another.

---

* Hoaxers frequently make references to Napoleon. *In Carrying a Gun for Al Capone*, Jack Bilbo described a totally fictitious scene in which Capone lectured his gang on Napoleon: 'We would have understood each other. He was an Italian like me.'

Perhaps both Ellis and Princess Caraboo started something on the spur of the moment and had to live with it until death or discovery.

Some of the differences in hoaxers' motivation can be seen by comparing three musical hoaxes. In 1961 Hans Keller and Susan Bradshaw, with the co-operation of the BBC, 'arranged' a programme of music by the contemporary composer Piotr Zak. The programme was broadcast on the Third Programme (now called Radio 3). Penderewski, an authentic contemporary composer, was told it was a hoax, but was invited to write a critique of Zak's work. The broadcast lasted roughly a quarter of an hour, and consisted of a wayward mixture of percussive and electronic sounds. Reaction to the hoax was mixed. Some saw it as proof that the musical establishment would fall for any rubbish that was presented as 'experimental music' – as Muriel Gray said, 'Why does Art labour under the delusion that to be great it has to be obscure?'[20] Others took the exact opposite view, pointing out that the music critics of *The Times*, the *Daily Telegraph*, and the *Listener* had all dismissed the music as worthless. Keller's reason for perpetrating the hoax was, however, genuine. He wanted to call attention to a situation where late-twentieth-century music was unlikely to be condemned for its inaccessibility.

Seventy years earlier, Fritz Kreisler used similar methods for a different reason. He was a brilliant violinist, too brilliant for the repertoire at his disposal. At that time Bach was not popular, and there were few occasions when a young performer had an orchestra at his disposal so that he could play one of the standard concertos. There was also the problem that the great violin sonatas of Beethoven and Schubert had such difficult parts for the accompanying pianist that it was extremely difficult to find competent players. Kreisler was a composer as well as a violinist, but he knew that the critics would not take kindly to a recital programme packed with his own music. 'I resolved to write a repertory of my own . . . to write music under other composers' names . . . like Pugnani and Louis Couperin, the

---

Clifford Irving, when faced with the possibility that there was a rival authorized biography of Howard Huges, said to his accomplice (Richard Suskind): '*De l'audace* – my right flank is crushed, my left flank is giving way, my centre is demolished. What do I do? I attack! *Chutzpah* – brass – balls – gall – audacity. *Toujours l'audace*. That was Napoleon's motto, and look how far it got him'.[19] Mary Willcocks rowed to St Helena to meet Napoleon.

grandfather of François Couperin'.[21] Kreisler took a risk, for he didn't consciously write in the style of the composers whose names he borrowed. 'A child could have seen Pugnani never wrote it. There was a semi cadenza in the middle of it completely out of style with Pugnani's period'.[22] Later, Kreisler branched out, and wrote 'Posthumous Waltzes' by 'Joseph Lanner'. These he claimed to have discovered, and gave their début performance at a recital in Berlin. 'The following day Leopold Schmidt, the critic of the *Berliner Tageblatt*, accused me of tactlessness. He raved about the Lanner waltzes. They were worthy of Schubert, he said. How dared I bracket my own little salon piece, *Caprice Viennois* with such gems?'[23] Kreisler finally confessed in 1935, forty-two years after he had started his fake compositions. His is a unique reason for hoaxing – professional need.

Until the late 1970s, catalogues of recordings of classical music included a Violin Concerto in D by Mozart, *The Adelaide*, K Anh 294a. There were several recorded versions, including two by Yehudi Menuhin. In 1977 Marius Casadesus claimed that he had composed the work and that it had nothing to do with Mozart. His claim was taken before the Court de Justice in Paris, who accepted Marius's claim after hearing performances of two viola concertos by his brother, Henri Casadesus, works previously attributed to J C Bach and Handel. Marius Casadesus's motives were very similar to those of van Meegeren when he began painting his first Vermeer – to deceive the experts and to prove to himself that he was as good as a recognized genius.

That still leaves a handful of hoaxers whose motives are unaccounted for. Pierre Dupont, who wrote *The Man Who Wouldn't Talk*, was simply a daydreamer whose fantasies got out of hand. Frances Wright and Elsie Griffiths may have created the Cottingley Fairies out of boredom, or for fun, or to make mischief. What makes analysis of their motivation extremely complicated is a remark made by Frances on her last television apperance. 'But,' she said, 'there *were* fairies at Cottingley.' Sixty years later we are back at square one. And what are we to make of Arnaud de Tilh? Outside Hollywood, few of us, if mistaken for another person, immediately assume that other person's identity. Life may well have been more of a hit-and-miss affair in sixteenth-century France, but basic instincts don't change in four hundred years. Unless we have planned to take up another identity, we wouldn't adopt one on the spur of the moment.

There is always the possibility that a hoaxer is simple-minded, not really hoaxing at all, but sadly believing in their own fantasy. That may well have been the case with Mary Tofts, the wife of a poor journeyman cloth-maker at Godalming in 1726. She was described as being of 'a healthy strong constitution, small size, fair complexion, a very stupid and sullen temper, and unable to read or write'.[24] Her hoax – fraud, trick, fantasy, whatever we should call it – was simple. She gave birth to rabbits. Her explanation for this 'monstrous deviation from the laws of nature' was that . . .

> as she was weeding in a field, she saw a rabbit spring up near her, after which she ran . . . this set her longing for rabbits, being then, as she thought, five weeks gone with child. . . . Soon after, another rabbit sprang up near the same place, which she endeavoured likewise to catch. The same night she dreamt that she was a in a field with those two rabbits in her lap, and awaked with a sick fit, which lasted till morning; from that time, for above three months, she had a constant and strong desire to eat rabbits, but being very poor and indigent could not procure any.[25]

The first to be persuaded that Mary Tofts was bearing rabbits was a Mr Howard, a medical attendant of thirty years' experience and 'man of probity', who helped her deliver nearly twenty rabbits. News of this wonder spread rapidly. George I sent his house surgeon, Mr Ahlers, down to Godalming. The surgeon returned to London convinced of the truth of Mary Tofts's story, having received 'ocular and tangible proof', and having promised to procure a pension for her. The King then sent Mr St André, his anatomist, to Godalming. He too believed Mary. Both Ahlers and St André brought back some of Mary Tofts's progeny with them. The rabbits were dissected in the presence of the King. Whether or not there was something strange about Mary Tofts, there was certainly nothing wrong with the rabbits.

Matters began to get out of hand. People came to believe it was wrong to eat rabbits, and the rent of rabbit warrens sank to nothing. A public row developed between those who believed Mary and those who thought the whole thing was a fraud. Something had to be done. Mary Tofts was brought to town. Sir Richard Manningham, an eminent physician and Fellow of the Royal Society kept her under close watch. Threatened with dangerous operations to discover the truth of her condition, Mary confessed. The idea for the hoax had come from a woman friend, who had said it would be a way of obtaining a livelihood without having to work, and who had supplied her with the rabbits. Mary was sent to Tothill Fields' Bridewell.

We may never know *why* any hoaxer does what he does, but we can at least work out *how*. The secret of success lies in Lustig's Nine Commandments and Brian Bethell's insistence that a good hoaxer never tells a lie, he simply gives his victims all the component parts of the lie and lets them put the pieces together. Added to this are the techniques of hoaxing: keep your victim waiting; when in doubt increase the stakes; be bold – the more outrageous a hoaxer's behaviour, the more easily he is believed; let the victim do the work. Irving saw the hoaxer as a ventriloquist, and the victim as his doll or puppet. 'One day the puppet starts to sing by himself and the ventriloquist merely listens and marvels'.[26] He also realized that it was the conspiratorial element in any hoax that appealed to the victims:

> The secrecy part – the thing that protects you and me – is what they love the most. That takes them out of the humdrum into another world, the world we all dream of living in . . . the greatest thing for them is that this way they can live in it part time. They're participating but they're protected by an intermediary. I'm their buffer between reality and fantasy.[27]

Irving describes the hoaxer as almost a therapist. To others, he is patient rather than physician. Sadly, there is only one recorded case of a psychologist's report on a hoaxer. Dr L van der Horst was called by the defence at van Meegeren's trial. The doctor's opinion was that 'the defendant's character leads to sensitiveness to criticism, fed by a revenge complex which explains his anti-social attitudes'.[28] As van Meegeren's career proceeded, this paranoia became worse. He believed that he was the victim of a sinister conspiracy. The forgeries were his attempt at revenge, not just on the art world, but on the entire world. 'I would describe him,' said van der Horst, 'as disequilibrated but fully responsible for his actions. A man of his personality would be greatly hurt by isolation; I would not advise imprisonment.'[29]

We could subject every hoaxer to a lie detection test, and then ask why he'd acted the way he did, but lie detectors were tried with Irving and yielded unsatisfactory results. The hoaxer is often in a highly charged state, which tends to interfere with the efficiency of such machines. For the moment, we have to take what the hoaxer does and what he says, and see what conclusions we can draw. Alan Abel seems to be out for fun, but even he has a more serious side. 'My aim, I guess, is just to shake people up – give them a verbal or visual kick in the intellect, so they are able to suddenly stop and look at themselves and laugh more, and to participate in life rather than just be passive bystanders – to get involved, to picket, to write letters of protest, to say "No, I won't go!" Or "I won't stand in line! I won't just be a drone any longer; I'm sick and tired of being sick and tired".'[30]

11

Victims

'The broad mass of a nation . . . will more easily fall victim to a big lie than to a small one.'

Adolf Hitler, *Mein Kampf*, 1925

As with hoaxers, so with victims – there's no one type. We are all potential victims, it is simply a matter of fitting the hoax to the victim. For we all have a weakness; a secret, a fantasy, an obsession, an ambition, a blind spot or a prejudice. And most of us approach life in a trusting and innocent way. If we order soup in a restaurant, we do not expect to be served a bowl of washing-up water. If we buy tickets for seats at a concert, we expect there to be an auditorium, and music, and something to sit on. If someone dressed as a ticket collector approaches us on a train, we give him our tickets because we do not expect him to be a lunatic or a practical joker. We make assumptions about people and situations. Usually we are right, but not always.

And it is this 'usually' that the hoaxer exploits. Our familiarity with situations breeds not contempt, but over-confidence. I recently saw a young man perform a highly successful and very simple hoax. He stood at an unmanned ticket barrier on Catford Bridge station, smiling, and with one hand cupped in front of him. A train pulled in. The first passenger through the barrier assumed he was a ticket collector, although there was nothing in the young man's appearance to suggest that he was, and handed over his ticket. Once the first passenger had done this, all the other passengers followed suit. The young man found it almost impossible to keep a straight face. He had said nothing, done nothing, but had collected thirty or forty tickets. Had there been fare dodgers on the train, he could presumably have collected money, simply by standing on a railway station and smiling at passengers. It beats begging, and doesn't seem to break the law.

Most victims of hoaxes are middle- or upper-class, for the simple reason that they have money, and a hoaxer is usually after money. Jeremy Beadle may shock and terrify the poor, but he is an exception. A random list of victims of some of the hoaxes covered in this book includes headmasters, scientists, artistic directors, admirals, mayors, writers, publishers, tourists, newspapermen, art gallery owners, museum curators, historians, music critics, business executives, public relations officers, and magicians. It isn't easy to see what all these people have in common, beyond a trained tendency to respond to certain stimuli, in the manner of Pavlov's dogs – which is what the hoaxer exploits.

With knowledge that the H Rochester Sneath letters were all a hoax, we can look at the contents of the letters (see page 69) and marvel at the naivety of the august academics he took in. Of the Heads he wrote to only those of Winchester and Wimbledon College saw through the hoax.

The majority tried to make sense of what they had received. The poor Head of Tonbridge who received this scurrilous letter –

Dear Rootie,
Imagine my surprise when I returned from India to be told that the man I had carried home, drunk as a coot, seven times a week, should have got a job . . .[1]

– assumed that Sneath himself had been the victim of some prank, having been hoaxed into believing that this miscreant 'Rootie' had been appointed to his own lofty position. He wrote back to Sneath asking him to divulge whence he had obtained this false information.

But before we sneer too contemptuously at the poor Heads, we should try to imagine why they were so taken in. Such people may well receive a great many letters, on a scale of eccentricity from the almost normal to the totally irrational. Each has to be answered. Invitations *are* issued to preach in school chapels, so it is not beyond the bounds of possibility that someone should genuinely seek such an invitation. Ivy-covered buildings may well have rat problems. The Head of Eton may well get letters from teachers asking how they may be considered his successor as he nears retirement. The world of the public school is shot through with ambition. The Heads to whom Berkeley wrote had long ago set their sights on the lofty positions that they subsequently held. They would assuredly take as authentic correspondence from those still struggling up the slopes – Berkeley often gave the impression that Sneath was trying to raise the status of Selhurst School. In a headmaster's office, any letter on headed notepaper, already opened by a secretary, may well seem as valid as the very principles on which the school is founded. And so, Sneath's letters had to be answered, as professionally as possible.

The victims of Ken Campbell's Royal Dickens Company hoax were similarly taken in by letter. In 1980, Campbell went to the Royal Shakespeare Company's production of *Nicholas Nickleby*. A friend in the cast told him that Trevor Nunn, the producer of *Nicholas Nickleby*, had encouraged the cast at rehearsals to adopt the style of *The Ken Campbell Road Show* in their approach to parts of the play. Although Campbell sat in the front row, and enjoyed what he saw, the link with his own *Road Show* escaped him. After the performance, he went backstage where one of the cast had a bowl of fruit in his dressing room. Friends were invited to help themselves from this bowl, but there was a catch in the banana. If anyone touched it, it turned into a penis. Campbell says that it was this that in some way inspired him to create his hoax.[21]

With the help of a couple of friends, Campbell had some headed writing paper printed, a perfect replica of the Royal Shakespeare Company notepaper, save for the replacement of 'Dickens' for 'Shakespeare', and 'RDC' for 'RSC'. He also discovered that Trevor Nunn signed his letters 'Love, Trev'. Campbell wrote dozens of individual letters to actors, writers, directors, producers, deisgners and composers, as well as Sir Roy Shaw of the Arts Council. A typical letter read:

Dear X,

As you probably heard there has been a major policy change in our organization.

Nicholas Nickleby has been such a source of real joy to cast, staff and audience that we have decided to turn to Dickens as our main source of inspiration.

So that'll be it for the bard as soon as our present commitments decently permit.

There followed a suggestion for the next production: *Sketches by Boz*, *Bleak House*, or *The Pickwick Papers*. Each letter ended with an individually tailored invitation. For Lindsay Anderson, Campbell signed off with: 'Thinking of you brings *The Old Curiosity Shop* to mind. What a coup if you could bring Sir Ralph and Sir John together again in a script by David Storey. I feel your cool, intelligent approach is going to be badly needed in these new times.' Max Stafford Clark was offered *Barnaby Rudge* as a production: 'I find this a compelling piece which could be admirably served by your sparse, clear directorial style – especially if the whole sweep of the book could be captured with the aid of no more than six chairs.' Norman St John Stevas, the Arts Minister, was told: 'The first production of the RDC is hoped to be *Little Dorrit*. Any thoughts you have on this will, as always, be treasured.' To accompany the letters and add punch to the campaign, the Aldwych Theatre was covered in RDC posters, in the style of the RSC, giving advance notice of the production of *Little Dorrit*.

The RSC production of *Nicholas Nickleby* was spread over two nights, and it was a few nights later that Campbell went to see the second half. He was told that the letter had not gone down well, and that Trevor Nunn had called in the Special Branch. There was no suspicion on Campbell, as Nunn believed it was an inside job. Newspaper reports of the hoax grandly exaggerated the affair, saying that 'thousands of sheets' of RDC notepaper had been printed, and that 'hundreds of letters' had been sent. Trevor Nunn was reported as saying: 'It is deeply embarrassing; a lot of people have written to me refusing, or, even more embarrassing, accepting the offers'.[3]

Some months later, while Campbell was working at the Everyman Theatre, Liverpool, he was phoned by a researcher from the BBC TV programme *Newsnight*, who accused him of being the RDC hoaxer. Campbell denied it at first, and consulted with his accomplices, who offered him mixed advice. He decided to come clean, and was asked to appear on *Newsnight*. In the television studio, where he made his confession, he was horrified to see himself, on a monitor, lit like a terrorist, a sinister, dark figure in silhouette. But the affair blew over with no harm done and no recriminations.

It was a brilliant, speedily executed hoax, that trapped its victims because it was so near the highly probable, and because it took people when their guards were down. For Campbell and Berkeley, like almost all hoaxers, bearded the victims in their own dens. Home, or our place of work if we enjoy what we are doing, is where we feel most safe, and therefore are at our most vulnerable. Balfour visited those he conned in their own houses. Cole's *Dreadnought* hoax took place on the flagship of the Commander-in-Chief Home Fleet. Oscar Hartzell's Drake legacy victims never left their homes, never once saw Hartzell. They were sworn to 'silence, secrecy and non-disturbance'. Irving went to the offices of McGraw-Hill time and time again, convinced that he would be welcome there. 'They're straight. They're the establishment,' he told his accomplice Suskind. 'They believe. They've got to believe or they'd never get a night's sleep'.[4] Reichenbach went to the Anti-Vice Squad offices. Orton faced Lady Tichborne in the Paris hotel room. Voigt marched his soldiers to the Kopenick Town Hall. Victor Lewis-Smith phoned the *That's Life* office, a home from home if ever there was one. Sophie Lloyd auditioned in front of members of the Magic Circle. Buck Henry, as J Clifford Prout, stalked into the television studios.

That there is a link between the success of the hoaxer and the gullibility of the victim is obvious. It seems amazing that it took so long to open one of Dr Abrams's occilloclasts and expose the fraud, and even more amazing that no one in Army medical circles ever bothered to open Sergeant James Shearer's box. Most amazing of all is that Professor Blondlot never suspected that his own box was a fake. Was the lab assistant always there? Did Blondlot never operate the box without him? The whole thing smacks of a very unscientific approach on the Professor's part. Kammerer, Smith Woodward and Beringer, the other scientists hoaxed by colleagues, show similar credulity. Granted that, once a scientist is in pursuit of evidence to support a theory, he or she may not always be on guard, all three fell for suspiciously easy pickings. Kammerer was so obsessional in his support for Lamarckian theories that Indian ink was enough to make him believe that the amphibians had responded as he hoped they would. He was also a very highly strung man, described by Arthur Koestler as 'brilliant but decadent', a man who spent his nights, after a long day in the laboratory, composing symphonies – while his assistant painted out the salamander's golden spots. Beringer's theory – that some stones were mysteriously able to imitate the forms of other bodies – was so outlandish that it is less wonder that he was duped so simply and for such a long time. Smith Woodward's is a different case, in that Dawson and Keith (or whoever) were themselves experts who planted the false evidence with care and precision. There was enough for Smith Woodward, and many other scientists, to draw their wonderful but wrong conclusions, not so much that it took on the quality of a fairy tale.

In all these cases we have to try to imagine how the hoax must have appeared to the victim at the time that it took place. The discovery of the Piltdown skull, by a labourer named Venus Hargreaves, fulfilled earlier evolutionary predictions. Some eighty years later, we can see how this served to set up the hoax, but at the time, to Smith Woodward, it must have seemed all the more likely that the skull was pukka. Piltdown Man was a piece in a jigsaw puzzle. It took nearly forty years to work out that he was, in Ronald Millar's words, 'the right colour but the wrong shape'.[5] The more unstable or preoccupied a victim's mind, the more tractable the victim. Many hoaxers found their prey in the shattered and unstable Europe that existed during and after the First World War. The inference is that Lincoln, Toplis, Stephane Otto, Bottomley, Lustig, Maundy Gregory and company would have had to tread more warily in other times and other places. The Hartzell Drake hoax, however, runs counter to this theory. Hartzell's victims were all American, living in peace and comparative security. Their society had not been shaken by the war, their homes had not been threatened, their land had not been fought over. Yet the number of Hartzell's victims ran to thousands, of whom no one appears to have asked the obvious question – if Francis Drake had an illegitimate child by Queen Elizabeth (or anyone else, for that matter), just how many potential heirs are we talking about? No wonder Hartzell kept raising the stakes.

Victims of art hoaxes have two ways of explaining how they were tricked. They can say that the hoaxer was brilliantly clever, or that they themselves were extremely foolish. They don't like to do either. If a hoaxer is clever enough to fool all the experts, then this must cast doubt on the authenticity of many more existing works of art. What contemporary hoaxers can do in the name of Chagall, older hoaxers may have done in the names of the Old Masters. Since Keating, van

Meegeren, Stein and company came along, the number of paintings unquestioningly attributed to Rembrandt, for example, has fallen dramatically. Where all was, if not black and white, at least a limited palette before, now all is doubt and half certainties. On the other hand, the experts are hardly likely to want to spread about the news that they are idiots who couldn't recognize a fake if and when it was held under their noses. (There is, of course, a third possibility – that the experts know the fakes are fakes, but choose not to say so and to take the money instead. This is a harsh accusation, and seriously complicates matters, because it would mean that the experts were not then the victims.)

To discover how to avoid being the victim of an art fraud, we have to examine a hoax of the late nineteenth century. In 1896 Shapschelle Hochman tried to sell a solid gold tiara (one pound in weight) to the Imperial Museum in Vienna. The tiara was said to have been found on an ancient site on the coast of the Black Sea. The story attached to the tiara was that it had been offered to King Saitaphernes of Scythia in 200 BC. The Viennese were not interested, so Hochman took the tiara to Paris, where he sold it to the Louvre for 200,000 francs. After two months on exhibition, it was claimed by a Russian to be a fake: the gold was real, the workmanship exquisite, but all the decorative scenes on the tiara had been copied from other pieces of jewellery. Seven years later, Israel Rouchomowski, from Odessa in Russia, admitted that he had made the tiara for 2,000 roubles in 1895 – nobody knows at whose request. At first few believed him, then an American entrepreneur offered to pay the Louvre exactly what they had paid Hochman if Rouchomowski could prove that the tiara was a fake. Rouchomowski produced some convincing work, but the directors of the Louvre wanted to hedge their bets. The Saitaphernes Tiara was removed to the Musée des Arts Décoratifs.

The whole episode provoked a long letter to *The Times* from Bernhard Berenson, who aimed his opening shot at the Louvre:

Sir,

Whether the famous Tiara of Saitaphernes turns out to be a forgery or not, the discussion will have done good in bringing before the public the general question of forgeries. That there is nothing impossible in the Louvre authorities falling victims to fraud is proved by at least one of their recent purchases. The body that could buy the obviously cinquecent copy of Desiderio's famous *Putto of San Lorenzo*, believing this statue of forms at once mincing and puffy to be Desiderio's own handiwork, would seem to be the natural prey of the clever forger . . .

Berenson went on to explain how the forgery business operated:

I feel that the public should be especially warned against some of the cleverest dealer-forgers whose centre of operations is in Florence. These 'artists' get hold of old ruined panels with just enough patches of original paint left on them to enable them, if suspicion is aroused, to experiment on these carefully chosen parts with solvents that would destroy modern work, and to point triumphantly to their resistance as 'scientific proof' of the picture's genuineness. The rest of the panel they fill in, with undeniable skill, in the style of Filippino Lippi, Ghirlandaio, Raphael – whom you will – according as they think they can spare their purchaser. The productions are rarely to be found in such a vulgar place as a shop; they are 'discovered' in old palaces and castles, sometimes in the most out-of-the-way villages in Tuscany, and they boast an undisputed pedigree, sworn to by some spendthrift scamp bearing an historic name. What wonder if the unsuspecting American or British buyer is taken in, especially if the dealer has the cleverness to hypnotize them by dangling the picture before their eyes as an un-heard-of bargain!

Given such villainous improbity, Berenson felt there was only one thing the well-meaning collector could do to escape falling victim: he or she had to develop a definite passion as well as talent for the subject, and devote as much time as possible to training his eye to distinguish quality. If we don't wish to become a victim, we must become an expert.

Nothing but a fine sense of quality and a practised judgement can avail against the forger's skill. Technical, documentary, stylistic standards may all be satisfied, but the one thing the forger cannot do is to satisfy the standard of a specially trained taste, and to avoid betraying himself by some mannerism of his own which the experienced eye can learn to detect.[6]

It is all very well for Berenson to advocate that collectors should develop a 'definite passion' and a 'talent' for whatever they are collecting, as a safeguard against being sold a forgery. If museum staff aren't passionate or talented enough, what chance has the layperson? The Saitaphernes Tiara is not unique as an example of a world-famous museum being fooled by fake craftsmanship. The Rospigliosi Cup was long held to be the work of Benvenuto Cellini, and a masterpiece of the Renaissance. In 1929, Charles Truman, curator of the Victoria and Albert Museum, discovered drawings by Reinhold Vasters, a German student from Aachen, which suggested that the Rospigliosi Cup was not what it seemed. Vasters had worked as a goldsmith in the treasury of Aachen Cathedral, maintaining and restoring gold and silver work collected there over centuries. Truman's investigations led to an article in *Connoisseur* magazine implicating Vasters in a series of Cellini forgeries. Alarm bells rang in many museums, particularly the Metropolitan Museum of Art in New York, where at least thirty 'Renaissance' fakes of Vasters were discovered. The Vasters hoax might never have come to light if Truman had not found the drawings, for gold, the medium in which Vasters worked, is impervious to carbon-dating and carries no watermark or tell-tale archaic pigments.

At about the same time, a Roman mason named Alceo Dossena was producing 'Ancient Greek' statues, 'Gothic' carvings and 'Renaissance' terra-cottas. One of his most successful fakes was a statue of the Pallas Athene. Having completed the work, Dossena knocked a few fingers off it, to give the impression of age, and presented it to Jacob Hirsch, an expert on Greek statues. Hirsch was convinced the statue was authentic. Dossena produced more forgeries. *The Tomb of the Savelli*, a High Gothic work, was planted in the ground near an old church. Dossena claimed to have found it, and sold it for 25,000 lire – it subsequently changed hands for 6 million lire. When news of Dossena's fakes came to light, several museums were troubled. The Cleveland Museum of Art had to accept that what they believed was a thirteenth-century carved wood *Madonna and Child*, was one of his works – an X-ray examination showed that the piece contained modern nails. It is said that the Museum replaced the fake with a marble statue of Pallas Athene, at a cost of $120,000, and that this, too, turned out to be a Dossena forgery. Just how talented and passionate does a museum have to be?

The situation is further complicated if we consider that it might be possible for an expert to be too vigilant, too suspicious, too critical, and dismiss a genuine work of historic and artistic importance. We still do not know for certain whether or not this is what happened in the case of Moses Shapira and the Dead Sea Scrolls.

Moses Wilhelm (formerly Benedict) Shapira was born in Kiev in 1830, but lived in Jerusalem for much of his life. He was small, vain, ostentatious, romantic and gullible; a man of vision, with enough furious passions for a dozen or more hoaxers, and enough weaknesses for a dozen or more victims. While in Jerusalem, he became a Christian and was received into the Anglican Church. He earned his living selling baubles to tourists: mother-of-pearl necklaces, camels and crucifixes carved from olivewood, flowers from the Holy Land, and pieces of parchment scroll that he bought from the poor Jewish community nearby. Shapira claimed that he was a 'Correspondent to the British Museum', and appeared in many ways more English than the English. He dressed in a dark frock-coat, a soft wide-brimmed hat, grey gloves and tight trousers, outdoing all his friends in his conformity to what he regarded as the respectable. This was one side of Shapira. The other was straight out of a romantic novel. Off with the frock-coat and tight trousers, and on with billowing robes and a silken headdress bound with golden cords – Shapira leapt on to his white Arab mare and galloped into the desert. Days later he would return to Jerusalem, in the company of a caravan of pack camels. He used this method to smuggle pagan statuettes and other *objets* into Jerusalem, hidden in sacks of wheat.

In 1868 Shapira's imagination was further stirred by the discovery of a black basalt stele inscribed with rows of ancient writing. The finder was a French diplomat and archaeologist named Charles Clermont-Ganneau. The writing was said to be a ninth-century BC account of Moab's revolt against the Israelites. Shapira was impressed. He began to look for similar finds of his own, and soon produced some fragments of ancient pottery. Clermont-Ganneau denounced these as forgeries and spoke scathingly of the 'poor bookseller of Bathsehba's pool who believes himself an industrious scholar'. Shapira was undaunted. He continued to trade with the bedouins in the desert, and in 1882 bought a bundle of parchment scrolls. To Shapira's delight, the scrolls appeared to be a hitherto unknown section of the Book of Deuteronomy, proably two thousand years older than any such documents ever seen before.

He sent the scrolls to Dr Konstantine Schlottmann, Professor of Old Testament Studies at the University of Halle. Schlottmann dismissed the scrolls as rubbish. Shapira humbly accepted this decision, but placed the scrolls in the vault of a Jerusalem bank. A few weeks later, Shapira learnt of the discovery of other parts of the text of the Pentateuch, and of their acceptance as genuine. His hopes rose, and by May 1883 he was convinced that Schlottmann had made a mistake. He gathered his scrolls and went to Berlin. Here a team of experts examined them for a considerable time, before deciding that they were a 'clever and impudent forgery'. Shapira was not told of this decision.

Meanwhile, he took the scrolls to London where he met Walter Besant, Secretary of the Palestine Exploration Fund. Besant was interested in the scrolls and introduced Shapira to Dr Christian Ginsburg, a converted Jew and an acknowledged expert on Old Testament texts. Ginsburg was impressed and his translations of the texts were published in *The Times* on 10 August 1883. Shapira's scrolls went on exhibition at the British Museum and he became hopeful that the Museum would purchase them. The price he asked was £1 million. Meanwhile, back in Jerusalem, Shapira's family was piling up credit both socially and financially.

At the same time, Clermont-Ganneau arrived in London. He may have wanted to outbid the Museum for the scrolls; he certainly wanted another and closer examination of them. This was denied him, and Clermont-Ganneau angrily announced that Shapira's manuscripts were fake, simply two- to three-hundred-year-old pieces of synagogue scrolls. Many other academics and the press joined voice with Clermont-Ganneau, but the public on the whole were on Shapira's side. Ginsburg, who had previously supported Shapira, then pronounced the scrolls to be forgeries. 'The compiler of the Hebrew Text was a Polish, Russian or German Jew.... There were no less than four or five persons engaged in the production of the forgery'.[7] On 23 August Shapira wrote to Ginsburg:

Dear Dr Ginsburg!

You have made a fool of me by publishing and exhibiting things which you believe to be false. I do not think that I shall be able to survive this shame, although I am not yet convinced that the manuscript is a forgery. . . . I will leave London in a day or two for Berlin.

Yours truly
M W Shapira.

The press were unpleasantly smug. *Punch* published a cartoon and a nasty little poem:

MR SHARP-EYE-RA
SHOWING IN VERY FANCIFUL PORTRAITURE, HOW
DETECTIVE GINSBURG ACTUALLY DID MR SHARP-EYE-RA
OUT OF HIS SKIN

Says Aaron to Moses, 'That GINSBURG is a bore,
And Clermont-Ganneau's far too fast with his linguistic lore
    That million will not come *his* way
    Learning our dodge discloses
    Archaic forgeries don't pay.'
    'No; hang it all!' says Moses.[8]

The Times reported that Shapira 'is so disappointed with the results of his bargain that he threatens to commit suicide. This, we venture to think, he will not do'.[9]

The Times was wrong. For a few months Shapira wandered around Europe, a broken man. In March 1884, in a room in a small hotel in Rotterdam, he shot himself. There is now some evidence that the scrolls may have been genuine. Undoubtedly, some of the shoddy treatment Shapira received had at its root anti-Semitism or racism. The higher echelons of society in late-nineteenth-century Berlin and London were no places for a Russian Jew, even if he had become a convert to Christianity. Shapira's story is a personal tragedy, but it also shows that there is no simple way to ensure that we can protect ourselves against art hoaxes without the risk that we throw away some genuine treasures. And it is one of those strange hoaxes where we cannot be sure who was hoaxer and who was victim. Shapira was a victim, to be sure, but not of a hoax – unless we believe that Ginsburg and Clermont-Ganneau reckoned all the time that the scrolls were genuine. On the other hand, if Shapira knew that the scrolls were fakes, then he became the victim of his own hoax. Either way, the case is unique.

12

The Psychology of Victims

'Do you think that the things people make fools of themselves about are any less real and true than the things they behave sensibly about? They are more true: They are the only things that are true.'

George Bernard Shaw, *Candida*

Nobody likes to be hoaxed. No matter how clever the trick, how polished the performance, there is the egg-on-the-face feeling that we should have seen through the hoaxer's ploy. Indeed, we often try to persuade ourselves that we *did* see through it – we thought there was something wrong – in fact, we weren't really hoaxed at all. This was certainly the attitude of most of the members of Cheam Cricket Club when the Brigadier fell from glory. We may seethe with rage that we have had money taken from us under false pretences, but what strikes just as deep and often lasts longer is the feeling that somehow a superior intelligence has got the better of us. Of course, it wasn't really a superior intelligence, but it will think it is, and that's almost as bad. We try to banish the whole episode from our minds.

It's also important to note that nobody *wants* to be hoaxed. Tourists do not set out for Trafalgar Square hoping that someone will sell them Nelson's Column. Curators of prestigious museums do not fall upon Pleistocene skulls and jawbones hoping that they are really bits of modern ape. Publishers do not accept biographies and memoirs hoping that they are complete and worthless fiction. Although there may be many weaknesses conspiring within us to make us easy prey, we do not consciously seek victimization. The initiative lies entirely with the hoaxer. He creates the fantasy world.

He invites us in. Our role as victims is, initially at least, a passive one.

What is surprising is how quickly this role changes. There is something of A A Milne's Tigger in many of us, and we race from 'What-Have-We-Here? to 'Being-Hoaxed-Is-What-Tiggers-Like-Best' in a few swift moves. When Conan Doyle first heard of the photographs of the Cottingley Fairies, he was sceptical. The pictures looked fake. He took them to Sir Oliver Lodge, who suggested that pictures had been taken of the fairies and superimposed upon a rural English background. Conan Doyle would not accept this, however, 'I argued that we had certainly traced the pictures to two children of the artisan class, and that such photographic tricks would be entirely beyond them'.[1] He had then reached the point of wondering if they were genuine, rather than assuming they were fake. His spiritualist friends were more suspicious, one calling the fairies 'Parisian-coiffed', and pointing out that the lens needed on a camera to take pictures of persons 'in rapid motion with clarity' would be f4.5 and would cost 'fifty guineas if a penny' - not the sort of camera one would imagine being available to children in an artisan's household. The more Conan Doyle investigated the matter, however, the more convinced he was that the children could not have faked the photos. He was given known fake photos to compare with those of Elsie and Frances, but 'clever as they were, there was nothing of the natural grace and freedom of movement which characterized the wonderful Cottingley fairy group'.[2]

By then, he was no longer wondering *if* the pictures were genuine, but how it could be proved that they *were* genuine. He displayed none of Holmes's intellectually suspicious nature. Far from it: Conan Doyle had an answer for every criticism. When someone remarked that the fairies were too conventional to be real, he explained that this was because the fairies were manifestations of 'thought-form', which would naturally be conventional. Thus he was unintentionally collaborating with the hoaxers, as is common among victims. He was seeing far more than was there:

> The elves are a compound of the human and the butterfly, while the gnome has more of the moth . . . the wings are more moth-like than the fairies and of a soft, downy, neutral tint. The music of the pipes held in the left hand can just be heard as a tiny tinkle sometimes if all is still. No weight is perceptible, though when

on the bare hand a fairy feels like a 'little breath'.[3]

Major Hall-Edwards of the *Birmingham Weekly Post* took a more jaundiced, military and realistic view. 'The picture in question could be "faked" . . . the little fairies were stuck upon cardboard, cut out and placed close to the sitter. . . .'[4] This is, of course, exactly what Frances and Elsie had done. There were those who thought it only too likely that the children were up to mischief, but Conan Doyle swept himself along in a surfeit of self-deception. To anyone who suggested the children were making the whole thing up, he replied: 'Children claim to see these creatures [fairies] far more frequently than adults. This may possibly come from far greater sensitiveness of apprehension, or it may depend on these little entities having less fear of molestation from children'.[5] It may also, of course, come from children being economical with the truth.

The executives of McGraw-Hill went through a similar process of unwitting collusion with Clifford Irving and the Howard Hughes autobiography. Early in the proceedings, when the Hughes Tool Company flatly denied that Hughes had entered into negotiations for such a book, this was seen by McGraw-Hill and *Time-Life* not as an indication that Irving was conning them, but as proof that Irving's claim was genuine. Much later in the sorry affair, when enormous doubt was being cast on the authenticity of the manuscript, Irving went to a meeting at McGraw-Hill and suggested to them that one theoretical explanation for what was happening was that he, Irving, was a fraud. 'This possibility I intend to discard,' he said, 'and I hope you do too.' They did, with great relief. At the sales luncheon for the book, Al Levanthal, general books vice-president, made a speech. 'We who have had the privilege of reading the book know that it would take a Shakespeare to invent such a work. And much as I admire our author, Clifford Irving, he is no Shakespeare'.[6] (Just as there were those who were convinced Chatterton was not Thomas Rowley back in the 1770s.) Everyone at McGraw-Hill laughed politely. Irving felt flattered and mildly annoyed. Later still, when it was clear that the Swiss bank account, into which the money for the book had been paid, was not in Howard Hughes's name, Irving expected trouble. It didn't come. 'Where I had expected unsmiling nervousness, I was greeted with warm handshakes and cordiality'.[7] The victims had become full-blown partners in the hoax, as Irving had anticipated: 'They've got to believe, or they'd never get a night's sleep.'[8]

Better than most hoaxers, Irving understood this lemming-like drive to complicity among victims. Suskind had reservations about some of the fictitious incidents that Irving was putting into the book, including the supposed meeting between Hughes and Spiro Agnew in a car park in Florida at five o'clock in the morning. Irving knew that the more it stretched the imagination, the happier McGraw-Hill would be with what he brought them. He knew that a hoaxer must approach his prey with confidence. Truth, reality, fact, solid evidence become irrelevant once the victims are drawn into the hoaxer's web of conviction. When Irving presented his first (appallingly bad) forgery of a Hughes letter, Ralph Graves, editor of *Life* Magazine, was at pains to prove the letter was genuine. He drew attention to a scratched and inked-in 'I': 'The way he writes the letter "I". You see here? How he's gone over it twice, scratched it with his fountain pen where he didn't get it right the first time? . . . That's a habit of his. I've seen it before in his other letters, the ones in our file. Very characteristic'.[9]

The same eagerness was displayed by victims during the Hitler Diaries hoax in the early 1980s. David Irving, a right-wing historian, believed the diaries were genuine at first because the handwriting deteriorated in them as the years went by. This would be compatible with the writing of a sufferer from Parkinson's Disease. Irving doubted that any forger would know that Hitler had Parkinson's Disease. What didn't occur to the Hitler Diaries Irving, was that the handwriting might have deteriorated for a quite different reason – that the forger was getting tired, bored or careless as he worked his way through twenty-six volumes. Another clear parallel between the Howard Hughes victims and the Hitler Diaries victims is that, just as the Hughes Tool Company's repudiation of the book increased the confidence of the McGraw-Hill executives, so, when Hugh Trevor-Roper eventually dismissed the Hitler Diaries as false, this caused not a tremor among the senior executives of *Die Stern*. They took Trevor-Roper's change of mind as proof that historians could not be trusted with the Diaries. 'They would either leak what they had seen or change their minds in public'.[10]

The problem is that once we are drawn into a hoax, we do not necessarily seek to discover the real truth, but look for support for what we *hope* is the truth. 'We perceive a situation, locate it within our experience and (perhaps unconsciously) look for clues to support our judgement'.[11] Once it had been established that *The Times*, rather than the *Sunday Times* would negotiate with *Stern*, Hugh Trevor-Roper travelled to Zurich with *Times* reporters, to examine the Diaries in the Handelsbank. He was impressed by the sheer weight of the material, the form of it, the handwriting, the style and Hitler's signature. He was '99½% certain' that the Diaries were genuine. There was no doubt of his abilities as an historian, but he wasn't a handwriting expert, and it's hard to see why the weight of the material should have been taken as evidence of its authenticity. Other experts, among them Professor Alan Bullock and Professor Gerhard Weinburg, doubted that Hitler had kept a diary, for three good reasons: he had no time, he detested writing, and he was too sick to write for much of the time. When the hoax collapsed, all the reasons originally given for believing that the Diaries were genuine were recycled as further evidence that they were false. The victim pays too little attention to what he is looking at, and too much to what he hopes to see.

Some hoaxers are lucky enough to be able to by-pass this process, for the ground has been prepared for them by their victims. In the Hitler Diary hoax, for years there had been reports of the existence of such diaries, written on very thin airmail paper and buried in zinc boxes. The Counter Intelligence Corps of the United States had looked into this, and had been told by the former head of the SS in Austria that he had seen the Hitler Diaries in the *Führerbunker* at Obersalzburg. Once rumours start that something may exist, it soon will, in one form or another. Kujau, like van Meegeren, Dawson, Ireland, Chatterton and others, profited from this anticipation; all dealt with victims who were predisposed to accept the fake that came their way for what they hoped it would be. Need or greed are the victim's worst enemies, the hoaxer's staunchest allies. Dr Bredius needed more Vermeers; Smith Woodward and others needed a major British palaeontological find to rival those of Germany and France; Britain, at war with Revolutionary France, may not have needed a new play by its greatest national hero, but was ready to welcome such a find and was going through one of its periodical obsessions with Shakespeare; Martin Guerre (even in the guise of Arnaud de Tilh) was needed back in Artigat.

And, once such finds have been made, and such needs have been met, and such vast sums of money have been paid, the victim often does the hoaxer's work for him. Smith Woodward supported the claims for the Piltdown Man to his dying day. Bertrande Guerre always insisted that de Tilh was Martin Guerre. Conan Doyle acted as chief publicity agent for the Cottingley Fairies. Lady Tichborne provided Orton with access to information that he so desperately needed to maintain his pretence to being her son.

One hoax which illustrates how determined a victim may be to prolong his misery is that of Denis Vrain-Lucas, a Parisian forger and conman. Vrain-Lucas was born in 1818 in the small town of Châteaudun, some twenty-five miles south of Chartres. His father was a peasant, but Vrain-Lucas left the country and went to Paris as a young man. Here he became a lawyer's clerk. He was ambitious, but lacked the background, qualifications and contacts needed to gain advancement. He did, however, have one very marketable quality – he was a skilled copyist of rare mauscripts. For a while he worked for a dealer, but the dealer died, and Vrain-Lucas discovered he could just as easily sell copies of old manuscripts as the manuscripts themselves.

In 1861, Vrain-Lucas was recommended to Michel Chasles, newly appointed Librarian to the Paris Academy. Chasles's predecessor had run down the Academy's collection of manuscripts, and Chasles was determined to rebuild it. His weakness was that he was obsessively patriotic. Almost everything he did was dictated by a passion to place France in the forefront of all nations. This was all Vrain-Lucas needed. He began to feed Chasles a series of forged letters. The first was from Molière, which Chasles bought for 500 francs. There followed letters from Racine and Rabelais (at 200 francs each). When Chasles asked Vrain-Lucas where the letters came from, Lucas was ready with his story. An eighteenth-century nobleman, he said, had been shipwrecked while emigrating. The nobleman's elderly descendant was now forced to sell this wonderful collection of ancient manuscripts. Vrain-Lucas was cunning – there had been such a nobleman – and he forced Chasles's hand by saying that there was another descendant who was opposed to the sale of the letters and papers. This standard hoaxer's trick increased Chasles's desire to buy and his fear that he wouldn't be able to.

The letters became older and older and stranger and stranger. There was one from Lazarus to St Peter; from Alexander the Great to

Aristotle, giving him permission to visit Gaul and study the Druids there; from Mary Magdalene to the King of the Burgundians ('You will find the letter I spoke of to you which was sent me by Jesus Christ a few days before His passion'.[12]); a letter from Vercingetorix to Trojus Pompeius; from a French doctor to Jesus; from Shakespeare acknowledging his debt to French authors.

Chasles bought them all in a frenzy of thoughtless enthusiasm. No matter that letters dating from 350 BC were written on paper, a writing material that became available for the first time several hundred years later. No matter that a letter from Galileo complaining of eye strain was ostensibly written three years after he became blind. No matter that a letter from Pascal contained a reference to coffee, and that coffee didn't arrive in France until seven years after Pascal's death. No matter that Archimedes and Attila unaccountably wrote in medieval French. Once ensnared in a hoax it is almost impossible for a victim to want to get in touch with reality. Chasles paid altogether some £6,000 for 27,000 fake letters.*

Vrain-Lucas's method was simple. He would feign ignorance of famous figures of whom Chasles spoke with reverence, and suggest that they together consult the *Biographie Universelle*, so that he would be better informed. Sure enough, a few days later, Lucas would produce a letter from the person concerned out of the collection of the nobleman's descendant. Eventually, Vrain-Lucas over-reached himself. He came up with a series of letters between Pascal and Isaac Newton, proving that Pascal had anticipated most of Newton's work. There were two problems: at the time of the alleged correspondence, Newton would have been only eleven years old, and the scientific information on which Pascal was supposed to have made his calculations in 1662 had not been available until 1726. The experts were called in. Some, notably the French academicians, sided with Chasles and declared the documents authentic. In 1869, the Paris Academy endorsed the letters, but Dr Grant, from the Glasgow Observatory, pointed out the numerous discrepancies in the correspondence between Pascal and Newton.

---

* I find it hard to accept this figure. Twenty-seven thousand letters assumes an output of something like fifteen a day (every day) over a period of five years. Perhaps we are once again being hoaxed by those who write about hoaxes.

Chasles and Vrain-Lucas were accused of conspiracy. Poor Chasles was able to convince the authorities that he was guilty of nothing more than immense folly. Vrain-Lucas alone was brought to trial. The legal proceedings were a nightmare for Chasles, as choice passages were read aloud from his vast collection of unlikely letters. Vrain-Lucas was sentenced to two years' imprisonment. Chasles was left to lick his wounded pride.

The tenacity with which victims cling to a hoax is also shown in the case of Lothar Malskat and Dietrich Fey. During the Second World War, incendiary bombs gutted St Mary's Church, Lübeck, and burnt the whitewash from the church walls, revealing scraps of thirteenth-century wall paintings. The authorities decided to commission 'experts' to restore the paintings. Malskat and Fey had worked together before the war, restoring parts of Schleswig Cathedral, some sixty miles away, and they had teamed up again in the chaos and confusion of the early years of peace. Malskat's speciality was faking paintings, including the inevitable Chagalls: Fey's speciality was selling them. Over several years they produced and disposed of some five hundred paintings before Malskat made the mistake of trying to sell on his own and not through Fey.

In 1948 Fey received the commission to restore the frescos at St Mary's in Lübeck, and the work there excited considerable interest. Fey claimed that he was using a miracle compound that somehow drew the murals out of the wall, but no one was allowed to see this take place. We are back in the naive, trusting world of Sergeant Shearer and Dr Abrams. By autumn 1950 there were reports that the frescos in the nave had been restored and that Malskat and Fey were now working on other parts of the church, especially the choir. To commemorate the work and the findings, a special 5-pfennig postage stamp was issued. Konrad Adenauer, Chancellor of the West German Republic, was given a conducted tour of the church by Fey. Praise was heaped on the restorers: 'After the fire the frescos were very badly exposed to the elements. However, it proved possible to save them by careful restoration which added nothing but merely preserved what had survived'.[13]

The church was reopened in 1951, to mark its 700th anniversary, and the 'restored' paintings were revealed to the public. There were scenes from the Bible, mythical beasts, images of the saints in purple and gold. The work in the choir was the subject of special praise, for here the frescos were complete with a border frieze and formed elaborate paintings. Fey received the Federal Cross of Merit, Malskat received nothing. He became embittered, and in May 1952, Malskat announced that the frescos were fakes. Few believed him. The main thrust of the argument against Malskat's claim was that he and Fey didn't have enough ability to create such beautiful works. They might be good restorers, but they were not fine artists. But what really made their victims refuse to accept that they had been hoaxed was the time and money that had been spent on the so-called restoration, and the prestige that had been attached to it.

It took Malskat a considerable time to convince his victims that he had hoaxed them. Eventually he was able to persuade the experts that among the figures in the thirteenth-century frescos in the choir of St Mary's were portraits of Marlene Dietrich, Rasputin, Genghis Khan and Malskat's own sister. Even then, it was argued that, though the paintings in the choir were fake, those in the nave were genuine. Malskat explained that such traces of the old work as had remained had crumbled away at the touch of a brush, and there had been nothing left to restore. Tests proved that what he said was true. Fey, Malskat and two others were arrested, charged and sent for trial. The trial lasted from August 1954 to January 1955, further evidence of the reluctance of the authorities to accept that they had been victims of a hoax. Malskat, seen as the humble but skilled artisan, became something of a national hero, but both he and Fey were sent to prison – Fey for twenty-two months, Malskat for just two months less.

The case of Malskat and Fey also shows how we are continually at risk from hoaxers because we try to make sense of any situation in which we find ourselves, and we are reluctant to backtrack in our thoughts to do so. We build a tottering structure on our past false assumptions. Our initial premise is that we are dealing with a world that is straightforward, if not honest, in what it presents to us. We do not believe we are living in Beadleland where nothing is what it seems and everything has been deliberately designed to trick us and make fools of us. We depend on the basic integrity of the outside world, and we presuppose each day that nothing has happened to turn it upside down. A Hollywood publicist, Al Horwitz, used to delight in sending struggling film actors a wire that read DISREGARD MY PREVIOUS

TELEGRAM. ZANUCK. All his victims accepted the wire in good faith, assuming that it came from Zanuck, and that there had been a previous wire. From that moment, life became a nightmare of hope and fear, anguish and disappointment for them.

Oscar Hartzell's thousands of victims repeatedly produced their own excuses for Hartzell's behaviour and for the non-payment of the Drake legacy. Rather than admit to themselves that they had been hoaxed, they were prepared to believe that the British Government were refusing to pay, since payment would bankrupt Britain; that the FBI and MI5 were secretly manipulating the affair; that pipes had been switched for bars of gold shipped out to pay them. Whatever happened, Hartzell's victims tried to make sense of the situation, but sense that was compatible with the concept of Hartzell being an honest man. What matters is not reality, but believability. Such is the essence of both tragedy and comedy. As victims, first we want to believe, then we *have* to believe, and an atmosphere of secrecy serves only to increase our faith in the process which is leading to our downfall. As Clifford Irving observed: 'A moment in time arrives . . . when the victim's willingness may lead him, consciously or otherwise, across the thin dividing line between gullibility and culpability'.[14]

And, once one of us has sought to make fool's sense out of the situation, the rest of us may blindly follow. In 1914, Paul Birault, a journalist living in Paris, noted that a member of the French cabinet unveiled statues of a musician and a philosopher on the same day, making similar fulsome speeches of praise at both ceremonies. It was the last great age of the statue: generals, poets, artists, industrialists, scientists – all received bronze and stone immortality. Birault invented Hegesippe Simon, 'precursor of modern democracy and martyr to the tyranny of the *ancien régime*'. He sent printed invitations to all the liberal and radical members of the French National Assembly to attend the unveiling of a monument to Simon of the occasion of the 150th anniversary of his supposed death. Fifteen senators and nine deputies accepted. Once one had done so, it was difficult for others not to. Nobody bothered to check Hegesippe Simon's history, though the date fixed for his death by Birault was as recent as 1764. As Joe Cooper wrote of another hoax,

If any great truth is to emerge from the curious case of the

Cottingley Fairies, for me it is this; that human beings are fallible, vain and consequently in social life prone to gloss over their imperfections and present themselves as favourably as possible to others . . . we don't know as much as we think we do, and we tend to delude ourselves and others in the cause of credulity and status.

Having put in such hard work to make fools of ourselves, it's hardly surprising that we become extremely angry once we are forced to accept that we have been hoaxed. When critic James Boaden was informed that William Ireland (and not Shakespeare) had written *Vortigern*, he wrote young Ireland a furious letter: 'You must be aware, sir, of the enormous crime you committed against the divinity of Shakespeare. Why the act, sir, was nothing short of sacrilege; it was precisely the same thing as taking the holy chalice from the altar and ******* therein!!!!'[15] Perhaps part of his anger was directed at himself for his own credulity. Before the 'discovery' of *Vortigern*, Boaden had predicted that one day 'a rich assemblage of Shakespeare papers would start forth from some ancient repository, to solve all our doubts and to add to our reverence and enjoyment'. After the exposure of the Hitler Diaries hoax, Hugh Trevor-Roper let fly in a review of *Adolf Hitler: The Medical Diaries – The Private Diaries of Dr Theo Morell*, edited by fellow victim David Irving, and published in May 1983. One week Trevor-Roper was on the front page as a great authority; the next, he was a humble reviewer on page 46. As soon as the headmasters of Britain's leading public schools learnt the truth about H Rochester Sneath, 'a cascade of Headmagisterial letters descended on Sir Montagu Butler, Master of Pembroke College'[16], and Humphry Berkeley was sent down for two years. The Magic Circle expelled Sophie Lloyd, even though it was then prepared to admit women. Officers of the Royal Navy wished to thrash Cole and others in revenge for the *Dreadnought* hoax. Ronald Dredge, one of Count Victor Lustig's victims, pursued his hoaxer across the United States for months.

With the anger often goes sadness, for victimization is a cruel art. When the body of Paul Kammerer was found on the Theresian hillside in Austria in 1936, there was a note in his coat pocket:

Dr Paul Kammerer requests not to be transported to his home, in order to spare his family the sight. Simplest and cheapest would perhaps be utilization in the dissecting room of one of the University institutes. I would actually prefer to render science at least this one small service. Perhaps my worthy academic colleagues will discover in my brain a trace of the qualities they found absent from the manifestations of my mental activities while I was alive.[17]

We are often caught up in a hoax, because we leap at the opportunity that the hoaxer seems to present to us. And once we have leapt, there can be no twisting in mid-air and turning back. And the further or the higher we have leapt, the longer the hoax will run and the more helplessly we shall be enmeshed in it. We all have our weaknesses, and we all have our dreams. We swallow what Jiminy Cricket tells us, that when we wish upon a star our dreams will come true. Hoaxers know this, consciously or sub-consciously. Life is like a monster jigsaw puzzle and we spend all our time looking for the right pieces. The hoaxer is the man who comes along and tells us that he had just the piece we are looking for. It may be a fossil or a fresco, a picture or a performance, a cure or a concerto, but the betting is that we will clutch at it, and then, in the words of Private Fraser: 'We're doomed! We're all doomed!'

13

The Prevalence of Hoaxing

'There are no such things as lies, only truths looking for new premises.'

Wolf Gort, *A Life of Deceit*

One of the wearisome features of the human condition is that we constantly search for the truth. Cats, ants and swallows don't. We do, and become increasingly afraid that the truth, whatever it is, is ever harder to find. Knowledge of how things work, how matter is constructed, how we can extract more and more from less and less, hasn't helped us to discover the truth about ourselves. We deceive and are deceived every bit as much today as two thousand years ago. We may not believe in the *bona fides* of someone who offers to read our palm, but we have total faith in someone who offers to read our electricity meter, and let such people into our homes, often with disastrous results.

At the time of writing this book, hoaxing has become a growth industry. There may not be many new ideas, but the old, old hoaxes are still going strong. For hundreds of years the bogus aristocrat has been so well identified as to be used as a staple character in farce and tragedy, but it was still possible in the 1980s for Rosemary Aberdour to pass herself off as Lady Aberdour, daughter of a Scottish earl, and be given a position of authority in the management of a hospital charity. In 1991 she was accused of stealing £2.8 million from that charity. In the 1920s, Maundy Gregory sold honours on behalf of himself and Lloyd George. In the 1980s seventeen peerages were awarded to 'private sector industrialists whose companies had donated more than £5 million to the Tory party or its front organizations. This works out at £300,000 a peerage'.[1] Maundy Gregory and Lloyd George charged a mere £100,000 – though, given inflation, the Tory offer does seem a bargain. In 1987 the activities of the Royal Knights of Justice were investigated, to the delight of some and the horror of others. This organization, which was linked to a religious sect who called themselves the Aetherius Society, successfully sold fake knighthoods. If it's hard to believe that such a hoax could work in our contemporary sophisticated society, it's worth remembering dear old Oscar Hartzell: 'The idea of an Iowa farmer setting himself up as the executor of one of Elizabeth I's sea-dogs must strike anyone as far-fetched, but in the hoaxing business, the more ludicruous the idea, the more successful it is likely to be.'[2] Art hoaxes may be in something of a rut, but it's a very profitable rut. In the 1950s, David Stein faked paintings and drawings by Chagall. In 1991 John Tetro of California was accused of the biggest ever art fraud, with over $100 million worth of fake paintings on the market, among them a host of 'Chagalls'. The jury has not yet reached a verdict in this case, but, just as many in the art world were not happy to admit they had been hoaxed when Keating's Sexton Blakes came to light, so it is proving difficult for the American police to find galleries who will admit that they have been fooled by John Tetro.

Juries are still out all over the Western world, deliberating the actions of hoaxers and would-be hoaxers. Mohammed Yehia Saed spent two years in the United States masquerading as the chairman of Harrods. All went well until a freelance photographer sent some photographs of Mohammed Yehia Saed with members of the pop group, Duran Duran, to the real head of Harrods, Mohamed Al-Fayed, accompanied by a note which read: 'Mo – here are a couple of prints from the Duran tour. Hope you like them. Denis.' The real head of Harrods had never accompanied Duran Duran on tour, and had never been addressed as 'Mo'. He spent half a million dollars tracking down the impostor, while bills from hotels, restaurants, car hire firms and airlines flooded in to the House of Fraser. Eventually, Mohamed Yehia Saed was discovered in a hotel in New Orleans. He was the son of a poor family from Alexandria in Egypt, and had spent his childhood not far from where the Al-Fayed brothers grew up. He worked as a merchant seaman and jumped ship some time in the 1980s in Panama. By the time he was arrested he was wanted by the police in Georgia, Virginia, Texas, California and Ontario. He slipped away while on bail but was subsequently recaptured in a night-club in Orlando, Florida. He is now on the receiving end of a $5 million lawsuit which he describes as 'absolute garbage'.

Joe Flynn, the self-styled King of Sting, is still operating from his base in Spain. Years ago he was paid £25,000 for a pair of shoes which he claimed belonged to Jimmy Hoffa, head of the Teamsters Union in the United States. Flynn claimed that the shoes proved that the Mafia killed Hoffa. On examination the shoes turned out not to be Hoffa's size. In 1991, Flynn was accused by the *Daily Mirror* of hoaxing Seymour Hersch and his publishers, Faber & Faber, over claims that Robert Maxwell and two journalists from the paper were involved in the Mossad kidnapping of Mordechai Vanunu. This was far less profitable, bringing in only £1,200. Flynn was happy to admit that the 'proof' he offered to substantiate his allegation was a hoax: 'It was all a sting – a one hundred per cent pack of lies'.[3] On this issue, questions flood the mind. Did Flynn really hoax Hersh? Did Hersh know he was being hoaxed, and did he thus in turn hoax Fabers? Did Fabers know they were being hoaxed? And on and on we go – how did Robert Maxwell die? Indeed, in the minds of some people, is Robert Maxwell dead? After all, John Stonehouse returned from the ocean a generation ago.

We are still searching for the truth about the phenomenon of crop circles, symmetrical patterns of flattened wheat or other cereals that unaccountably appear overnight in the fields from the plains of Wessex to the Prairies of Canada. Some of the circles are known to be hoaxes; the Wessex Sceptics ('Skeptics' to the *Guardian*) from Southampton University have created crop circles as a way of exploding, or at least diluting, some of the more fanciful theories advanced as to how such patterns are formed. A simple circle takes roughly two hours, a length of rope and a garden roller to make. How the more complicated patterns are formed, we don't know. We do know, however, that there are people who have falsely claimed to be responsible for the circles. Several British papers carried reports in September 1991 of the work of two Sussex men, Doug Bower and David Chorley, who made a circle to order, using a wooden board, a piece of string and a siting device attached to a baseball hat. The demonstration was impressive, but Bower's and Chorley's so-called admission that they had invented crop circles in 1978 and had been solely responsible for the great crop circles hoax of the last thirteen years was not accepted. Both men were in their sixties, and though fit, could not have produced twenty circles in a single night. Other theories that have been advanced are that the circles are produced by wind, or atmospheric vortices, or underground energy sources, or electro-magnetic or electro-static forces, or plasma fire, or alien beings from another planet, or a whole army of hoaxers. We may never know which. What is surprising is the lack of concern on the part of science or society; perhaps if more money was involved we should be more worried.

But the most disturbing feature of hoaxing is that it is a way of gaining and using power. While such power is in the hands of a Horace Cole or an Alan Abel, maybe we have little to worry about, but the last twenty or thirty years have seen a vast increase in the known cases of duplicity or dirty tricks on the part of democratic governments all over the world. Hoaxing has become a common political weapon. There seems to have been a rise in the recorded incidence of our leaders and their subordinates being 'economical with the truth', which is a long-winded way of saying that we have been hoaxed. In the 1950s, the governments of Britain, France, Turkey, Norway and Formosa knew about the American U2 plane and its spying missions over Soviet territory. Among those who did not know were the American people, and they were not supposed to know, and President Eisenhower took considerable pains and told several lies to keep the truth from them. The lies were not the hoax – the hoax was the pretence that any one form of government conducts its affairs in a totally honest way.

There is an allegation that when Harold Wilson became Prime Minister in 1964, his office was bugged by MI5 at the request of the Conservative Central Office. The justification for this was that Wilson had visited the Soviet Union in 1949 with his secretary, and might therefore have become a target for blackmail and thus a security risk. In other words, the Prime Minister's office was bugged for the sake of the country. None of this was public knowledge at the time, for there is much secrecy in politics, and we cannot be sure of the facts even now. But, again, the bugging (if it took place) is not the hoax. The hoax is the spurious reason given for bugging, since it would obviously be of enormous advantage to any opposition party to know what was going on in the inner sanctums of government.

Watergate, *Spycatcher*, *Death on the Rock*, the sinking of the

Belgrano, Westland, Oliver North and Irangate – the list of political hoaxings is depressingly long and frighteningly complicated. But we tend to admire liars, if they are daring enough, just as we tend to be suspicious of those who try to tell us the truth. To quote H L Mencken: 'A Galileo could no more be elected President of the United States than he could be elected Pope of Rome. Both high posts are reserved for men favoured by God with an extraordinary genius for swathing the bitter facts of life in bandages of soft illusion'.[4] Nor are our leaders immune from being hoaxed by their subordinates or other, lesser folk. The Princess of Wales visited a hospital in Ottawa during a visit to Canada in October 1991, to open a new heart ward. The ward wasn't ready to receive real patients, so bogus patients were brought in and plonked into the beds. Most of them were ex-patients who were asked to return to the hospital for what one of the doctors at the hospital described as 'cosmetic reasons' – to make an empty ward appear full. Seeing may be believing, but it isn't necessarily believing in the truth.

It's impossible to tell whether life has been ever thus, whether hoaxes were as commonplace in the past as they appear to be now. What may be new, however, is our knowledge of the prevalence of hoaxes and the corresponding weak hold that we have on the truth. We know that newspapers can lie, television can lie, our leaders can lie. We have learnt to be sophisticatedly on guard in the way we interpret what is going on around us. If we see two men fighting in the street, we are as likely to believe that there is a TV, video or cine camera nearby as that we are witnessing a life-or-death struggle. If we see someone set fire to a car on a piece of wasteland, we are as likely to believe it's the work of Jeremy Beadle as that of an arsonist. If we see a youth running up behind an older man in the street, we are as likely to believe it's part of an advertising campaign for the police as an imminent piece of snatch thievery. The trouble is that we may become *too* aware of the possibility that someone is out to trick us, and adopt an over-sophisticated attitude. We become hesitant to run to the assistance of someone who desperately needs our help, because it may all be a hoax.

We are on our guard, but it may not be enough, for the initiative always rests with the hoaxer, who has some new trick up his sleeve, or a variation on an old one, or who times his hoax well. Few would accept a series of newspaper articles announcing the discovery of man-bats on the moon today, but a great many might start to accept video film advertised as taken by a camera from a satellite in space, whatever it supposedly recorded. Thanks to Shakespeare, we believe in the villainy of Richard III. Thanks to Hollywood, we believe in the heroism of General Custer. Thanks to Leonardo da Vinci, we believe in the serenity of the Madonna. Hoaxing has for ever been all around us in one form or another. The artist is no more than a legitimate hoaxer, someone who has presented us with a revered and expensive version of the truth. We accept this, we glorify it – no colour photograph of sunflowers will ever approach the value of van Gogh's Impressionist painting. We may say that we have a different attitude to science, and that we expect the truth from scientists. But often, they don't know what that is any more than we do, and we certainly don't wish to give them *carte blanche* in their search for it.

The problem is also that we all have the potential to be hoaxers. 'No healthy man,' wrote H L Mencken, 'in his secret heart, is content with his destiny.' We embroider the truth in our lives. We tell our friends that our car does a little more to the gallon than anyone else's, our purchases are a little bit cheaper (or more expensive), our allotment a little more productive (or infertile), our highs are higher, our lows are lower. It is impossible to be one hundred per cent honest – thank goodness, for that would make life deadly dull. Most of the time our deceit doesn't mater, for nobody is asked to give money or to make important judgements on the exaggerated information that we give them. And yet we hope that our standing in the community will benefit from such decoration – why else do we do it?

Maybe hoaxers and victims come together because they have so much in common. A hoaxer is no more egocentric than his victim, no more absorbed in how he presents himself to the outer world. Both are trying to make life fit a design of their choice, whatever the sacrifices. To a degree all life is a hoax, and we are all hoaxers.

Which leaves us with the unpleasant conclusion that we must all be victims, too.

References

Introduction

1 The *Guardian*, 17 September 1991
2 Harry Reichenbach, *Phantom Fame*, Noel Douglas (London, 1932) 67
3 *Ibid.* 68
4 Clifford Irving, quoted in Stephen Fey, Lewis Chester and Magnus Linklater, *Hoax*, André Deutsch (London 1972) 17
5 Adrian Stephen, *The 'Dreadnought' Hoax*, Chatto & Windus (London, 1983) 21

1 The Inspiration and Origin of Hoaxes

1 Adrian Stephen, *The 'Dreadnought Hoax'*, Chatto & Windus (London, 1983) 23
2 *Ibid.* 22
3 *Ibid.* 24
4 *Ibid.* 22
5 Quoted in Norman Moss, *The Pleasures of Deception*, Chatto & Windus (London, 1977) 27
6 *Ibid.* 28
7 *Ibid.* 168
8 Quoted in Andrew Mound, *Heroic Hoaxes*, Macdonald (London, 1983) 9
9 Quoted in Fey, Chester and Linklater, *Hoax*, André Deutsch (London, 1972) 5
10 Stephen, *op. cit.* 35–6
11 Joseph McCarthy, 'The Royal Canadian Navy's Mystery

Surgeon, *Life Magazine* (1952)
  12 Stephen, *op. cit.* 48
  13 Quentin Bell, *Virginia Woolf, Vol. 1: Virginia Stephen 1882-1912*, Hogarth Press (London, 1972) 159
  14 Stephen, *op. cit.* 32
  15 *Ibid.* 34–5
  16 *Ibid.* 38
  17 *Ibid.* 39
  18 *Ibid.* 45–6
  19 Bell, *op. cit.* 157
  20 *Hansard*, 24 February 1910
  21 Stephen, *op. cit.* 59
  22 Bell, *op. cit.* 163
  23 *Ibid.* 160
  24 Stephen, *op. cit.* 61
  25 Lord Kilbracken, *Van Meegeren*, Nelson (London, 1967) 4

2 Puffers and Bluffers

  1 James Thurber, 'The Owl Who Was God', *New Yorker*, 29 April 1939
  2 Quoted in Norman Moss, *The Pleasures of Deception*, Chatto & Windus (London, 1977) 99
  3 *Ibid.* 10
  4 *Ibid.* 26
  5 Harry Reichenbach, *Phantom Fame*, Noel Douglas (London, 1932)
  6 Andrew Mound, *Heroic Hoaxes*, Macdonald (London, 1983) 75
  7 Alan Abel, *Yours for Decency*, Elek Books (London, 1966)
  8 *Ibid.*
  9 *Ibid.*
  10 *Ibid.*
  11 Quoted in Richard Saunders, *The World's Greatest Hoaxes*, South Yarmouth Press (Massachusetts, 1980)
  12 Quoted in Moss, *op. cit.* 28
  13 Mark Pauline, quoted in Andrea Juno and V Vale (eds), *Pranks*, Re/Search Publications (San Francisco, 1987) 17
  14 Boyd Rice, quoted in *Ibid.* 33
  15 Thomas, Tenth Earl of Dundonald, *Autobiography of a Seaman*

(London, 1869)
16 Westminster Popular No. 5, *The Story of the Liberator Crash* (London, 1896)
17 *Ibid.*
18 A J P Taylor, *England 1914-1945*, Oxford University Press (London, 1965)
19 *Daily Sketch*, 22 February 1933
20 *Ibid.*

3 Never Give a Sucker an Even Break

1 Harry Reichenbach, *Phantom Fame*, Noel Douglas (London, 1932)
2 *Ibid.* 246
3 *Ibid.* 29
4 *Ibid.* 118
5 Fey, Chester and Linklater, *Hoax*, André Deutsch (London, 1972)
6 Bill Sloan, *The Seventy Thousand Heirs of Sir Francis Drake*, Crowell, Collier Publishing Co. (USA, 1950)
7 *Ibid.*
8 Quoted in Andrew Mound, *Heroic Hoaxes*, Macdonald (London, 1983) 15
9 James F Johnson, as told to Floyd Miller, *The Man Who Sold the Eiffel Tower*, W H Allen (London, 1962) 11

4 Habitual Masquerade

1 Adrian Stephen, *The 'Dreadnought' Hoax*, Chatto & Windus (London, 1983) 35-6
2 Victor Lewis-Smith, 'My Life as a Hoaxer', the *Sunday Correspondent*, 25 November 1990
3 Victor Lewis-Smith, interview with the author, 29 January 1992
4 Victor Lewis-Smith and Paul Sparks, interview with the author, 29 January 1992
5 The *Sunday Correspondent*, 25 November 1990
6 Jenny Winstanley and Sophie Lloyd, interview with the author, 2 December 1991
7 *Ibid.*
8 The *Guardian*, 27 September 1991

9 Humphry Berkeley, *The Life and Death of Rochester Sneath*, Davis-Poynter (London, 1974) 19
10 Andrew Mound, *Heroic Hoaxes*, Macdonald (London, 1983) 13
11 Natalie Zemon Davis, *The Return of Martin Guerre*, Penguin Books (London, 1985) 37
12 *Ibid*. 44
13 *Ibid*. 89
14 *Ibid*. 59–60
15 *Ibid*. 103
16 Quoted in Richard Newnham, *Fakes, Frauds and Forgeries*, Guinness Publishing (London, 1991) 20
17 Quoted in Norman Moss, *The Pleasures of Deception*, Chatto & Windus (London, 1977) 172
18 Jack Bilbo, *I Can't Escape Adventure*, Cresset Press (London, 1937) 32
19 *Ibid*. 62
20 *Ibid*. 71
21 Jack Bilbo, *Carrying a Gun For Al Capone*, Cresset Press (London, 1943) Preface
22 *Daily Express*, 21 June 1929
23 *Ibid*.
24 *Independent on Sunday*, 22 July 1990
25 *Ibid*.

5 Not What They Seemed

1 *News of the World*, 20 June 1920
2 *Ibid*.
3 William Allinson and John Fairley, *The Monocled Mutineer*, Quartet Books (London, 1979) 23
4 *News of the World*, 20 June 1920
5 Bernard Wasserstein, *The Secret Lives of Trebitsch Lincoln*, Penguin Books (London, 1989) 30
6 *Ibid*. 63
7 George Smith (ed.) *Dictionary of National Biography: From the Beginnings to 1900*, Oxford University Press (Oxford, 1903)
8 *Tichborne in Prison, Being an Account of Interviews Had with Him* 'by Lady T, Lord Rivers, G. Onslow Esq., A. Biddulph Esq., J.S. Helsby Esq., and Dr Kenealy MP', Englishman Office, 63 Fleet Street,

London, 1874
9 *DNB, op. cit.*
10 Ibid.
11 R M Gunnell (ed.), *The Tichborne Almanack for 1877*, Tichborne Papers, British Library
12 *Ibid.*
13 *Ibid.*
14 *Tichborne in Prison, op. cit.*
15 *Ibid.*
16 *Ibid.*
17 *The Tichborne Times*, Tichborne Papers, British Library

6 The Fairy Tales of Science

1 Arthur Keith, *The Antiquity of Man*, Williams and Norgate (London, 1925)
2 Arthur Smith Woodward, *Geological Magazine*, 1916, Vol 3, 477–9
3 *Sussex Express*, 1 January 1954; quoted in J S Weiner, *The Piltdown Forgery*, Oxford University Press (London, 1955) 194
4 Ronald Millar, *The Piltdown Men*, Gollancz (London, 1972) 123
5 Quoted in *The Times*, 21 November 1953
6 Teilhard de Chardin, quoted in Frank Spencer, *Piltdown, A Scientific Forgery*, Natural History Museum Publications (London, 1990) 202
7 J S Weiner, *op. cit.* 105
8 Millar, *op. cit.* 195
9 *The Times*, 21 November 1953
10 *Ibid.*
11 F J M Postlethwaite, letter to *The Times*, 25 November 1953
12 *The Times*, 26 November 1953
13 Millar, *op. cit.* 210
14 Quoted in Edward L Gardner, *A Book of Real Fairies*, Theosophical Publishing House (London, 1925)
15 Quoted in Joe Cooper, *The Case of the Cottingley Fairies*, Robert Hale (London, 1990)
16 *Strand Magazine*, March 1921
17 *Manchester City News*, 29 January 1921
18 Quoted in Cooper, *op. cit.*

19 *Ibid.*
20 *Ibid.*
21 *Ibid.*
22 Elsie Griffiths, interviewed by Austen Mitchell on Yorkshire Television's *Calendar*, September 1976
23 Quoted in Cooper, *op. cit.*
24 *National Geographic* Magazine, August 1971; quoted in June Southworth, 'The Great Stone Age Tribe Hoax', *Daily Mail*, 19 August 1988
25 John Edwards, quoted in *Daily Mail*, 19 August 1988

7 True Colours, False Canvases

1 Quoted in Richard Saunders, *The World's Greatest Hoaxes*, South Yarmouth Press (Massachusetts, 1980)
2 Zad Rogers, interviewed by the author, 7 January 1992
3 *Ibid.*
4 Quoted in Lord Kilbracken, *Van Meegeren*, Nelson (London, 1967) 81
5 *Ibid.* 3
6 *Ibid.* 4
7 *The Times*, 10 September 1984
8 *The Times*, 11 September 1984
9 *The Times*, 20 August 1984
10 Brian Sewell, interviewed in 'Portrait of a Master Faker', *Omnibus*, BBC TV, November 1991
11 Eric Hebborn, *ibid.*
12 *Ibid.*
13 *Ibid.*
14 *Ibid.*
15 The *Mail on Sunday* 20 October 1991
16 *Evening Standard* 24 October 1991

8 There Must be a Man Behind the Book

1 Quoted in Norman Moss, *The Pleasures of Deception*, Chatto & Windus (London, 1977) 115–16
2 Quoted in Richard Newnham, *Fakes, Frauds and Forgeries*, Guinness Publishing (London, 1991) 45
3 *Ibid.*

4 Quoted in Moss, *op. cit.* 121
5 *Ibid.* 124
6 Clifford Irving, *The Hoax*, Mandarin Books (London, 1989) 145
7 *Ibid.* 362
8 Dr Johnson, letter to Sir Joshua Reynolds, January 1775
9 Quoted in Gwyneth Lewis, *Eighteenth Century Literary Forgeries*, PhD thesis, Oxford University, 1991, 48
10 Quoted in *Ibid.* 82
11 Quoted in *Ibid.* 86
12 *Ibid.* 86
13 Quoted in Moss, *op. cit.* 107
14 Quoted in Philip Kerr (ed.) *The Penguin Book of Lies*, Penguin Books (London, 1991) 196
15 Quoted in Andrew Mound, *Heroic Hoaxes*, Macdonald (London, 1983) 19
16 Walter E Traprock, *The Cruise of the Kawa*, George Putnam, Sons (London, 1921) Introduction
17 *Ibid.* 136-7
18 Neville Cardus, *Full Score*, Cassell (London, 1970) 134

9 Growing Weary, Growing Wary

1 Quoted in Kenneth Newnham, *Fakes, Frauds and Forgeries*, Guinness Publishing (London, 1991) 204
2 Andrea Juno and V Vale (ed.), *Pranks*, Re/Search Publications (San Francisco, 1987) 109
3 David Freedman, quoted in Epilogue to Harry Reichenbach, *Phantom Fame*, Noel Douglas (London, 1932) 256
4 G K Chesterton, *Autobiography*, Hutchinson and Co. (London, 1936) 315-16
5 Jack Bilbo, *I Can't Escape Adventure*, Cresset Press (London, 1937) 191-2
6 *Ibid.* 223
7 Dr Thomas Kenealy and others, *Tichborne in Prison*, Englishman Office (London, 1874)
8 Jabez Spencer Balfour, *My Prison Life*, Chapman and Hall (London, 1907)
9 *Ibid.*

10 The Psychology of Hoaxers

1 Quoted in Andrew Mound, *Heroic Hoaxes*, Macdonald (London, 1983) 9
2 Clifford Irving, *The Hoax*, Mandarin Books (London, 1989) 63
3 *Ibid.* 339
4 *Ibid.* 359
5 Eric Hebborn, interviewed in the *Mail on Sunday*, 20 October 1991
6 Eric Hebborn, interviewed in the *Evening Standard*, 24 October 1991
7 Joey Skaggs, interviewed by Andrea Juno, *Pranks*, Re/Search Publications (San Francisco, 1987) 43
8 *Ibid.* 59
9 Lord Kilbracken, *Van Meergeren*, Nelson (London, 1967) 139
10 Kenneth Williams, *Back Drops*, Futura (London, 1983) 70
11 *Ibid.* 30
12 *Ibid.* 31
13 Humphry Berkeley, *The Life and Death of Rochester Sneath*, Davis-Poynter (London, 1974) Introduction
14 Brian Bethell, interview with the author, 24 November 1991
15 Quoted in Norman Moss, *The Pleasures of Deception*, Chatto & Windus (London, 1977) 179
16 Bernard Wasserstein, *The Secret Lives of Trebitsch Lincoln*, Penguin Books (London, 1989) 63
17 *Ibid.* 102
18 Irving, *op. cit.* 34
19 *Ibid.* 182
20 Muriel Gray, *Art is Dead, Long Live TV*, Channel 4 TV, October 1991
21 Quoted in Klein (ed.), *Grand Deception*, Faber (London, 1962) 149
22 *Ibid.* 149
23 *Ibid.* 151
24 Philip Kerr (ed.), *The Penguin Book of Lies*, Penguin Books (London, 1991) 155
25 *Ibid.* 156
26 Irving, *op. cit.* 181
27 *Ibid.* 259

28 Kilbracken, *op. cit.* 13
29 *Ibid.* 180
30 Alan Abel, interviewed by Andrea Juno, *op. cit.* 107

11 Victims

1 Humphry Berkeley, *The Life and Death of Rochester Sneath*, Davis-Poynter (London, 1974) 71
2 Ken Campbell, interview with the author, 5 November 1991
3 *The Times*, 31 July 1980
4 Clifford Irving, *The Hoax*, Mandarin Books (London, 1989) 260
5 Ronald Millar, *The Piltdown Men*, Gollancz (London, 1972) 205
6 Bernhard Berenson, letter to *The Times*, 4 April 1903
7 Dr Ginsburg, *Report on Mr Shapira's 'Manuscript of Deuteronomy'*, (London, 1883)
8 *Punch*, 8 September 1883
9 *The Times*, 27 August 1883

12 The Psychology of Victims

1 Arthur Conan Doyle, *The Coming of the Fairies*, Hodder & Stoughton (London, 1922) 18
2 *Ibid.* 52
3 *Ibid.* 38-9
4 *Ibid.* 55-6
5 Arthur Conan Doyle, *The Edge of the Unknown*, John Murray (London, 1930) 170
6 Clifford Irving, *The Hoax*, Mandarin Books (London, 1989) 20
7 *Ibid.* 317
8 *Ibid.* 260
9 *Ibid.* 69
10 *Sunday Times*, 8 May 1983
11 Joe Cooper, *The Case of the Cottingley Fairies*, Robert Hale (London, 1990) 48
12 Quoted in Kenneth Newnham, *Fakes, Frauds and Forgeries*, Guinness Publishing (London, 1991) 117
13 Hans Jürgen Hauser, quoted in Andrew Mound, *Heroic Hoaxes*, Macdonald (London, 1983) 40
14 Irving, *op. cit.* 362
15 Quoted in Gwyneth Lewis, *Eighteenth Century Literary*

Forgeries, PhD thesis, Oxford University, March 1991

16 Humphry Berkeley, *The Life and Death of Rochester Sneath*, Davis-Poynter (London, 1974) 95

17 Arthur Koestler, *The Case of the Midwife Toad*, Pan (London, 1975) 1

13   The Prevalence of Hoaxing

1 *Observer* Magazine, 29 December 1991

2 Andrew Mound, *Heroic Hoaxes*, Macdonald (London, 1983) 19

3 *Daily Mirror*, 18 November 1991

4 H L Mencken, 'The Art Eternal', reprinted in Philip Kerr (ed.), *The Penguin Book of Lies*, Penguin Books (London, 1991) 321

Index

Abel, Alan, 12, 24, 34–8, 156, 158–9, 174
Abel, Jeanne, 35
Aberdour, Rosemary, 205–6
Abnagale, Frank, 11, 158, 160, 167, 174
Aborigines, Australian, 78–81
Abrams, Dr Albert, 107–8, 109, 173, 184
Abyssinia, Emperor of, 15–22, 52, 65
Adams, Caswell, 31
Adenauer, Konrad, 200–201
Adolf Hitler: The Medical Diaries, 203
Aetherius Society, 206
Afghan princess, 58–9
Agincourt, Robert, 69
Agnew Spiro, 143, 196
Ahlers, Mr, 177
Alaska, 29
Al-Fayed, Mohamed, 206–7
Allen, Herb, 31
Allen, Major-General H T, 87
Allinson, William, 92, 93
Ambassador Club, 47
American Express Revue, 84
American Medical Association, 108

Amin, Idi, 159
Ampleforth, Head of, 70
Anahareo, 82
Andaman Islands, 78
Andersen, Hans Christian, 125
Anderson, Lindsay, 183
Andre, Michele, 34
Anglo-Texan Friendship Society, 40–41
April Fools' Day hoaxes, 24–5, 39
Arnstein, Nick, 61–2
ART IS DEAD – Long Live TV, 126–8
Ashe, Penelope, 142
Ashkin, Julius, 59
Ashton, Lord, 87
ASPCA, 168
Associated Press, 31
At the Edge of the Unknown, 119

Bach, Charlotte, *see* Hadju, Karoly
Bacon, Francis, 56
Baigent, Mr, 97
Baker, Mary, *see* 'Caraboo'
Balfour, Jabez, 43–5, 158, 165, 172, 174, 184
'Ballad of Chevy Chase', 147
Ballantine Books, 169

Ballantine, Sergeant, 98
Bambula, 163
Barnum, Phineas T, 29
Baruch, Hugo, 12, 64, 83-7, 89, 129, 156, 160-63, 172, 173, 174fn
BBC, 83, 115, 145; Radio 3, 175
Beadle, Jeremy, 181, 209
Beadle's About, 67
Beazley, Samuel, 39, 40
Beckford, William, 153
Belaney, Archibald, 11, 82-3, 88, 174
Bella, 96
Bennett, Arnold, 58
Berenson, Bernhard, 186-8
Bergler, Edmund, 26
Beringer, Dr Johann, 116-17, 174, 184, 185
Berkeley, Humphry, 65, 69-70, 157, 170, 173, 182, 203
Berliner Tageblatt, 176
Bernard, Gertrude, 82
Berner's Street, 39-40
Berry, Clifford, 59
Bertram, Charles Julius, 152
Bertram, PC, 93
Besada, Ashem Muhammad, 145
Besant, Walter, 190-92
Bethell, Brian, 170-71, 173, 178
Biafra, Jello, 168
Bickerstaffe, Dr Isaac, 174
Bickerstaffe's Almanac, 174
Bilbo, Jack, see Baruch, Hugo
Billi, 161-2
Biographical Memoirs of Extraordinary Painters, 153
Birault, Paul, 202
Birkett, Norman, 47
Blackhouse, Sir Edmund, 8
Blondlot, Professor René, 106-7, 174, 184
Blundells, Head of, 70

Blunt, Anthony, 173
Boaden, James, 203
Bogle, 97, 164
Bogus letters, 66, 170-71
Bonaparte, Napoleon, 158, 174fn, 175fn
Bonnard, fakes, 133
Book of Real Fairies, 119
Bottomley, Horatio, 8, 13-14, 45-8, 91, 158, 165, 174, 178, 185
Boucher, Madeleine, 34
Boult, Sir Adrian, 70
Bower, Doug, 207-8
Bradley-Hudd, Richard, 127
Bradshaw, Susan, 175
Bredius, Dr Abraham, 130, 172, 197
Bristol, 147-8
British Medical Journal, 109-112
British Museum, 105-6, 116, 136, 190
Bronstein, Yetta, 35
Brook, John, 162
Brueghel, fakes, 136, 137
Brussels marathon, 1
Bullock, Alan, 197
Burt, Sir Cyril, 12, 122, 173
Bushman, Francis X, 27-8
Buxton, Anthony, 15-22
Bynner, Walter, 153, 168, 173

Cabbage hoax, 7
Calendar, 120
Campbell, Ken, 157, 182-4
Candid Camera, 6
Candidus, George, 75, 76
Canynge, Master, 147-8
Capital Radio, 25
'Caraboo', 13, 76-7, 82, 88, 89, 158, 174, 175
Cardus, Neville, 155-6
Carrying a Gun for Al Capone, 85-6, 160, 175
Casadesus, Henry, 176

Casadesus, Marius, 173, 176
Castle of Otrano, The, 145
Catch Me if You Can, 11, 160
Cellini, Benvenuto, 188
Chabas, Paul, 28
Chagall, fakes, 131, 133, 174, 200, 206
Chappell, George S, 154, 156
Charles Dennehy and Company of Chicago, 4-5
Chasles, Michel, 198-200
Chatterton, Thomas, 147-9, 150, 156, 173, 197
Cheam Cricket Club, 49-50, 193
Chesterton, G K, 77, 161
Cheung, Johnny, 31, 32
Children's Hour, 83
Ching, Cheng, 75
Chorley, David, 207-8
Christ at Emmaeus, 130
Christies, 134, 136
Chronicles, 151
Churchill, Winston, 39
Clarion Call to Youth, A, 70
Clark, W E Le Gros, 114
Clermont-Ganneau, Charles, 189-90, 192
Cleveland Museum of Art, 188
Coburn, Sir Alexander, 99
Cochrane, Thomas, 42-3
Cocteau, fakes, 131
Cole, Horace, 7, 9-12, 13, 15-22, 38-40, 53, 57, 65, 116, 158, 173, 184, 203
Collins, David, 134
Colnaghi's auction house, 136
Complete System of Geography, 76
Compton, Henry, 74
Comstock, Anthony, 28
Conan Doyle, Sir Arthur, 103, 113, 116, 118-19, 120, 123, 158, 194-5
Congdon, James, 144-5
Constable, fakes, 133

Conway, J, 122
Cooper, Joe, 202-3
Cottingley Fairies, 14, 52, 117-20, 123, 176, 194, 198, 203
Country Life, 83
Coxinga, Emperor, 75
Cronkite, Walter, 37
Crop circles, 207-8
Crosby, Doc, 49, 51
Crosse and Blackwell, 170
Croyden, Jerry, 31, 32
Cruise of the Kawa, The, 154-5, 169
Curie, Pierre, 107

Daily Chronicle, 81
Daily Express, 19, 87
Daily Mirror, 12, 19, 207
Daily Telegraph, 19, 175
Daily Worker, 70
Daly, Denise, 39
Dancing Ducks, the, 3-4
Daumier, President, 86
Dave Garroway Show, 36
Dawson, Charles, 110-16, 158, 173, 174, 185, 197
Dead Sea Scrolls, 189-92
'Dean of all Twentieth Century Charlatans', 108
De Berenger, Captain, 43
De Chardin, Teilhard, 112, 114, 116, 158
De Coras, Jean, 72-3
Deepdene Hotel, 47
Defence Diaries of W Morgan Petty, 170
De Hory, Elmyr, 53, 132-3, 142, 158
Demara, Ferdinand Waldo, 59-61, 160, 174
De Rougemont, Louis, 13, 23, 65, 78-82, 89, 124, 156, 158, 174
De Tilh, Arnaud, 72-3, 82, 158, 176, 197

De Voogt, Anna, 129
Dew-fish, 155
Diary of a Good Neighbour, The, 144
Dictionary of National Biography, 96, 97, 98, 164-5
Die Stern, 196-7
Dietrich, Stanley, 143
Dimbleby, Richard, 24-5, 157
Disumbrationist School, 126
'Doctor Weyman', 57-8
Dossena, Alceo, 174, 188-9
Drake Fund, 52-5, 184
Drake Legacy, 202
Drake, Sir Francis, 53-4
'Dr Cyr', 60
Dreadnought, 7, 10, 11-12, 15-22, 52, 57, 65, 184, 203
Dredge, Ronald, 62, 203
Dufy, fakes, 131
Dupont, Pierre, 138-9, 176
Duvan, George, 61-3

Ebel, Peter, *see* Congdon, James
Edward VII, coronation of, 4-5
Edwards, John, 124
Eiffel Tower, sale of, 62-3, 173
Elinoure and Juga, 148
Elizabeth I, 151, 152
Elizalde, Manda, 123-4
Ellis, Reverend Wilfred, 77, 88, 174-5
Emperor's New Clothes, 125, 126, 127
Encyclopaedia Britannica, 153
Englishman, The, 99, 164
Eoanthropus dawsoni, 112
ERA, 108
Esau, 1-2
Étaples, mutiny at, 8, 91
Evening Mail, 26
Evolution, theory of, 121-2, 123
Ewing, Frederick R, 169
Exaltation, 126

Eynesso, Martin, 76, 77

Faber & Faber, 207
Fairley, John, 92, 93
Fake's Progress, The, 137
'Fall of Silence', 83
Father Philip, 161-2
Fatu-liva bird, 154-5
Ferdinand, Tsar of Bulgaria, 85
Fey, Dietrich, 200-201
Filbertese, 155
Filbert Islands, 154-5
Film Buhne, 84
Fingal, an Ancient Epic Poem in Six Books, Composed by Ossian Son of Fingal, 146
Fisher, William, 15
Five Golden Wrens, 33
Flint Jack, *see* Simpson, Edward
Flynn, Joe, 207
Forgeries, letter, 198-200
Formosa, 74-6, 77, 78
Fragments of Ancient Poetry Collected in the Highlands of Scotland, and Translated From the Gaelic or Erse Languages, 145
French, Robert Linton, 60
Fulton, PC Alfred, 92, 93
Furguson, Arthur, 56, 158, 174
Futura, 144-5
Fyleman, Rose, 117

Gainsborough, fakes, 133
Gansebrust, Gretchen, 34
Garden, Dr Thornley, 121
Gardner, Edward L, 118, 119, 148
Garland, HMS, 162
Garroway, Dave, 36-7
Genesis, book of, 1-2
Geological Society, 112, 113, 115
Geologists' Association, 106
Ghost Artists, 41
Gifford, Major, 120-21

INDEX

Ginsburg, Dr Christian, 190–92
Glasgow Observatory, 199
Goering, Field-Marshal Hermann, 129, 130
Goethe, 146
Goldetsky, Jacques, 35
Gorguloff, 86, 160
Gort, Wolf, 205
Goya, fakes, 133
Grant, Duncan, 15–22
Grant, Major, 21
Grant, Mrs, 21
Grantaire, Pierre, 27
Graves, Ralph, 196
Gray, Muriel, 126–8, 175
'Great Imposter', 59–60
'Great Reynard, The', 28
'Greatest Liar of All Time', 78
Greene, Graham, 40–41, 173
Gregory, Maundy, 13–14, 46–7, 74, 160, 172, 174, 185, 205–6
Grey Owl, 11, 82–3, 174
Grien, Henri Louis, *see* De Rougemont, Louis
Griffiths, Anne, 118
Griffiths, Elsie, 14, 117–20, 123, 157, 176
Guardian, 13
Guerre, Bertrande, 72–3, 198
Guerre, Martin, 72–3, 197, 198
Guinness, Samuel, 40–41

Hadju, Baron Karl, *see* Karoly, Hadju
Haggard, Sir Henry Rider, 79, 81
Hall-Edwards, Major, 195
Halliwell, Kenneth, 169–70
Harding, President, 58–9
Hardinge, Sir Arthur, 16
Hargreaves, Venus, 185
Harris hoax, 120–21
Hartzell, Canfield, 56
Hartzell, Oscar, 52–6, 158, 174, 184, 185

Hat, Bruno, 126
Hathaway, Anne, 151
Hazlitt, William, 24, 146
Hebborn, Eric, 135–7, 156, 167, 173, 174
Hehn, Niklaus, 116, 117
Hehn, Valentin, 116, 117
Henry, Buck, 36, 37, 65
Henry Root Letters, 66, 170, 173
Hersch, Seymour, 207
Herschel, Sir John, 104–5
Hewitt, Martin, 59, 160, 174
Hewlett, Maurice, 119
Hirsch, Jacob, 188
Historical and Geographical Description of Formosa, An, 74–5
History of English Painters, 148
History of English Poetry, 149
History of Hastings Castle, 111
Hitchcock, Alfred, 119
Hitler Diaries, 8, 53, 138, 144, 174, 196–7, 203
Hoblitzel, Ralph 'Hurry Up', 31, 32
Hochman, Schapschelle, 186–7
Hoffa, Jimmy, 207
Holker, Sir John, 99
Holmes, Florence, 82
Hollywood hoaxes, 51–2, 62, 201–2
Honours, sale of, 47, 205–6
Hook, Theodore, 39, 40, 173
Hopkins, Mr, 97
Horwitz, Al, 201–2
Hoskins, Cyril, *see* Kuan, Dr
Howard, Margaret, 122
Howard, Mr, 177
Hughes, Brian, 34
Hughes, Howard, 11, 13, 23, 52, 119, 134, 141, 142–4, 159, 173, 175fn, 195–6
Humours of Prison Life, 165
Hutchinson, Kenneth, 127
Huxley, T H, 103

Ice Worm festival, 29
I, Libertine, 169
Inheritance of Acquired Characteristics, The, 121
Innes, Reverend Williams, 74
Inquiry into the Validity of the Papers Attributed to Shakespeare, 151-2
Ireland, Samuel, 150-51
Ireland, William, 150-52, 156, 160, 172, 174, 197, 203
IRS, SINA and, 37
Irving, Clifford, 11, 13, 14, 22, 23, 31-2, 119, 142-4, 156, 158, 172, 173, 174, 175fn, 178, 184, 195-6, 202
Irving, David, 196-7, 203
Irwin, John, 140
Isaac, 1-2

Jack Paar Show, 36
Jacob, 1-2
Jesus, Society of, 75, 100
J'irai Cracher Sur Vos Tombes, 165
John Blunt, 165
John Bull, 45, 165
John O'London's Weekly, 119
Johnson, Dr, 76, 146, 147, 149
Johnson, James, 157
Jones, R V, 27
Jordanovitch, Pavel, 126
Journal of Commerce, 105
Jumping Jean, 154

Kammerer, Paul, 121-2, 123, 174, 184, 185, 203-4
Karoly, Hadju, 13, 88
Karoly, Michael, *see* Karoly, Hadju
Keating, Tom, 53, 128, 133-5, 137, 156, 168, 174, 206
Keith, Arthur, 110, 112, 113, 116
Keller, Hans, 175
Kemble, Fanny, 81
Kemble, John, 152

Ken Campbell Road Show, 182
Kenealy, Dr Edward Vaughan Hyde, 98-100, 163
Kilbracken, Lord, 23
'King of Imposters, The', 87
King Solomon's Mines, 79, 81
Klondike Nugget, 29
Kopenick, Captain of, 70-71
Kreisler, Fritz, 166, 174, 175-6
Kruger, Wolfgang, 86
Kuan, Dr, 139-41, 156, 166, 173
Kujan, Konrad, 8, 174, 197

Lamarck, Jean Baptiste, 121-2, 123
Lamprecht, Thomas, *see* Lincoln, Trebitsch
Lanner, Joseph, 176
Lauder, James, 146
Leake, Lieutenant Commander E W B, 47
Legros, Fernand, 132
Leicester, Earl of, 152
Les morts ont tout la même peau, 165-6
Lessing, Doris, 144
Leventhal, Al, 195
Lewis-Smith, Victor, 65-7, 184
Liberator Society, 44-5
Life, 196
Lincoln, Trebitsch, 8, 12, 13-14, 65, 74, 94-5, 159-60, 172, 174, 185
Listener, 175
Lithographiae Wirceburgensis, 117
Lloyd George, David, 205-6
Lloyd, Raymond, 65, 67-9, 70
Lloyd, Sophie, 65, 67-9, 88, 89, 158, 173, 184, 203
Locke, 104-5, 172, 173
Locker-Lampson, Oliver, 38-9
Lockwood, Colonel, 19
Lodge, Sir Oliver, 194
Longford, Thomas, *see* Lincoln, Trebitsch

Lorincz, Thomas, *see* Lincoln, Trebitsch
Los Angeles Chronicle, 37
Los Angeles Exposition, 52
Los Angeles Times, 126
Louvre, museum, 186
Lübeck, St Mary's Church, 200–201
Lustig, Count Victor, 61–3, 74, 157, 158, 171, 172, 173, 174, 178, 185, 203
Lusus Naturae, theory of, 116–7
Lyell-Manson, Daphne, 88

MacDonald, Ramsay, 38
Macpherson, James, 145–6, 149, 150, 156, 174
Maeterlinck, Maurice, 87
Magic Circle, the, 67–9, 203
Magna Carta Society, 99
Majorca, 160–61
Malone, Edmond, 151–2
Malskat, Lothar, 200–201
Manchester City News, 119
Manchester Guardian, 112, 155–6
Mandeville, Sir John, 78
Manningham, Sir Richard, 178
Man Who Wouldn't Talk, The, 139, 140, 176
Marcos, President, 123, 124
Mardi Gras, *see* New Orleans
Marlborough, Master of, 69
Marsh, Othniel Charles, 8
Marston, Dr, 115
Mason, Laura, 127
Mavrides, Paul, 42
Maxwell, Brigadier, 49–50
Maxwell, Colour-Sergeant, 50, 70
Maxwell, Robert, 207
May, Vice-Admiral Sir William, 15–22
McGrady, Mike, 141–2, 156, 168–9, 173
McGraw-Hill, 11, 13, 14, 23, 52, 119, 142–4, 184, 195–6
'McGubbin, The', 119
McKenna, Mr, 19, 20, 22
McKenna, Mrs, 20
'Melancholy Reflections', 26
Mencken, H L, 26, 209, 210
Men of the Last Frontier, 83
Mercier, Cardinal, 87
Mercury Theatre, 166
Metro Pictures, 27–8, 51–2
Metropolitan Museum of Art, 136, 188
Meyer, Stanley, 143
Michael Joseph, 144
Miller, Robert, 61–3
Mindanao, 123–4
Miscellaneous Pieces Relating to the Chinese, 147
Mitford, Tom, 126
Modigliani, fakes, 131, 132
'Monacled Mutineer', *see* Toplis, Percy
Morganwg, Iolo, 149–50, 174
Morris, Harry, 113
Mosley, Lady Diana, 126
Moss, Norman, 27, 138–9
Mossad, 207
Mozart, fake compositions, 176
Müenchener Illustrierte Presse, 85
Museum of Modern Art, New York, 32–3
Mussolini Diaries, 53, 144
My Prison Life, 165

Naked Came the Stranger, 141–2, 169, 173
National Gallery of Denmark, 137
National Geographic, 123, 124, 155
NBC, 36, 123, 124
'Neglected Anniversary, A', 26
Negri, Pola, 58
Nelson was a Nance, 170
Newburger, Morris, 30–32, 158, 169, 173

228	HOAXERS AND THEIR VICTIMS

New Orleans, 3-4
New York City Annual Cat Show, 34
New York Herald-Tribune, 31
New York Post, 31, 35
New York Times, 31, 33, 40, 158, 169
Newsday, 141
Newsnight, 183
News of the World, 90, 93
Nicholas Nickleby, 182-3
Nine Commandments, 171, 178
No Priest, No Parson, Liberty, Peace and Truth, 150
N-rays, 107
Nuclear-proof cockroaches, 42
Nunn, Trevor, 182-3

Oakley, Dr K P, 114
Observer, 13
'Ode on Converting a Sword into a Pruning Hook', 150
Oderic, 78
Of Truth, 56
Oil and Drilling Trust of Roumania, 95
Ojibway, The, 82
'Only Living Brazilian Invisible Fish', 51, 173
Onslow, Guildford, 98
Ooza snake, 154
Operation Parallax, 25
Oratory, Headmaster of, 70
Orton, Arthur, 65, 95-102, 158, 163-4, 172, 184, 198
Orton, Joe, 169-70, 173
Ossian and the Poetry of the Ancient Races, 146
Otto, Stephane, 87-8, 158, 174, 185

Padgham, Mrs Florence, 111
Paine, Ralph Delahaye, 27, 158
Palmer, Samuel, 133-4

Pannani Galleries, 136
Paris Academy, 199
Partridge's Almanack, 174
Patrizzio, Hannah, 127
Penderewski, 175
People, 163-4
Percy, Bishop Thomas, 146-7, 149, 150, 174
Philippines, 123-4
Picasso, fakes, 131, 132
Pilgrims of the Wild, 83
Piltdown Hoax, 14, 23, 109-116, 158, 172, 173, 185, 197-8
Piranesi, fakes, 137
Plainfield Teachers, 31, 169
Pleasures of Deception, The, 22, 138
Poisson, André, 62-3
Polynesia, 154-5
'Posthumous waltzes', 176
Priestless Society, 150
Profession of Faith, 151
Prout, G Clifford Jr, 36-8, 184
Psalmanazar, George, 13, 23, 73-6, 77, 88, 147, 156, 157, 174
Public monuments, sale of, 56-7
Punch, 117, 191
Putnam, George Palmer, 154, 156, 169

Rampa, Lobsang, *see* Kuan, Dr
RCA records, 59
Reader's Digest, 138, 139, 140
Rebekah, 1-2
Redmond, William, 19
Rees-Bunce, Sir Clint, 65-7, 70
Reichenbach, Harry, 2-4, 27-9, 33, 42, 50-52, 62, 156, 159, 172, 173, 184
Reliques of Ancient English Poetry, 147
Rembrandt, fakes, 133
Renoir, fakes, 133
'Return of Martin Guerre, The', 72

INDEX

Revenge, The, 149
Reynolds, Quentin, 139
Richard of Cirencester, 152
Ridley, Guy, 15–22
Ritchie, Inspector, 93
Ritz Hotel, 170
Rivers, Lord, 98
Roberts, Lloyd, 83
Robinson Crusoe of Australia, 65, 79–81
Robinson, Sir William Cleaver, 81
Rochester Sneath, H, 65, 69–70, 157, 181–2, 203
Roderick, Ignatz, 116–17, 158, 174
Rogers, Zad, 127–8
Romanian Consul-General, 57
Root, Henry, *see* Henry Root
Rosebery, Lord, 43–4
Rospigliosi Cup, 188
Rouchomowski, Israel, 186
Routh, Jonathan, 6
Rowley, Thomas, 148–9
Royal College of Surgeons, 112
Royal Dickens Company, 157, 182
Royal Knights of Justice, 206
Royal Shakespeare Company, 182
Rugby, Headmaster, of, 69–70
Rushton, Edward, 149
Rustom, Christopher, 144–5
Ryan, Rocky, 13

Saed, Mohammed Yehia, 206–7
Saitaphernes Tiara, 186–8
Sanctuary, The, 91
San Francisco Chronicle, 35
Saunders, Esther, 148
Scandal, 124
Schlottmann, Dr Konstantine, 190
Schmidt, Leopold, 176
Scott, Sir Giles Gilbert, 69
Secker and Warburg, 139–40, 141
Selassie, Haile, 162
Selhurst School, 69–70, 157
Selhurst Symphony, 70

September Morn, 28, 173
'Sexton Blake', Picassos and Renoirs, 53, 206
Shakespeare, fakes and, 151–2
Shanghai, Buddhist Abbot of, 95
Shapira, Moses, 158
Shaw, George Bernard, 70
Shawcross, Sir Hartley, 40–41
Shearer, James, 23, 108–9, 158, 184
Shearer's Delineator, 108–9
Shepherd, Adna, 53–4
Shepherd, Jean, 169
Sheridan, Richard, 151, 152
Shiloh, 150
Simon, Hegesippe, 202
Simpson, Edward, 105–6
SINA, 36–8, 41
Sinatra, Frank, 35
Sitwell, Dame Edith, 82
Skaggs, Joey, 42, 168
Smith, Paul Jordan, 126, 173
Snelling, Harold, 118
Soldier for Eden, A, 144–5
Somer, Jane, 144
Somerset Maugham, William, 90
Songs of the Cell, 165
Sotheby's, 132, 136
Southcott, Joanna, 150
South Kensington Museum, 110, 113, 115
Spaghetti hoax, 24–5, 157
Sparks, Paul, 66–7
Spectrist School of Poetry, 153, 168
Stafford Clark, Max, 183
Stalin, biography of, 138
Stein, David, 53, 131–2, 134, 158, 186, 206
Stephen, Adrian, 7, 9–12, 15–22, 65, 156
Stephen, Virginia, 15–22
Stevas, Norman St John, 183
Stone, L T, 30, 173

Stonehouse, John, 207
Stowe, Headmaster of, 69
Strachey, Lytton, 126
Strand Magazine, 14, 119
Stranger than Naked, Or How To Write Dirty Books for Fun, 142
Stuart, Lyle, 141–2
Styles, Kenneth, 118
Sun 104, 105
Sunday Sport, 24–5
Sunday Times, 85–6, 122, 145, 197
Surrender diplomas, 51
Sutro, John, 40–41
Swift, Jonathan, 174
Sweeny, Estelle, 62

Tales of an Empty Cabin, 83
Tandler, Leo, *see* Lincoln, Trebitsch
Tasady Tribe, 123–4
Tehami, Abbes, 1
Telephone hoaxes, 41–2, 66
Tennant, Professor, 106
Tetro, John, 174, 206
That's Life, 66, 184
'Theatre of the Five Thousand, The', 84
Theosophical Society of Bradford, 118
'There are Fairies at the Bottom of My Garden', 117
Third Eye, The, 139–41, 166
Thomson, Brigadier-General Andrew, 41
Tibet, 139–41
Tichborne Almanack, 100
Tichborne Bonds, 97
Tichborne Gazette, 164
Tichborne, Sir Henry, 95
Tichborne, Sir James Francis Doughty, 96
Tichborne, Lady, 96–7, 98, 163–4, 172, 184

Tichborne, memorabilia, 164
Tichborne, Roger, 95
Tichborne Times, 101–2
Time, 31, 32
Time-Life, 23, 143, 195
Times, The, 40, 104, 114, 115, 134, 135, 164, 165, 175, 190, 191, 197
Toad-in-the-Hole, 110–11
Today, 36
Tofts, Mary, 174, 177–8
Tomb of the Savelli, The, 188
'Tommies' Ambassador', *see* Bottomley, Horatio
Tonbridge, Head, of, 181
Topless String Quartet, 34–5
Toplis, Percy, 8, 11, 65, 90–94, 158, 174, 185
Toronto Presbyterian Church, 91
Tottenham, Mrs, 40
Traprock, Walter E, 154–5, 173
Travels, 78
Trelford, Donald, 13
Trevor-Roper, Hugh, 8, 146, 196–7, 203
Tronchet, Maria, 34
Troy, Hugh, 13, 32–3, 41, 156, 159, 172, 173
Truman, Charles, 188
Truman, Harry S, 26
Truth, 119
Turner, fakes, 133
Twisaday, Reverend, 164

U2 spy plane, 208
Ultra-Violet School of Poetry, 153
United Press International, 42
US Air Force, 41

Valentino, Rudolph, 57–8
Vallance, Jeffrey, 42
Van Beuningen, D G, 130
Van der Horst, Dr L, 178–9
Van der Vorm, W, 130

INDEX

Van Gogh, Vincent, 32–3
Vanishing Frontier, 83
Van Meegeren, Hans, 22, 23, 128–31, 134–5, 142, 158, 168, 172, 174, 178, 185–6
Vanunu, Mordechai, 207
Vasters, Reinhold, 188
Venice, 39
Vermeer, 23, 130, 147, 172
Vespertilio homo, 104
Vian, Boris, 165–6, 174
Vidal, John, 13
Village Voice, 168
Villegas, Count Alain de, 23, 174
Virgin of Stamboul, The, 52
Voigt, Wilhelm, 70–72, 82, 88, 174, 184
Von Elkhart, Georg, 116–17, 158, 174
Vonnegut, Kurt, 138
Vortigern and Rowena, 151, 152, 160, 203
Vrain-Lucas, Denis, 174, 198–200

Wales, Princess of, 209
Walpole, Horace, 148
Walpole, Hugh, 145
War of the Worlds, 166
Warton, Thomas, 149
Washington Post, 13, 33
Wasserstein, Bernard, 172
Watters, Edward, 2–3, 33, 42, 174
Waugh, Evelyn, 126, 173
Weinburg, Professor Gerhard, 197
Weiner, Dr J S, 114, 116
Welles, Orson, 166

Wellthorpe, Edna, 170
Wessex sceptics, 207–8
Weyman, Stanley, 11, 53, 57–9, 158, 160, 172, 174
White, E J Stroller, 29, 30, 173
Whiteaker, Sudie, 53
Whitehall Gazette, 47
Wikiki Bar, 161
Willcocks, Mary, *see* 'Caraboo'
Wilson, Colin, 88
Wilson, Harold, 208
Winstanley, Jenny, 67–9, 89, 158, 173
Winsted Liar, The, 30
Wizard of Sussex, *see* Dawson, Charles
Wood, R W, 107
Woodward, Arthur Smith, 110–16, 184, 185, 197, 198
Woodward, Bob, 13
Woolf, Virginia, *see* Stephen, Virginia
World Wide Magazine, 78, 80
Worrall, Samuel, 76–7
Wright, Frances, 14, 117–20, 123, 176
Wright, Polly, 118
Wyoming USS, 57

Yamba, 79–81
Yates, Kenneth, 59

Zaenger, Christian, 116, 117
Zak, Piotr, 175
Zanuck, Darryl, 201–2
Zanzibar, Sultan of, 10